Men for All Seasons

Men for All Seasons

How Australia Shattered England's Ashes Dream

CHRISTOPHER MARTIN-JENKINS

SIMON & SCHUSTER
A VIACOM COMPANY

First published in Great Britain in 2001
by Simon & Schuster UK Ltd
A Viacom company

Some sections of this book are included as they appeared in *The Times* newspaper during 2001, with no changes made in hindsight.

PICTURE CREDITS
All pictures courtesy of Allsport
1, 7, 8, 15: Laurence Griffiths
2, 9, 10, 14, 16, 19, 20: Hamish Blair
3, 17, 18: Tom Shaw; 4, 5: Craig Prentis
6, 11: Adrian Murrell; 12, 13: Mike Hewitt

1   3   5   7   9   10   8   6   4   2

Simon & Schuster UK Ltd
Africa House
64–78 Kingsway
London WC2B 6AH

Simon & Schuster Australia
Sydney

A CIP catalogue for this book is available
from the British Library.

ISBN: 0-7432-2023-4

Typeset by Palimpsest Book Production Limited,
Polmont, Stirlingshire
Printed and bound in Great Britain by
The Bath Press

To the writers and inside sports staff on *The Times*, who produce, day in and day out, the best cricket coverage by any newspaper.

Contents

Introduction

'SIR, This Australian side is so good they win even when they lose. At Hampshire and Headingley the declarations showed both self-belief and a recognition that if you only draw when you could have won, you, the game, the crowd, lose.

'It is one of those charming ironies of life that it takes such a team of supreme professionals to remind us that it is a game not a business. Eschewing negative bowling and defensive field placings they well deserve the tag "greatest ever".'

Thus, in a letter to *The Times* shortly before Australia won the fifth Test in the old-fashioned way, by mounting a huge total and bowling their opponents out by a combination of high-class fast bowling, wrist spin and fielding, did Jeremy Harrison from Swanmore in Hampshire make the case for the 2001 Australians to be the best of all teams.

What is certain is that they had raised the level of Test cricket in a number of ways, the most important of them all being the philosophy that everyone who plays for Australia should leave the game in a better state than it was when he started playing. To that end Steve Waugh and the senior members of his side have begun to turn back the trend towards foul-mouthed aggression as a means of winning cricket matches, restoring some of the game's traditional generosity of spirit. Since it was Australian sides who had themselves been in the vanguard of the win-at-all-costs mentality that became prevalent in all professional cricket after the Packer Revolution of the late 1970s, they owed the game the correction that seemed to be taking place under Waugh's inspiration throughout their tour.

His intentions were positive from the outset of the tour to England: 'Already it seems like the place to play,' he said at the opening press conference at Worcester. At the end he wrote in his column in the *Sunday Telegraph*: 'Even though it was my fourth tour of England it felt like my first. It's like being reborn as a cricketer. You can sense this is the place to play and the energy and enthusiasm that it brings recharges the battery instantly.

'From day one we wanted to be known not only as a very good team, but one that would go home with its image enhanced by excellent behaviour both on and off the field. Our goal was to be positive in attack and to back ourselves and each other at all times.'

It was this enlightened approach, coupled with an attempt to persuade his players that they should use cricket to enlarge their minds and touch their souls, that made this a team of genuine trendsetters. Already they had established that, with the talent at their disposal, the best way to win matches was to attack with bat and ball from the start to the finish of every game. Scoring at four runs an over had become a habit that entertained crowds, increased the fun and confidence of the batsmen themselves and bought the bowlers time to do their job.

John Buchanan of Queensland, the broad-minded, rather quirky coach of the side, who knows the basics of bowling and hitting straight, keeping fit, eating the right food and fielding better by working harder, also made it his business to try to stretch the minds of his young charges. It is Waugh, however, the intelligent family man who must surely be one of the best and toughest batsmen of all time, who first encouraged the notion that players travelling the world should not cocoon themselves within the confined circle of one cricket team, but get out to meet people, see the sights and expand their horizons. All this has been part of Australia's success.

On their way to England for the tour the players diverted via Istanbul to southern Turkey, to Gallipoli, to see where so many of the young Anzac soldiers – an estimated 36,000 Commonwealth troops in all – had died between February 1915 and January 1916 in the failed campaign to force a way through to Russia via the Dardanelles. It was a team-binding exercise with a difference, the result of a conversation at a dinner between Waugh and a senior Australian army officer. It gave all the cricketers a better under-standing of a tragic part of their country's history and a better perspective on their own lives. Theirs is a privileged existence and to share in a team success only enriches it. No Australian is ever left in any doubt about that, nor feels anything less than deep patriotism.

Jason Gillespie later wrote in the *Cricketer International* of how it had affected the players: 'Some of us went to Gallipoli not really knowing what to expect but came away with all sorts of different emotions, sadness and pride probably the main two.' He went on to relate how 'good old Gilly' (Adam Gilchrist) had got 'a bit choked up' when thanking Waugh on the coach on behalf of the players. Later, the team's fitness trainer, the son of immigrants from the Lebanon to Australia, had them all close to tears again when he told them how deeply the visit had touched his sense of national pride.

Here, in a nutshell, was one reason for the extraordinary ability of Australian sportsmen to rise to the national cause. It did not matter that this young 'new Australian', Pat Farhart, had no direct connection whatsoever with the tragic events of 1915. He was a fair dinkum Aussie; and so they all were; in it together for the pride of their homeland. Advance Australia Fair. It is a distant land and sport puts it on the map.

The team's Welsh press officer, Brian Murgatroyd, had, in a sim-ilar role, tried to paper over occasional splits in England dressing-rooms before being offered much better terms, taken into the enemy camp and embraced as one of their own. He spoke later in the tour of the camaraderie between the players as being, some-times, 'the nearest thing to a religious experience'. He referred as an example to the moment that Justin Langer, who had lost his place in the Test team to Damien Martyn, surrounded him with an emotional hug when the man who had superseded him got back to the dressing-room after making his maiden Test hundred.

Shortly before the final Test ended, there was another startling demonstration of their extraordinary togetherness. Mark Waugh had to go off the field at The Oval to have some stitches sewn into a severe cut to the webbing between his thumb and index finger. It would no doubt have kept most England players off the field for at least the rest of the game. Waugh was soon back but one of his substitutes, for a few overs only, was the reserve wicket-keeper, Wade Seccombe. When he ran on, bursting with keenness from every pore of his skin, team-mate after team-mate touched him on the hand as he came past them; wishing him luck; passing on the ethos that goes with the baggy green cap.

No other country is so successful at assimilating its talented young players so quickly and thoroughly into the team's culture. All of them have been bred for moments like this since they were first spotted as small boys in a system of recognition and phased development that is the envy of all rivals.

If the success does not go on for ever it will be because not even a system that breeds excellence or a nation that encourages total patriotism can guarantee that cricketing genius will emerge from each generation. The mighty Australian team of the 1970s possessed great players in the Chappell brothers, Dennis Lillee and Rodney Marsh, around whom several very good players excelled. The same was true of the 2001 side, based around the brilliance of five men in particular: Steve and Mark Waugh, Glenn McGrath, Shane Warne and Adam Gilchrist.

It seemed obvious in retrospect that a spine as unbendable as this would withstand anything the England team could do to try to break it. Just before the Ashes series, however, three epic Tests in India had proved both the wonderful unpredictability of cricket and the fact that no side is infallible. Taken together with results elsewhere on the subcontinent, India's glorious victory raised the stock of English cricket at just the right time.

Contemporary life is dictated and dominated by the technological revolution of the second half of the twentieth century. Television and computers have changed society even more radically than railways and the other products of the Industrial Revolution two centuries before. Amongst the consequences in sport, as in politics, is instant news, leading to the need for instant opinion and hence a gross over-simplification of events as portrayed in the media.

English cricket is a fine example: like Tony Blair or George W. Bush, it is a good thing one moment, a national disaster the next. In 1999, according to the media (by which in this case I mean mainly the headline-makers of radio, television and the newspapers), English cricket was hopeless; in a state of crisis; moribund. Having lost to New Zealand at home, regardless of the strength of a visiting side that has never hit such a peak since, England, according to the front pages, were officially the worst team in the world. Twelve months later – notwithstanding the shattering exposure throughout the summer of a match-fixing scandal which, though it was centred elsewhere, might have been expected to dampen enthusiasm for the game – they were national heroes, conquerors of the West Indies, whose teams of the 1980s and '90s had invariably carried all before them.

England sustained their form and enhanced their status during winter tours of Pakistan and Sri Lanka in 2000/01. Few were under any illusions about the size of the challenge that followed but when the Australians, world champions in Test cricket and holders of the one-day World Cup, arrived in the United Kingdom in late May, there was real hope that their run of six successive series dating back to 1989 might at last be brought to a halt.

It had been one of the bleakest periods for England since the first official Test in 1877 and one of the most triumphant for Australia. A change of fortune now would be all the more extraordinary for the speed of England's improvement in a single year and because Australia had seemed for a time to be almost invincible. Six Ashes wins in succession was a remarkable achievement, but winning sixteen successive Tests against six different opponents between October 1999 and March 2001 was utterly astonishing. Twelve in a row by the West Indies in the 1980s had been unprecedented and, it seemed, unlikely to be repeated by anyone.

During their record sequence, Waugh's side, adaptable, but based on the same set of players, won four matches by an innings, two by ten wickets and two more by margins of 180 and 285 runs. Only at Hobart, when they beat Pakistan by four wickets from an apparently hopeless position at the start of the last day, had they been seriously threatened by defeat until 27 February 2001, two days after the death of their greatest cricketer and sporting icon, Sir Donald Bradman. Then, at Bombay, they collapsed to 99 for 5 in the first innings of the first Test against India. They were rescued by Adam Gilchrist and Matthew Hayden and went on to win with deceptive comfort.

In the following epic match at Calcutta in the middle of March they lost against the head, victims of wonderful performances by V. V. S. Laxman, Rahul Dravid and the young off-spinner, Harbhajan Singh. India's second innings of 657 for 7 declared led to only the third instance of a side winning a Test after following on. It was the first crack in the carapace and supreme English optimists saw an additional grain of hope for England in that they had provided the other two instances, also against Australia, once in the nineteenth century, once in the twentieth.

Now, everyone with a stake in the forthcoming Ashes series in England watched in fascination as the deciding games of simultaneous Test series in India and Sri Lanka came to the boil. On 17 March England beat Sri Lanka at Colombo to win their fourth successive Test series. On 22 March India beat Australia in Madras to record their third successive home win in a series against Australia. They managed it by a mere two wickets but it was only Australia's second defeat in any series since Mark Taylor's side had also lost on the subcontinent four years previously.

The fact of its coincidence with England's comeback from losing the first Test of a three-match series was doubly significant, because the only defeat under Waugh was in Sri Lanka. If Australia's rare defeats on the subcontinent only showed that a brilliant side was not unbeatable, England's four wins in four series against Zimbabwe, West Indies, Pakistan and Sri Lanka proved not only that they had become hard to beat, but that they had learned how to win.

Since losing to Australia last time England had acquired a determined and methodical coach, Duncan Fletcher; a successful captain, Nasser Hussain; an authentic all-rounder, Craig White; an effective pair of opening batsmen, Michael Atherton and Marcus Trescothick; a consistent pair of opening bowlers, Darren Gough and Andrew Caddick; a settled team; and a belief in themselves.

Australia remained favourites, until proved otherwise the best side in the world, but the consequence of recent events meant that the 2001 series, sold out long before the tour started for most days of the five Tests, was the most eagerly anticipated since the Coronation year of 1953.

One

Winter of Content

If England were to have any chance of winning back the Ashes in 2001 following home victories against Zimbabwe and the West Indies the season before, they had to believe, deep down, that Australia could be beaten. For that to happen and a deep-seated inferiority complex to be banished, they somehow had to get through two demanding winter series with their honour and credibility intact. In the event, they did more than that.

This is an account, in diary entries and reports for *The Times*, of two unusually enjoyable tours of the subcontinent.

Monday, 6 November 2000
The start of a five-week trip to Pakistan which I was contemplating with far less trepidation than previous visits. Wearying travel, frustratingly bad communications and food which my digestive system simply does not appreciate have soured my view in the past of a part of the world that is in many other ways fascinating; but in all these respects things have greatly improved.

I left for Heathrow in a car provided by Emirates Airways, with whom I was travelling to Peshawar via Dubai. Getting to the airport after yet more heavy rain was no simple matter but I was lucky to get a driver who knew an alternative route via Cobham when a deep flood prevented us from getting on to the A3 at Ripley. There were only minor dramas after that: a two-hour wait for air-traffic clearance at the very start and then two more hours hovering over Peshawar in the early morning because the pall of dust and pollution was bad enough to deter the pilot, who sounded South African, from landing. Eventually he went for it, with no mishap. It brought back memories of a BBC trip to Belfast years ago when the pilot made four or five attempts to land in thick fog, only to think better of it when almost at runway level, swooping up again like a dolphin. That really was unnerving.

Once settled in at the old Pearl Continental hotel – the furnishings in my room were a bit drab but it was all clean and comfortable and the food not bad at all – I got straight to work, catching up on news, attending a press conference with that feeling of grey weariness that always follows long flights and before writing a preview of the second of England's two first-class matches before the first Test in Lahore.

Tuesday, 7 November

England start an important four-day match today and Alec Stewart the final phase of his long career. Ever the pugilist, he is in the appropriate place to prove he can refocus his mind and energy on playing cricket: Peshawar on the North-West Frontier, where fighting comes naturally. His task is to prove that the last harrowing week, during which he has had to defend himself against the claim that he took money to give information to an Indian bookmaker, will not prevent him from performing at his best in the first Test against Pakistan next week.

If he cannot convince Nasser Hussain and Duncan Fletcher that he is in the mood to do himself justice, he would be omitted and Paul Nixon, with whom he worked closely in practice yesterday, included in his stead. The odds, if that is not an insensitive word to use, are that Stewart will rise to his latest personal challenge: for all Nixon's qualities, England will clearly be the weaker if he does not. It will not have been forgotten by Nasser Hussain, however, that in his first match as a Test captain at Edgbaston in 1999, immediately after Stewart's summary dismissal following the World Cup, the deposed leader was sufficiently distracted to have comfortably the worst of his 102 Tests.

It is, on the other hand, equally relevant that, resilient character that he is, Stewart quickly found his feet again. In fifteen Tests since making 0 and 1 as an opening batsman and highly fallible slip-fielder in that first Test against New Zealand, he has scored 900 runs at an average of 36 with two hundreds, finally settled at number five in the England order, reclaimed the wicket-keeping gloves from Chris Read and, as his thirty-six victims suggest, consistently performed with aplomb. The nightmare of the past few days has been quite different from the one he suffered during those gloomy days in June last year but Hussain said yesterday that Stewart was 'back to himself and in a mood to focus his mind on the cricket after a tough week'.

He takes his place, therefore, in a side which has been chosen with a view to clarifying as many options as possible before the first Test, as distinct from being the side which will actually play in Lahore. Both the specialist spinners, Ashley Giles and Ian Salisbury, play again in this second first-class match, against a largely inexperienced team playing under the imposing title of the North-West Frontier Province Governor's XI. Michael Atherton and Michael Vaughan, neither of whom was able to spend long in the middle in Rawalpindi in their only innings so far, both play again and Craig White will do so too because the selectors, worried about the hamstring strain which affected him last week, want to be sure that he can bowl flat-out. If he does so, Dominic Cork, a hero on his home pitches last season, seems certain to be the one who will make way for a spinner in Lahore. He has been left out of this game after an ineffective first match.

Quite rightly the management has not ruled out playing both Giles and Salisbury next week if the pitch merits it. It is more likely, however, that this game will serve as an eliminator between the two. Hussain admitted that he has no really close personal knowledge of either and that he wants to see 'the look in their eyes' when he captains them together for the first time in this game. The snag is that they can bowl only so many overs when other bowlers, not just Darren Gough and Andrew Caddick, but also the part-time off-spinner, Vaughan, all need preparatory work. Jeff Dujon, now the West Indies assistant coach, pointed out in Australia this week that preparation by touring sides for Test series these days is hopelessly inadequate and this tour is certainly no exception. It is often a mixed blessing to win provincial matches too easily in the preparatory stages of a tour, as England did in Rawalpindi.

Rashid Latif, one of the first whistle-blowers in the long saga of cricket corruption, captains the home side, which contains three other players with Test experience, although none of them is likely to play in Lahore. The pitch is grassy enough to give whoever bowls this morning some movement off the seam, especially as there will be dew about if the match starts at the appointed hour of 10.30. Light at the other end of the day may be a problem, too: a thick pall of dust hung over Peshawar all day yesterday with no wind to disperse it.

Wednesday, 8 November

Shahi Bagh Stadium, Peshawar (first day of four; England won toss): North-West Frontier Province Governor's XI have scored 174 for 5 against England.

England put their opponents in to bat yesterday on as green and lively a pitch as they are likely to encounter in Pakistan but they bowled more like a West Indian attack of old, peppering youthful batsmen with short balls for much of a first day limited by the weather to 56 overs. It was a hostile approach, but not one which made the best use of decent conditions for seam bowlers. Had it not been for the two wickets taken in three balls by Ashley Giles in the first over after tea, the decision to field first, obvious though it was after a wet morning, might have appeared seriously flawed.

It is true that the most experienced batsman, Wajahatullah Wasti, will take no further part in the game after breaking his left thumb when Darren Gough got a ball to lift sharply in the half-hour's play possible before lunch, but batting conditions improved and the local team recovered with some spirit from 113 for 5 in the third session by means of two young players willing to counter-attack the quicker bowlers and to move their feet against Giles and Ian Salisbury. In the end none of the bowlers will remember events with great affection, certainly not Gough, the pack leader, who had one of those days on which he looked disgruntled with himself, the umpires and life in general. No doubt the smile will soon be back.

Even before the rain, Nasser Hussain would have been tempted by the look of the pitch to bowl first. The alternative would have been to subject his top-order batsmen to a seaming ball, which might have done nothing for their confidence. He knows how precious match practice is going to be for everyone in advance of next week's Test and it was better that Gough, Andrew Caddick and Craig White should make their errors of length and direction here than in Lahore.

The six specialist batsmen playing in this game are all certain to play in the first Test, with Thorpe and Vaughan swapping places at four and six, so performances now as much as the condition of the Test pitch will determine which of Hick, Cork, Giles, Salisbury and Hoggard will occupy the last two places. There are those who argue that England would be wiser to stick to the plan which worked well towards the end of the West Indies series, playing seven batsmen and four quick bowlers; but these are different opponents in very different conditions.

Once a local band dressed in smart red waistcoats had signalled the presentation of both teams to the Governor, Gough began yesterday's business with six balls which Wasti either left alone or could not reach. Wasteful to Wasti; wasteful of the new ball. Caddick at once bowled straighter but despite having the left-handed Imran Farhat badly dropped by Thorpe at third slip in his third over, he was rather too concerned with getting the ball to lift. Cuts and hooks brought Farhat five fours before White, who proved his fitness by bowling genuinely fast, had him caught behind, cutting again.

This was the first of two catches for Alec Stewart, who was at his slickest all day; very much his usual ebullient self. He claimed a third catch, vehemently, with the sixth ball bowled by his Surrey colleague, Salisbury. Had the appeal been upheld, as bowler and keeper clearly thought it should have been, it might have made a lot of difference to Salisbury but it would also have nipped in the bud what became an attractive innings by Yasar Hameed, a neat and correct 22-year-old right-hander playing in his home city.

Hussain sensibly gave his leg-spinner a chance to settle by putting a man deep on the square boundary on either side. If Mark Taylor could do that for Shane Warne in India there was no reason why Salisbury should not be given similar protection. It was not long before the deep cover moved to silly point and the deep square-leg to forward short but he induced few errors after his early misfortune and it was Giles who broke through instead, first having the stylish Naumanullah caught at silly point off bat and pad and then removing the left-handed Akhtar Sarfraz second ball when he top-edged an attempted pull.

When he pushed the ball through, Giles demanded respect on a pitch still giving everyone some surprisingly generous bounce but as he slowed in an attempt to spin the ball more, he was played more easily. Gough cheered himself momentarily by having an always uncomfortable-looking Rashid Latif caught in the gully off an edge on to his pads, but Hameed and Mohammad Hussain, yet another left-hander, brightened an overcast, almost chilly evening with some handsome strokes. Hameed had six fours in his fifty and Hussain played the stroke of the day, a searing cover drive on the up against White. The lesson was clear, or ought to be. If England's bowlers do not get their length right against better batsmen next week, the punishment will be much more severe.

Sunday, 12 November
To Lahore by air this evening after six generally enjoyable days in Peshawar. The changes in this country really are significant and I do believe they will get an increasing number of tourists if only they can make it easier for them to get visas (it had taken me all day to get mine) now that there are such things as purified drinking water and menus to suit sensitive stomachs. Peshawar certainly has as much to offer as various more vaunted cities in India. The journalists were all asked on Wednesday night to the lavish house of Waqar Zaman, whose father, Abid Ali, fat and full of honeyed words, welcomed us with a splendid buffet, served relatively early – 10pm. The food was preceded and accompanied, in this Muslim country where drinking alcohol is forbidden, by as much as anyone wanted of a gallon bottle of Johnnie Walker Black Label or, for those who preferred, finest Danish lager. A Pakistan Test player was also a guest and knew better, asking for wine: a 1996 Bordeaux was duly produced.

There is no such thing as a free dinner, however. The sales patter which followed from the ubiquitous Waqar in the carpet shop at the Pearl from then on was relentless and by the end of the week most of the guests at the party had bought carpets, myself, slightly guiltily, amongst them. I had had it in mind to buy one more for the house but did not intend to spend as much as I did when father and son accompanied me to the 'largest and finest carpet palace' in Pakistan to see 'not cheap modern carpets made in Pakistan' but 'highest quality, hand-made Boukharas from "Affanistan" which you will treasure for the rest of your life. What is money compared to these beautiful things from which you will always remember your visit to Peshawar?' Once the minions began rolling out carpet after carpet, the old ones superseding the brash modern examples, it was almost impossible not to succumb, especially when such a very, very special price was offered to our honoured visitor. He would have persuaded Scrooge to go home with something.

Derek Pringle has bought eight carpets from the charming Waqar on previous visits and was determined not to be beguiled again. He was tempted by one carpet when he went with John Etheridge to give him the benefit of his experience, however. He refused all entreaties until Waqar said: 'Here is the calculator. Please give me your own price for the carpet.' Derek said he couldn't: the only amount he was prepared to offer would be an insult. 'Mr Pringle,' said Waqar, 'it would be an honour to be insulted by you.'

England won the match on the fourth day after a clash between a local umpire and Andrew Caddick had opened old wounds, eagerly exacerbated, naturally, by the English press corps. I played a round of golf on Saturday, half a day off at least, with the *Guardian*'s Mike Selvey, defeating him for a change, although playing with only half a set of clubs. The weather was lovely and the course in good condition. It was remarkably peaceful walking round – very few people on the course – considering the teeming streets of the old town not far away and the even more teeming bazaars.

I had dinner that night at the Khan Club, a tall old building dating from the Moghul era which was renovated five years ago by an Irishman. It is now an atmospheric restaurant with good food served on low stools to customers sitting on not very soft cushions on the floor. There are a few rooms shrewdly modernised for discerning tourists.

Even more likely to bring the visitors in future is the journey through the Khyber Pass by 'antiquated steam mechanism'. At present it runs once every three weeks and we were lucky enough to coincide with one of the trips. Since the flight to Lahore did not leave until the evening and I had done most of my piece for Monday's paper on Saturday, I went with Pringle and Michael Henderson. For 4,000 rupees (£50) one chugged slowly up the historic valley on the line skilfully engineered by the British at different stages between 1905 and 1926. The scenes outside were fascinating: rugged hills and low houses in the tribal villages made of mud and stones. The train is obviously still a novelty for both children and adults amongst the tribesmen because they peered and waved at the two carriages, pulled at one end and pushed at the other by locomotives built in England before the First World War. The train stopped at intervals to switch lines, proceeding to 3,500 feet by a succession of forward and reverse rails, on the principle of switchback roads.

We were entertained by a bagpipe band at Jamrud, tea and Pathan musicians at Shaghai Fort, and then taken from the end of the line at Landi Kotal by minibus to hear a brief history of the Khyber Rifles by a smart young officer who pointed out various landmarks in the valley below which led to the Afghanistan border two miles away and on to Kabul. Lunch, too spicy for me, was then served in the gardens of the splendid Mess at Michini. The collection of photos of visiting dignitaries was extraordinary: mainly military and political but also including the Queen, Princess Anne, Jackie Kennedy, and, in 1992, Diana, Princess of Wales. As the *Insight* guidebook says, 'Anybody who is anybody' has been to the Khyber Pass.

Wednesday, 15 November

First Test, Gaddafi Stadium (first day of five; England won toss): England have scored 195 for 4 against Pakistan.
Almost exactly a year ago Nasser Hussain lost his first toss as captain in an overseas Test match, England were put in to bat on a shamefully wet pitch in Johannesburg and three overs later had lost four wickets for two runs, a position from which there was no realistic hope of recovery. Twelve months on Hussain won a

scarcely less crucial toss and with under half an hour to go before tea on the first day the opening pair of Michael Atherton and Marcus Trescothick was still batting on a slow, dry turner which can only get more difficult for the batsmen of both sides. It was the ideal start for the touring team, a worrying one for Pakistan.

The wonderful skill and accuracy of Saqlain Mushtaq pulled them back into the game in the third session, however, and left England, 195 for 4 at the close, still a long way from the total of 320 or more which would give them every chance of exploiting the pitch if their bowling, especially their spin bowling, is good enough. It was an intriguing start to the series, a day on which honours finished more or less even, but cricket being so much a game of initiatives much depended on the ability of the two remaining specialist batsmen, and the bowling all-rounders who followed, to make the Pakistan spinners really toil for the remaining wickets.

Apart from Hussain, who took a calculated, somewhat uncharacteristic gamble against Saqlain and lost it (as gamblers do, more often than not), England played the bowling on its merits but the positive way in which Atherton and his young, talented, phlegmatic partner looked for their scoring opportunities was a pleasure to witness. It made their eventual stand of 134 every bit as valuable as the partnership of 159 with which they launched the final Test against the West Indies at The Oval at the end of August.

Playing with great composure but refusing ever to get bogged down, either during the ten overs from Wasim Akram and Abdur Razzaq with the new ball, or when Saqlain and Mushtaq Ahmed began wheeling away in eager expectation, they managed a rate of three an over before lunch. Trescothick soon dissuaded Razzaq from trying to bounce him out, twice hooking him meatily in front of square, but fast scoring is difficult in these conditions, especially as the ball gets softer. The outfield is a vast expanse of thick green grass – 80 yards all round – and it tests alike the strength of the fielders' arms and the stamina of the batsmen.

Atherton had no fewer than eight threes but only one four in his first fifty runs. Each was a well-timed stroke which would have gone to most boundaries. Trescothick, blessed with equally natural timing but younger and stronger, hit five fours in his own fifty, reached in the thirty-third over of a day of flawless weather in which the temperature was just about perfect for cricket. But the spinners, especially Saqlain, shuffling in over after over with that run-up which suggests that his legs are loosely tied together at the ankles, gradually reined them in.

In the end Atherton actually faced three fewer balls than his partner for the same number of runs. It was pleasing that in the innings in which he joined Hammond, Hutton, Cowdrey, Boycott, Gooch and Gower as the only Englishmen to have scored more than 7,000 runs, he should have played so well. He let the ball come to him and, like the boys who drive the donkey through the teeming but increasingly well-organised streets of Lahore, made it do his work for him, steering it into the gaps on either side. He is obviously relishing his partnership with Trescothick and the unfamiliar challenge of batting against the spinners. 'It's a different game from playing fast bowling when you get about two minutes between each ball,' he said in contemplation later. 'It's rapid fire and you've got to make sure your concentration is good, have a game plan but not be too pre-determined in the way you play.'

Pakistan's desperately-needed breakthrough, after much frenzied appealing which failed to convince either umpire, came twenty-five minutes before tea when Trescothick, aiming a sweep without quite getting to the pitch, top-edged a catch to backward square-leg. Had Saqlain now followed up with Graham Thorpe's wicket as he should have done, the recovery which followed might have been still stronger. For some reason, however, Pakistan had been switching their slip fielder to the spinners all day and it was the fifth of them, Qaiser Ahmed, who on his first day of Test cricket at an age variously estimated between eighteen and twenty-four, dropped a quickish knee-high edge. Officially the new all-rounder, who bowled a couple of tidy overs before the end to get him into the game, was born on 7 May 1982.

Thus reprieved when only on two, Thorpe settled in valuably during the last session without being able to dominate. Graeme Hick accompanied him calmly for the last half-hour, but he saw three partners disappear in the space of four overs from Saqlain, the first, Atherton, top-edging a paddle sweep to backward square.

Stewart's nets against his Surrey colleague were no insurance against a swift execution as he pushed no more than a few inches forward to a quicker off-break; but it was the one that spun the other way which defeated Hussain, who had delayed his entry in order to have more treatment on his stiff back. The captain's first foray down the pitch produced a classical drive back over the bowler's head but the second lobbed to cover off a thick outside edge.

This was either rash or enterprising batting depending on the charity of your opinion. What is certain is that it was defeated by wily bowling. All day Saqlain had changed his pace and the angle of his feet and body at the crease, not to mention mixing the floating off-spinners with his special, Ramadhinian front-of-the-hand leg-break. It was good cricket on both sides, played by subtle bowlers and batsmen in old-fashioned caps and hats. So far, too, the pitch had held together tolerably well.

Sunday, 19 November
Gaddafi Stadium (final day of five): Pakistan drew with England.
When the selectors announced their touring teams for this winter in September they reserved for themselves the right to add an extra spin bowler for the second assignment in Sri Lanka after Christmas. If, however, they want to be sure that they are giving themselves every chance of bearding the Pakistan tiger in his den, the lesson of a First Test which defied all logical predictions by ending yesterday evening in a draw is that they should cover the possibility of two more dry, turning pitches in Faisalabad and Karachi by sending immediately for a second specialist finger-spinner.

Dominic Cork's back injury, serious enough for his early return to England to be a probability, gives the management a practical reason, if it is necessary, to send for an extra bowler, besides which the presence in Lahore of the ECB's chief executive, Tim Lamb, removes any possible administrative delay. To have a realistic chance of being considered for either of the last two Tests, which are to be played back-to-back in Faisalabad and Karachi from next Wednesday, any replacement bowler would have to arrive in Lahore in time to play in the three-day match against a Pakistan Cricket Board XI which starts here on Thursday.

It is by no means certain that had they brought three spinners in the first place, and a specialist off-spinner had played along-side Ashley Giles and Ian Salisbury, in place of Andrew Caddick or the impotent Darren Gough, England would have been able to enforce the follow-on here and thereby give themselves a chance of winning in Pakistan for only the second time in seven tours. Thanks to Giles, who bowled well throughout, and to Craig White's ability to reverse-swing an old ball, they came within two wickets of the first objective on Saturday; but the pitch remained too slow for Salisbury to raise even a suspicion of the flutter he regularly causes in the dovecotes of opposing sides at The Oval.

It was not until after lunch on the fifth day that the bowlers could remove Pakistan's heroes, Saqlain Mushtaq, indubitably the man of the match, or his ninth-wicket partner, Yousuf Youhana, whose fourth Test hundred was impressive both technically and temperamentally. They put on 127 for the ninth wicket. Significantly, most of Salisbury's bowling was done after the follow-on had been averted by Youhana and Saqlain.

His analysis of 0 for 71 from 31 overs, although it made his already mildly embarrassing Test record even less attractive, did not compare all that unfavourably with the more highly regarded Mushtaq Ahmed's match figures of 1 for 164 on a pitch which lacked not the turn but the bounce which wrist-spinners need to be really effective. Whether he will get another chance depends, clearly, on the pitches prepared in the next two Tests. Faisalabad is expected to lose time to the anticipated combination of indus-trial smog and winter mist, so England may well prefer to play an extra batsman and hope to be more positive again in Karachi. For maximum flexibility, however, an additional finger-spinner makes sense.

If they should come to the same conclusion, David Graveney, Duncan Fletcher and Nasser Hussain, who faces a second X-ray today after being hit painfully on the right wrist by his third ball in England's second innings, will have to choose quickly. Chris Schofield, who goes on the 'A' tour to the West Indies after Christmas, can hardly be promoted above Salisbury now (Schofield and Phil Tufnell were the reserves for Salisbury and Giles), but

Jason Brown, the 26-year-old off-spinner from Northampton, has also been required to get fit in preparation for that tour, so he is one possibility. The others are the seasoned pair of Robert Croft and Peter Such. Croft is an official reserve for England's one-day team in Sri Lanka in March and would relish the chance to prove the selectors were wrong to ditch him after last summer's Old Trafford Test, but Such took five wickets in his last Test for England at Sydney early last year and could be relied upon, not least by Hussain, to give a professional performance.

In the end neither Pakistan's four spinners nor England's two, augmented by Graeme Hick, could strike sufficient spark from the wholly deceptive Lahore pitch on which I had confidently and erroneously predicted anything but a high-scoring draw and a probable win for the side batting first. It was the shifting nature of the cracks, rather than the familiar cracks themselves, which proved so misleading, not least to the two captains, who both said after the game that they had been surprised by the amount of time batsmen had had to adjust.

England had finally bowled Pakistan out for 401, six overs after lunch when Youhana, scorer of centuries in successive Tests against the West Indies' fast bowlers earlier this year and now proving himself no less authoritative a player of spin, at last got an outside edge to Giles, and Mushtaq Ahmed was trapped in front of his stumps to complete another outstanding all-round performance by White.

What followed was deflating for an England team which, having had the good fortune to win the toss, had made all the running for four days. Wasim Akram ran in at a purposeful sprint and banged the new ball hard into the worn surface as if determined to remind his coach, Javed Miandad, and captain, Moin Khan, who between them call the strategic shots for Pakistan, that proper 'cricket wickets' with some grass on them might actually suit the home team every bit as well as a dried-up river bed.

Marcus Trescothick had already failed to control one sharp lifter which lobbed safely clear of a close fielder before he was given out leg before. Then Hussain tried to hook his third ball and took it flush on the wrist. The first examination last night showed no fracture but severe bruising. He returns to the same doctor today

for a cortisone injection in his sore back and another precautionary X-ray.

The batting that followed against Saqlain and Mushtaq was
much less composed than in the first innings. Graham Thorpe,
who would captain England should Hussain be ruled out, sliced
a full-blooded drive to backward point, Mike Atherton was lbw
on the back foot and Graeme Hick, who struggled for most of
his forty-eight minutes before being last out, was bowled round
his legs aiming a sweep at a ball of the wrong length for the shot.
Alec Stewart, moving his feet decisively, alone retained some initiative in a game which did not end nearly so badly for Pakistan
as had at one time seemed likely. It would be a shame if England
have already given their best performance and Pakistan their worst.
It is possible, but the eventual conclusion of this game is that these
are well-matched sides with a firm respect for each other.

Monday, 20 November
After the first Test, in which England gave all of us a pleasant surprise by dominating the first four days and finishing rather disappointed not to win, there was an official party last night in the
Escort Gardens.

It was not the best-chosen of dates because everyone was tired,
in my case after writing when I got back to the hotel, still feeling
under the weather. I felt obliged, however, to go and did so at
about 9pm. It was a half-hour journey in a hotel car, a small
Toyota but driven by a chauffeur in a peaked cap. Some of the
journalists were only too pleased to take my car back when I
arrived, because there had been a succession of speeches around
the presentation of 'lifetime achievement awards' to several prominent Pakistan players, most of whom are brilliant cricketers but
have been alleged to have been guilty of taking bribes from bookies
to fix aspects of international matches.

There were more speeches to come when I arrived but first
there was a truly spectacular and very, very noisy firework display.
The whole scene was charming: fairy lights in the trees, carpets
on the ground, row upon row of wicker chairs on which to sit
and braziers burning to give warmth on a very cold, clear evening.

The Governor of Sind gave a hackneyed speech about the great and glorious game and its ability to unify people, slightly ironic in view of the recent decision by the Indian government to call off the tour of Pakistan which was supposed to take place when the England team leaves. Relations between the cricketers and cricket officials of the two countries are fine, but they continue to bicker and skirmish over the disputed and beautiful area of Kashmir which forms a buffer between the two countries. It has already caused one war between them since Partition, and now that both countries have nuclear bombs and missiles, everyone watches anxiously whenever the armies permanently placed either side of the border start firing at one another.

On matters of moment to cricketers, happily not of life and death, Tim Lamb spoke eloquently and formally on behalf of the England and Wales Cricket Board and Malcolm Gray, the relaxed Australian, gave a more informal speech in his role as chairman of the ICC, uttering platitudes about match-fixing but risking a joke or two and getting away with it. 'When I heard those fireworks going off I've got to tell you I thought the Indians were coming,' he said.

Thursday, 23 November
I cheered inwardly this evening soon after returning from the day's cricket at the Bagh-e-Jinnah: I passed a solid stool. It is precisely eight days since I last did so and in the intervening week I have had not only the runs, but a sore throat and stuffed-up nose. Who knows the cause? All but those of robust constitution in the press party have had some sort of tummy bug and the cold has been, as it is supposed to be, common to all. Dust or the air-conditioning in a hotel which has no windows that open are the most likely reasons for the snuffles, but whether the stomach upset is caused by food, water or germs in the air I have no idea. I have attempted to carry on as normal, having starved and slept for the first twenty-four hours of the bug. There has, of course, been work to do every day but the five hours' time difference make this the ideal part of the world from a working point of view. There is no hurry, but you don't have all night as you do in Australia and New Zealand.

The hotel could hardly be more comfortable. I have a large

enough room in which to swing a golf club, although I did knock the plastic casing of the fire warning device on the ceiling with a two-iron one night. I have repaired it and concentrated on my chipping and pitching technique since then. There is a large television with BBC World Service churning out repetitive news bulletins – America hadn't decided between Al Gore and George W. Bush when I arrived in Pakistan and they still haven't done so three weeks later – and several alternative channels, some of which show a variety of sports from round the world (including, somewhat incongruously, South African provincial cricket on the Star network) and others a mixture of films, either Bollywoods with Indians gyrating gymnastically to a background wail, or Hollywoods of various vintages.

Since the Test there has been both a Press v. Players golf match and an English Press v. Pakistan Press cricket match. We lost the first to more talented players – in my case a 4 and 3 defeat in partnership with Vic Marks against Andrew Caddick and Marcus Trescothick. They both played to their handicaps of 12. I was steady except for missing three putts within range which would have made it closer. Vic was off-colour, in the first stages of his personal dose of the Lahore collywobbles. He still managed to appear for the Press XI against what turned out to be XV of Lahore: a throwback to colonial days indeed.

The good will and hospitality of the Pakistanis is amazing. They had given each player a blue shirt and trousers for the occasion – they, of course, were in green – and the Test pitch at the Gaddafi Stadium was re-prepared for our benefit, with dressing-rooms presented clean and ready for use. We were expecting a side full of wristy stroke-players and unplayable spinners but in fact they were rather poor cricketers with very few exceptions. We took all fifteen wickets inside their allotted thirty-five overs. I claimed three for about fifteen runs, despite my first ball going for five overthrows, with a stumped, a bowled and a caught-and-bowled. We had knocked off most of the runs by the time I batted, however, and, as usual when I don't open, I could not concentrate. I made a rather undistinguished six or seven in singles before plunging forward to a ball which would have missed leg stump by about nine inches and being instantly triggered by an umpire very much on the home side.

Having suddenly taken a few wickets at that stage they were all chattering like starlings and appealing for everything and I could easily understand as I walked out, miffed, how the professionals lose their cool. Shades of Lord Tennyson telling his players in 1936/37 that they must take any bad decisions in their stride, only to explode when yet another appalling lbw was given whilst he was the non-striking batsman: 'Good Lord, man, don't tell me you're deaf as *well* as blind.' Still, we won on this occasion without recourse to the experience of Marks and Derek Pringle, who had both taken their share of the wickets.

Lahore is more orderly than it was when I last visited in 1993. The temperature has been lovely but the sun has seldom broken through the grey winter air, again an amalgam of mist, dust and exhaust fumes. Once off the fastish-moving wide roads of the new city, the old one looks much as it must have done when Kipling wrote *Kim* (1901. I know because I'm reading it). There were no motor trishaws then, of course, nor scooters, but there are still the crowded, narrow bazaars and the streets teem with donkeys and carts, ponies and traps and men in their *salwar kameez*, hurrying past the endless roadside booths. They either offer goods for sale or to repair whatever on earth might need mending, especially anything to do with transport.

Friday, 24 November

Most unexpectedly there was rain last night accompanied by thunder and lightning. This morning was wonderfully fresh and sunny; chilly at first but ideal, about 75°F, once the sun was up. The cricket was called off, so although a report of some kind had to be knocked together out of very little (never an exercise that bothers me much on tour – there is always something to talk about) there was time for some reading and advance packing. This has been as long a stay in one hotel as one gets anywhere and I am sick of it. Talking of which, I had more stomach cramps today and decided to take the Supproxin tablet which Mike Dickson gave me several days ago. Thinking I was all but over the bug, I had not taken it because antibiotics kill one's own antibodies as well as the invader. But enough is enough.

Saturday, 25 November

Feeling fine again, I played an enjoyable four-ball at the gymkhana with Mike Selvey, David (Toff) Lloyd and John Etheridge before watching the last two sessions of England's match with the PCB XI, which they dominated but, because of the loss of the second day, did not win. Matthew Hoggard bowled exceptionally well again but Ian Salisbury, sadly, was again innocuous. The ground, formerly Lawrence Gardens, now called Bagh-e-Jinnah (Jinnah Park) is lovely, with mature trees which were wondrously washed by the rain, their leaves, hitherto caked with thick dust, shining again.

Sunday, 26 November

The bus for Faisalabad was due to leave at 9am for those journalists, like me, who book their travel in winter through John Snow, once of Sussex and England, now making a good living out of looking after the air and hotel bookings of both the media and private clients wanting to support England overseas. By the time all the bags were aboard it was ten o'clock but a delay of half an hour by the experience of past tours is miraculously punctual.

The driver was intent on getting to Faisalabad as quickly as possible and to hell with anyone in his way on the mainly narrow road. His 'luxury coach' was absolutely filthy. It stank like a drain and the grime was visible. The two-and-a-half-hour journey through the clamour and squalor of outer Lahore took us on a grey morning on to the flat plain of the Punjab. With the well-tended and irrigated fields of vegetables, the landscape was much like East Anglia, except for the frequent brick kilns and the rather different look of the market towns through which one passed. The illiterate workers of Pakistan really do have a miserable life and so do their beasts of burden. The luckiest lot in this land, apart from the wealthy and educated, are the milk-producing cows, sheep and goats, who generally seem to have somewhere to graze, even if it is only a fenced-off portion of the grass in the middle of the passing traffic.

Wednesday, 29 November
Second Test (first day of five): Pakistan have scored 243 for 5.
A riveting opening day of the Faisalabad Test concluded with the
outstanding partnership between Yousuf Youhana and Moin Khan,
which restored the advantage Pakistan had gained when Moin
won the toss. England, with Ashley Giles again to the fore, com-
peted so well in the first two sessions of the match that they came
close to taking command of the game, but one close lbw appeal
against Moin before he had scored went against them and a second,
when he had made only 18 of his eventually dominating 57 not
out, did so too. It was as plumb as they come and it changed the
fortunes of the day.

England were obliged to start again this morning having at one
stage had a genuine chance of bowling their opponents out in a
day. It was limited to 75 overs by the unnecessary fussiness of the
umpires over the so-called bad light at half past four and by
England's slow over-rate, itself the result of Nasser Hussain's restless changes of field and a six-minute delay for excessive noise
during the first hour when someone, presumably accidentally,
turned on Pakistan's version of 'C'mon Aussie, C'mon' so loudly
that it reached even higher decibels than the relentless horn-
blowing. Steve Bucknor, the respected Jamaican umpire, wisely
stopped the game until the din stopped. He said he had heard
worse noise – in Dacca, Antigua, even Auckland – but that music
over loudspeakers during play was unfair on cricketers and umpires
alike.

Deafening though their clamour was, it was an ingenuous and
excited local crowd which filled at least three-quarters of this
neat, circular ground on a mercifully clear, sunny day. Their enthusiasm was contagious but it might have contributed to the haste,
and sometimes the carelessness, with which Pakistan's batsmen
proceeded to try to take advantage of their good fortune in getting first use of a pitch on which the ball has spun a little more
sharply, and bounced more generously, than it did in Lahore. The
level head, both mentally and technically speaking, of the per-
sistently impressive Youhana came to their rescue not a moment
too soon.

Giles was and will remain the key bowler but England paid for their reluctance to send for an extra finger-spinner last week. They would have been more combative still had Peter Such, Phil Tufnell, or Robert Croft – even Jason Brown or Graeme Swann – been playing instead of either Andrew Caddick or Darren Gough. It is a different game on the subcontinent and although they might yet become dangerous if the top of the bare pitch goes later in the match, even match-winning fast bowlers are innocuous in these conditions.

Ian Salisbury, rightly preferred to Andrew Flintoff, the only available extra batsman, again let himself down to an extent by bowling one short ball an over. He only bowled from over the wicket and was reluctant to use his dangerous googly; but here, as at Lahore, he was denied an early lbw, this time when he hit Moin on the knee in line with middle and off when he was right back on the stumps in the over after Pakistan's fifth wicket had gone down. A leg-break, the ball might conceivably have missed the off stump but there was no such doubt when Giles also hit Moin, then 18, on the back leg with a ball which pitched on the wicket and would have hit the off stump. If the umpire, the seemingly calm and collected Mian Aslam, remains consistent, England will not complain and the game will last longer, but it is hard on the bowlers.

Giles, wheeling accurately away, mainly from round the wicket, with small but not elaborate variations, was a credit to himself as he has been throughout the tour and he must have given heart to all those struggling finger-spinners in the county game. He has proved himself already to be an accomplished craftsman, which says much for his ability and character but also something for Warwickshire's policy of giving him deliberate assistance at one end of the Edgbaston pitches. So long as these things are not overdone they help to keep a badly needed balance in the game. So, of course, does cricket in Asia provide a welcome contrast to the pace-dominated game elsewhere.

The new-ball bowlers still had their moments during the ear-splitting first hour when Saaed Anwar played his usual enterprising, wristy game and Shahid Afridi his rather more reckless one. In the seventh over, immediately after the lacuna, Afridi was hit on the upper arm by Gough, pulled the following short ball for four through mid-on but then drove at the length of the next one and edged it to third slip.

Gough tried similarly to throw the gauntlet down to Anwar and Salim Elahi but they rose to the challenge with better judgement and many a fine stroke. The spearhead had to retreat with 1 for 38 from his first six overs and the total had already reached 78 when Giles came on for the sixteenth over. Off his sixth ball he missed a firmly driven return catch from Anwar, then 46. Imagine the relief of Giles when in his fourth over, with lunch approaching, he beat Anwar sufficiently in the air for a whipped on-drive to be spooned to mid-wicket. Two balls later he claimed Inzamam too as a tentative stroke spun back on to his stumps.

Elahi is a good, compact player but something of an obsessive cutter. He looked a candidate for the arm ball but it was in fact to an orthodox delivery that he drew back and carved to cover point just as he and Youhana seemed to be settling into a substantial partnership. When Craig White, who again looked the most dangerous of the quicker bowlers, produced a late reverse inswinger to hurry inside Abdur Razzaq's intended off-drive, England had reached their highest point.

Once into his stride Moin began to enjoy himself with that natural hand–eye co-ordination which makes his batting so dangerous. Youhana was impeccable at the other end, driving powerfully wide of mid-on when the chances came and playing everything with the full face and his body behind the line. By the close he had been batting for more than four hours without fault; the Catholic respected by the Muslims around him; the coolest cricketer in the side and a future captain.

The present leader, Moin, lifted White with perfect timing over mid-on for six and reached his fifty with another, straight-driven off Giles. The past one, Wasim Akram, was not yet needed, happy to admire the 22-carat gold plaque with which his team-mates had presented him in honour of his 100th Test cap.

Sunday, 3 December
Yet another unjust decision against the England captain, Nasser Hussain, in a second Test that was drawn yesterday in Faisalabad thanks to a stoical innings by Mike Atherton, has inevitably

rekindled the debate about the proper role of the television umpire. These matters are not best judged in the heat of the moment but it is a fact that Hussain's rating as a Test batsman has plummeted alarmingly this year in no small part because of a series of unfortunate – and, as he phrased it yesterday, 'honest' – umpiring errors.

Coming in with a game to save, he had made a fidgety start to what for himself and his side was an important innings when he was given out caught behind by the Pakistan captain, Moin Khan, from a ball bowled by the tall off-spinner Arshad Khan which clearly missed the bat and struck only the pad.

I say 'clearly' but the truth, of course, is that it was *crystal* clear only after several slow-motion replays had confirmed one's instinctive doubt. In the first innings Hussain had been given lbw to a ball which hit the bottom of his bat before going low into his pad. It was as clear as daylight on the replays but to Steve Bucknor, standing some twenty-two yards away in light that was starting to fade, with a noisy and excited crowd in the background, it was obviously a blur: otherwise he would have said 'Not out'. To him it seemed only that the ball had kept low and made a direct hit.

The double point here is that Bucknor was in the best position – better than any camera – to tell whether the ball would have hit the stumps; but also that it was, self-evidently, difficult for him to hear the nick and even, apparently, to spot the deflection. John Gayleard, producer for Sky Television of TWI's wonderfully thorough coverage of this series, admits that the cameras are rarely perfectly positioned and that they can, sometimes, give a false impression. Nor will he guarantee that the innovative three lines down the pitch, used by both Sky and Channel 4 to indicate where the ball has pitched, are precisely in line with the stumps.

Any idea that the third umpire should adjudicate on lbws, therefore, should be firmly resisted, unless the umpire in the middle wishes to consult him, on the possibility of the ball having hit the bat. Decisions on where the ball pitched, whether a batsman has played a shot and whether the ball has hit his pad in line with the stumps (as it must if he has indeed tried to play a shot) are all best reserved for the men in the middle.

Where there is now a case for consultation is on the notoriously difficult bat/pad decisions and, perhaps, also on the snicks (or otherwise) to the wicket-keeper. Generally speaking – but by no means every time – television replays lend added evidence to caught-behind decisions. The Channel 4 'snickometer' remains, as far as I can tell, in the realms of gimmickry, however, and until it can more quickly or definitely prove whether the bat had made contact with the ball, its evidence should be ignored. The principle should be, surely, that when an umpire in the middle feels he can better make a fairer decision by recourse to replays – as is now the case with line decisions and half-volley catches – he should ask for guidance.

Careers are at stake – of umpires no less than of players – and it is in everyone's interest that justice should wherever possible be done and be seen to be done. It is by now, alas, a truism that by appealing for everything players really only deserve the mistakes from which they sometimes suffer. On lbws at least, the umpires in the middle must continue to do their best and cricketers to accept their decisions as the law and the spirit of the law demand. Hussain took his latest setback with mature resignation again yesterday.

Monday, 4 December

It has been a long week here but not through any fault of the locals or of the Serena Hotel, which is a delightful piece of architecture. The hotel was built on only two storeys about ten years ago in rust-coloured brick around beautiful gardens with an abundance of slightly dusty roses. It reminds me of Fitzwilliam College, Cambridge. My room – 111, easily remembered – must be cool in summer but it is dark and jolly cold at night; definitely a pyjama-and-two-blanket temperature. It looks on to a courtyard with a little pond where the great grey kites came for a drink one afternoon. There are hoopoos too on the cricket ground behind, and wagtails which make a pleasant change from the jackdaws and kites one sees all the time.

There is a cold, small pool but also two tennis courts and a squash court. Also an interesting-looking table game played by the Pakistanis with a slate and sliding counters aimed into pockets by hand. Abdur Razzaq, a charming young fellow, looked to be the master player. I had one game of tennis on the day before the Test, whilst Mike Atherton and Graham Thorpe were enjoying what looked like a ding-dong battle on the other court. Since then, apart from one early-morning circuit of the just about playable nine-hole golf course beside the cricket stadium with Mike Dickson this morning, it has been all work and trying to find some reasonably appetising food in the evenings. If only I liked curry, or chillies and garlic liked me, it would actually be excellent food. Still, home cooking awaits once the deciding Test in Karachi has been played.

Thursday, 7 December
National Stadium (first day of five; Pakistan won toss): Pakistan have scored 292 for 3.
Three Pakistan wickets for 64 in the first 23 overs of the match gave England the sort of start to the final Test that sides dream about when they have lost the toss on a flat pitch. The reality of their situation by the end of the first day, however, was that they will have to find at least two batsmen to play as well as Inzamam-ul-Haq and Yousuf Youhana did yesterday – that is to say very well indeed – if they are to make this the eighteenth draw in thirty-five matches since Test cricket was first played at the National Stadium. Pakistan have won the other seventeen and barring gross negligence they can be utterly confident that the unbeaten record will continue.

They have the chance today to build the sort of mountainous score which by itself creates pressure on opponents no matter how benign the pitch. By the time England get their chance, moreover, it might not be quite such a pleasure to bat on as it was yesterday. The ball turned and it also swung when it was new, as it tends to in the greater humidity of Karachi, where sea breezes give bowlers the sort of assistance which bare pitches like this one invariably do not.

England, well as they bowled for most of the day and excellently as they fielded throughout, almost certainly waved goodbye to their dream of beating Pakistan away when another umpiring misjudgement, again pivotal to the fortunes of the day, went against them. The reprieved batsman was the Maharajah himself, Inzamam.

The somewhat unlikely bowler was Marcus Trescothick, purveyor of gentle swingers in one-day matches for Somerset, who took only two first-class wickets in 53 overs for his county last season but played a genuinely useful role yesterday and gained his first Test wicket with what he modestly described as a wide half-volley. If he can develop a 'golden arm' he will prove an even greater asset to the side than he already is.

He had every right to feel that he legitimately claimed a second victim, this time with a floater of full length which wobbled late on to Inzamam's instep on the popping crease and would certainly have bowled him. Inzamam, four not out at the time in only the 22nd over of the morning, said later that he had got a faint inside edge, but carefully examined slow-motion replays showed no touch. What is more, the umpire, Nazir Junior, told the bowler that in his opinion the ball would have missed the leg stump. If so, it was only because it would have hit the middle one.

The pattern for the series seems to have been that the 'home' umpires give everything not out, at least until they start to warm up by about the fourth day. They seem almost to be under military instruction not to be as trigger-happy as their counterparts of old. Again, so long as they are consistent in turning appeals down for both sides, complaint will be muted. Far better this extreme caution than the opposite; but it is hard on bowlers. Had some Pakistani umpires of the pre-satellite television era been standing in this series there would have been positive results one way or the other at both Lahore and Faisalabad. As for the Duncan Fletcher 'referral' proposal, if it had been applied yesterday a beautiful innings would have been nipped in the bud.

Luckily for a disappointingly small crowd, Inzamam played himself in with a responsibility not shown by two of the youngsters above him in the order and played for the rest of the day with 'unperturbed pace, deliberate speed, majestic instancy'. He and Youhana have established themselves as the engine room of a Pakistan team which is being shrewdly reshaped by Javed Miandad, and their colleagues were again indebted to the class and calm both of them exuded from the early stages of a partnership which started ten minutes before lunch and seldom looked like being interrupted.

Inzamam became the highest scorer in Test cricket this year

and by the close last night had reached 1,044 runs from eighteen innings. He scored 86 and 138 in Pakistan's last Test in Karachi in March and this was his twelfth Test hundred and second against England. Yet Youhana, technically and temperamentally already Inzamam's equal, has been even more prolific in this series. Having warmed up with three thirties in the one-day internationals he has scored 124, 77 and now a second century in three innings, reached with a force past gully off Andrew Caddick with the second new ball shortly before the close of what turned out to be a great day for Pakistan.

Apart from one purple passage by Inzamam in mid-afternoon, when he surged towards his first fifty with three offside fours in an over from Ashley Giles, it was Youhana whose quick feet created the scoring opportunities, as opposed simply to taking them as they were offered. He hit thirteen fours and a glorious straight-driven six off Giles in his fifth Test hundred, while Inzamam, who saw no need to lift the ball above a smoothly grassed outfield, had hit eighteen fours by the close.

Despite the lost toss, it had all started so promisingly for England after an exchange of teams that revealed an unchanged England side again, but two surprises in Pakistan's: the dropping of Wasim Akram to make way for the return of the dangerously determined Waqar Younis (officially Wasim was withdrawn because of a back spasm) and the inclusion of Shahid Afridi despite his omission from the original squad of fourteen.

Saeed Anwar was lbw in Darren Gough's third over when half-forward to a ball which cut back to hit him in line with middle and leg before Imran Nazir and Salim Elahi put on 38, mixing some fine shots with rash ones. Imran drove a catch to short extra; Elahi dragged a drive on to his stumps off the inside edge. These were rewards for sensible bowling to a full length by all four of England's swing bowlers but the nearest the spinners came to a wicket was when Youhana, then 19, cut the generally tidy Ian Salisbury in the air past Hussain's hands at slip. It was the sort of brilliant reaction catch that Colin Cowdrey might have taken and then, literally, pocketed. He would have relished the batting of Inzamam and Youhana yesterday and appreciated the black arm-bands which England wore in his memory.

Monday, 11 December

An extraordinary day and a very long one. I was up at dawn in order to pack most of my belongings for tomorrow's departure home from Karachi. The Test match looked destined for a quiet end and a third successive draw. That would have made it the eighteenth draw in twenty-one Tests in Pakistan between these two countries.

I got to the ground a little late (well, this *was* going to be a draw) because Bilal Ahmad had agreed to take me to see a maker of cane furniture, following an abortive journey last night when the shop was shut. (Hardly surprisingly, because it was 9pm by the time that I had finished and dispatched my report.) Bilal is a friendly, bearded little fellow who says he has been trained in hospitality and is therefore there to serve at all times. He has worked tirelessly as the local travel agent assigned to the press party – actually only to half of it, but he and his colleague Khalid have been only too happy to help anyone who has asked. He took me in one of the hotel buses, which are excruciatingly uncomfortable and may be responsible for the fact that my back has seized up as never before, to a shop down an alleyway past goats, sheep and local men hurrying about their business on a hot morning.

The furniture was of the highest quality and the prices offered were as for Pakistanis, as Bilal put it, not as for tourists. The shipping and duties will no doubt bump up the eventual price to much what I would pay, if not a fair bit more, for imports to England, but having gone to the trouble I hardly hesitated before making an order for our new Garden Room, roughly equating, I hope, to what Judy had specified over the telephone. Besides, I really didn't want to disappoint the furniture-maker: he was so desperate for a sale and simple to please.

Listening to the commentary in Urdu on the slow crawl to the National Stadium through heavy traffic, it was evident that Ashley Giles had got the night-watchman, Saqlain Mushtaq, early, which was essential if England were to have even the remotest chance of pulling off a win. Two more fell before lunch but it still looked odds-on the draw and even when Pakistan lost their last four wickets in the first 17 overs of the afternoon, all of us in the press box felt that although England now obviously had a chance of scoring four runs an over to get the 176 they needed to win, the strong probability was that Pakistan would slow things down sufficiently for the light to run out.

Well, they did slow it down, by every device they knew. Out and out cheating, as opposed to pragmatic gamesmanship, just is not possible any more with independent umpires and intensive, worldwide television coverage, but the umpires, absurdly, were not able to apply the five-run penalties prescribed in the new laws of cricket because the ICC in their foolishness had extracted from them anything likely to be controversial in Test cricket. Yet the changes had been specifically designed for Test cricket. I despair sometimes at the feebleness of our administrators.

Pakistan bowled eleven overs in the first hour, twelve in the second of England's innings. They are supposed to average fifteen an hour, but this still gave England a better chance than the one they had had in Trinidad in 1990 when Desmond Haynes managed to waste so much time that the West Indies bowled eight overs in one hour and eventually the light ran out.

Mike Atherton, whose first-innings century had made the game safe and made sure that the tour was going to be deemed a success whatever happened on the last day, played some brilliant shots in the early overs, but the loss of three wickets quite quickly left Graham Thorpe and Graeme Hick with much still to do. They played superbly, running between the wickets so well that at one point they got a single off ten balls in succession. Gradually, gradually, the target was hunted down. But it was getting very dark indeed when Hick slogged and missed at Waqar Younis. Nasser Hussain came out and wasted no time in hitting out at everything, knowing that soon it would be pitch dark. The luck and the moral force were with him as edges flew everywhere. Thorpe kept on finding the gaps and the umpires remained firm in keeping the players on the field, although, as anyone who has played evening cricket in England knows, it is harder for fielders to see the ball in twilight than batsmen who are well set. The last boundary of the day went through extra cover without a fielder moving. They might all have been blind, but Moin Khan, who had been protesting for ages that the match should end, had been hoist by his own petard. (Of course any Test captain of any country would have tried to slow it down just as he had.) A final snick from Thorpe's inside edge and it was all over. Two batsmen leaping for joy in the darkness and a warm glow for everyone who had followed England on the tour and admired their spirit, determination and capacity for hard work.

Naturally it meant a hard night for the journalists. After the interviews at the Stadium and the bumpy ride back to the Pearl Continental I received my orders from David Chappell, the Sports Editor. It amounted to three pieces for tomorrow's paper and another two of large proportion for the following day because I would be travelling and unable to deliver them. One by one I churned them out, trying to do justice to everyone and everything. Michael Henderson had mercifully unburdened himself of a couple of spare beers – apart from our end-of-tour dinner on Saturday, the first alcohol for weeks – and they kept my throat from drying up but there was no time for more than an accompanying omelette. The last article made its way miraculously through the modem and the mobile phone at 3.15am. On the last tour I would have to have dictated the copy in a pool of sweat and in days gone by it would have meant a journey to the telex office.

I set my alarm for 7.30 and rang Judy before putting the lights out, blissfully happy to have all the work done and at the thought of being home tomorrow.

Two

The Second Leg

Wednesday, 31 January 2001

I started packing for Sri Lanka today but also responded to a last-minute request to provide a brief imaginary commentary for a full-length feature film with Pauline Collins in the starring role, to be called *Mrs Caldicott's Cabbage War*. It certainly has an arresting title and the brief snatch of film I saw at Pinewood Studios to give me an idea of what was wanted looked promising. Terence Rigby, playing Mr Caldicott as pompously as possible, was listening to the start of ball-by-ball commentary in his kitchen before leaving to watch the Test match whilst his frustrated wife (Pauline) was getting his precious sandwiches ready.

My job was to provide the background commentary, which I did from my head, imagining Gough getting Steve Waugh out in one of the Tests this summer. Easy, really, but is it wishful thinking?

Pinewood Studios on a rainy day was as far from one's image of Hollywood as could be imagined: it looks like a run-down and long out-of-date industrial estate, with a hotch-potch of tatty buildings ranging from 1930-ish prefabs to portakabins. It obviously works, though, and everyone knows that creativity is possible in the most insalubrious surroundings.

Thursday, 8 February

The first day of straight match reporting felt like a long one after the inevitably fitful sleep following my arrival in Colombo. It was hot but not impossibly so watching the first day of the match at the P. Saravanamuttu Stadium, sitting under the asbestos roof of a Press Stand liberally endowed with electric fans. The view is pleasant to the Wimbledon-like ivy-clad scoreboard and a typical variety of lush Sri Lankan trees, but one has to shut out the stained concrete water tower and a block of yellow flats straight out of one of the grottiest European estates. They have plans to smarten up the ground to get Test cricket back to the club, the Tamil Union CC where MCC used to call in for a match to break the sea voyage to Australia (and the Aussies vice versa). There is a nice dedication on the wall of our stand to the past hero M. Sathasivam: 'The bat was a magic wand in his hand.'

My memories of the Taj Samudra are of a rather pleasant hotel with a torpid atmosphere governed by the heavy air seeping over the coconut palms from the sea. The snag this time is that few of the bedrooms have been refurbished for a long time (probably since the place was built): the carpets are stained and the bathrooms have a long-outmoded mosaic decor. What is more, I had been given a room on the city side, where the choice is either to open the window to let in steamy, mosquito-laden air and the din of hooters, enhanced at dawn by muezzins who put their Lahore counterparts in the shade, or to leave it shut and suffer air-conditioning which is reasonably adaptable as to temperature but has a rather unhealthy scent.

I made a determined attempt to change to a room on the seaward side this evening, making frequent calls to the front desk in between writing my report. Eventually someone came up with the key to a door almost directly opposite, which seemed too good to be true and was. It was a smaller room on the sea side but even as the porter closed the door after helping me move all my clobber – a laborious business since my belongings were already quite scattered – I realised that the windows would not open. So I had a distant view of the sea but no ozone. Having ascertained that they had been deliberately stuck fast to prevent anyone from jumping out (an obsession with hotels the world over) I was eventually conducted at about 10pm to a third room, back on the city side but bigger and with a view over the swimming pool and a large outdoor balcony. This one reeked at first of cigarette smoke, but I opened the French doors wide, risking mosquito bites and resolved not to be a wimp. There was room for me to swing a golf club and I practised shots with a bag full of soft rainbow balls, as usual in these circumstances convincing myself that my swing is now perfection itself.

Saturday, 10 February
A day off already! But it is always six days of work a week on tour and by no means all Saturdays are free, so I have learned to take them when I can. I went for a swim at Dehiwala beach and had a beer and a piece of grilled tuna for lunch before coming back to read by the pool for a while before having the traditional sundowner at the old Galle Face hotel with Selvey. The large orange ball dutifully plopped over the horizon but there was no green flash. Clearly I should have been on pink gin rather than 'Three Fountains draught'. Sitting on the lawn immediately beside the sea one could see a rather disconcerting-looking fixed gun on the nearest high roof-top (several High Commission offices are nearby) and the whole area was swarming with police. Why, I asked one. 'Because our President is going to see our Prime Minister this evening.'

There was a nice gesture from the team management tonight: the team entertained the press to supper and beer at The Cricketer's Café. All very relaxed and convivial. I was placed next to Duncan Fletcher with Nasser Hussain on my other side. Nasser asked me whether I thought Graeme Hick or Michael Vaughan should take the one disputed batting place. He said he thought Hick's weight of stroke could be valuable on the slow pitches here but I said that my vote would go to Vaughan because he has shown his mettle several times already in tight situations. Duncan was a lot more forthcoming than usual: *in vino veritas*.

Sunday, 11 February
The final day at Colombo and England won well. The 165-run margin would have been greater but for the umpires bending over backwards to give the batsmen the benefit of the tiniest doubt sometimes. No evening out tonight, alas, because I was asked for an extra piece on the ICC's decision to make all Tests in future

part of a World Championship. It is spurious and there is going to be no respite now for anyone on the international circuit, be he player or scribe.

Monday, 12 February

One of the depressing evenings tonight. The hotel between Galle and Matara that we reached at about 5pm is small and on the primitive side. After dark the dim lighting and dark wood got everyone down, especially as the food in the restaurant was a poor buffet – tepid and greasy – and there were mosquitoes everywhere. My room has a lovely view of blue sea and fishing boats but the sea itself looks too shallow and murky to swim in (and the guide books don't advise it). I had consoled myself with ten lengths – 200 strokes – of a pleasant enough L-shaped pool, watched by a few East European holiday-makers, but Henderson at his glummest announced on his arrival at the bar that the first thing he had seen from his room was a large snake slithering out of the pool. The vision of it towelling down and putting on sunglasses and sun-tan cream was briefly amusing but I wonder now whether I shall be diving in before breakfast as I had planned. There are smoke coils in the rooms to keep the mossies at bay but I know they tend to give me a headache; and the sheets on the thin bed are the size of large handkerchiefs. Nor was writing easy, with no desk and a mobile phone signal that came and went. I managed to file to my relief after about fifteen aborts.

The drive earlier in the day to Weligama near the southernmost tip of the island was a pleasant length – five hours – but colourful and only occasionally hair-raising. Everyone on this leg of the trip is travelling in twos in cars supplied by the Travel Club at the Taj, by pre-arrangement with John Snow. Colin Bateman has the delicate task of pairing off compatible journalists and placed me with Selvey, presumably because we both have golf clubs, although Mike eschewed the chance to play this morning and I did so instead with the club pro, Nandasinha, a marvellous little player of well over sixty with spindly, bandy legs. It was still cool and misty and the course was in good condition, with several new greens and the rest due to be reconstructed over the next two years under Donald Steele's guidance.

Tuesday, 13 February

It's amazing how morale rises with daylight, especially in glorious weather like this. I duly woke with a headache after a restless night but I don't seem to have been bitten and I had a pleasant swim before an excellent breakfast with not a snake in sight. Only monkeys in the bread-fruit trees. After looking at the Test ground – magnificent setting by the grass and stone ramparts of the old Dutch fort – and talking to Craig White at the player's much grander hotel, I am ready to write on my balcony in the dusk.

Wednesday, 14 February

The writing took far, far longer than anticipated. The worst thing that can befall a journalist on tour, bar illness or accident, occurred when I had finally finished the piece after the computer had frequently frozen, obliging me to switch off all power and start again. I realised after a while that the freezing was due to moving the machine in order to shift my position, since it is impossible to find a comfortable one for writing in the dimly-lit room. Therefore I had to finish the work stuck rigidly in one position for fear of moving the laptop. At last all was ready and turning in relief for the mobile I caught the wire with my leg and sent the computer crashing three feet from the bed to the tile floor. All went absolutely dead. I tried to keep calm; had a shower; poured myself a small malt whisky and began writing the story afresh in longhand in order to dictate it. Most of what I had written came back to me but halfway through I switched the computer on again just in case. To my intense relief the screen lit up and I was able to join the rest of the journalists holed up in this outpost for what remained of their fish supper at a local café.

It really is a delightfully unsophisticated area. Fish is the staple diet, caught every night from the narrow boats with their high prows (or by the single stick fishermen perched on poles driven into the shallow water and hooking their catch on the end of rods). It is then sold by the roadside and cooked at night, much as it is in Greek tavernas, only far cheaper because the sea is far better stocked, mainly with seer and tuna.

I swam twice today at the beautiful Paradise beach, a few miles east of Weligama, driven by the eccentric Cyril with many a close shave guaranteed as he weaves slowly about the road, never changing gear unless he absolutely has to do so. Later he had to take us back to Galle for another press conference at the Lighthouse. Duncan Fletcher was rather mean, I felt, in justifying their decision not to give Jason Brown a game.

Thursday, 15 February

A long, muggy, humid day, ending in a tropical storm. Ashley Giles aggravated an old Achilles heel injury and the local side recovered from a bad start by batting very well. Once again I had technical problems and it was dark by the time I left the ground in pouring rain.

Tuesday, 20 February

After a few days of having to write my copy in longhand – illegible longhand most of the time – I had the luxury of typing it instead today on a new – or newish – Dell computer, kindly brought out for me by Stephen Brenckley of the *Sunday Independent*. How the old one failed is really a mystery. Simon Wilde – alias Oscar – of the *Sunday Times*, whose own News International machine has also seized up, helpfully took mine to the Dell shop in Colombo where he was collecting his own after a service. Apart from regularly freezing, mine had recently refused to come to life at all. Yet when the man in the shop turned it on it apparently started up as if it had never failed anyone in its life. Three or four times it did the same. Conclusion: nothing wrong with it. 'I don't believe it,' I said to Simon and switched on in his presence. Sure enough the opposite of the Midas touch applied: the machine tried to start, spluttered and died. I begin to think I impart some electrical impulse inimical to all computers.

It was really oppressively hot watching the nets at Galle this morning. I spent ten minutes with the delightfully keen and ambitious Paul Nixon, who talked with guileless animation about what he has learned from his first two tours at the age of thirty and his hopes of taking over from Alec Stewart as England's wicket-keeper/batsman. I shall write about it tomorrow but today's job was the match preview, tapped out in my muggy, lofty room overlooking the coral reef after which this hotel is named. It is a big improvement on the previous one but as I write the ants go to and fro across the wall in front of me in their thousands and I am forever scratching some insect bite or other. This is, after all, the tropics, and you have to pay more for your hotel than we are doing for this one to be isolated from the realities and discomforts. Insects abound, the vegetation is wonderfully lush and there is a slight air of danger about every step one takes.

I went swimming today close to the area where a tourist drowned last week: I was looking, with goggles on and earplugs in, for the 100-year-old turtle I had seen over the reef from a glass-bottomed boat yesterday with Chris Broad, Michael Henderson, Mike Walters and Tim Abrahams, but could only see a few rainbow and parrot fish. Tomorrow I shall be warier still, because Derek Pringle reported seeing a stingray the size of a coffee table. Even walking along the street has hazards less obvious than the swaying lorries and the Leyland Lanka buses with their black exhaust fumes. A little man in a sarong came wheedling up to establish my nationality before saying that he could supply anything I wanted. Did I, for example, like girls? Yes, but not the sort he was about to offer. I sped away disdainfully before he could offer boys instead, but there is no doubt that he would have done.

Tuesday, 20 February
Andrew Caddick has played in every Test in the recent period of England success under Nasser Hussain and Duncan Fletcher. He and Darren Gough have opened the bowling together in the last fifteen Tests, Caddick taking forty-nine wickets while Gough has had fifty-eight. Yet, unless there is a last-minute change of heart, England are planning to ignore the trusted American theory that 'if it ain't broke, don't fix it' by leaving out Caddick, with his nasty bounce and hostile mien, when they take on Sri Lanka tomorrow in the first Test on the spacious ground set beneath the ramparts of the massive sixteenth-century fort.

It is hard to believe that the Sri Lankans will be more apprehensive about Graeme Hick or Michael Vaughan getting a mountain of runs against them than they would have been about Caddick with the new ball, for all his three wickets at 94 runs each in Pakistan. Ever since the tour started, however, Hussain and Fletcher have been expecting a dustbowl at Galle, based on South Africa's experience here in the most recent Test on the ground last summer.

In fact the pitch, prepared by Jayananda Warnaweera, whose dubiously bowled off-breaks did much to beat England in 1993, has been liberally watered, but there is no doubt that its grass covering is sparse, nor that the little mosaics of earth below are crusty. Despite the regular recent evening thunderstorms in this area, a weather pattern that the BBC forecaster Philip Eden expects to continue, the sun is so hot by day that the moisture rapidly evaporates. Having anticipated difficult turning pitches in the first two Tests in Pakistan and been deceived by appearances, England would do well to be cautious here, but this time expectation seems to be confirmed by appearance. The conclusion has to be that the pitch will turn almost immediately and become increasingly difficult for batsmen.

Both Muttiah Muralitharan and Ashley Giles are fit to play. Whereas Murali has 303 Test wickets and turns the ball as far as any finger-spinner ever has, it would be unreasonable to expect too much of Giles on the basis of one outstanding series in Pakistan. Yet it is on him and Robert Croft that England are pinning their hopes of winning here, if indeed they are not rather more concerned with not losing, biding their time for different conditions at Kandy and Colombo.

Murali has taken twenty-five wickets in five innings in Galle Tests but still has a problem with 'a little joint in his groin that has become damaged due to overuse', as the Sri Lankan physiotherapist, Alex Kontouri, expresses it. He has been advised to cut down on practice between matches in order to ease the strain that he puts on his slim but agile body, although the pain he felt in his left leg in South Africa and his right in New Zealand, the result of the same injury, occurred on both occasions when he was fielding.

Giles admits he was worried last Thursday when he came off the field with his permanently stiff left Achilles tendon 'sorer than normal'. To his and the rest of the team's relief, however, he has recovered well and he now feels, as also does the coach, that to return to his form in Pakistan he needs to try to forget his subconscious fear of overstretching the weak tendon and concentrate on bowling. His other problem, apart from the difficulty of keeping a grip on the ball in the intense heat when hands, trousers and shirt are all soaking and there is nothing on which to dry the ball, is to find a gap in England's intensive future programme to give the injury the long rest it needs.

Hick's calf strain has recovered sufficiently for him to continue, barring any late change of heart about Caddick, at number six. This is obviously an important match for his future, as it will be for Vaughan's, if he plays. Sri Lanka are also contemplating playing seven batsmen, meaning that they, too, would have to use two occasional off-spinners in Russell Arnold and the 35-year-old Aravinda de Silva. The latter has looked increasingly vulnerable around his off-stump against the quicker bowlers, but if he plays it is likely to be at five, following the dashing Jayasuriya; his patient opening partner, Atapattu, who made a mere 54 of an opening stand of 193 against South Africa here last July; the gifted Sangakarra and the accomplished Jayawardene. After some harrowing experiences against South Africa's fast bowlers, the Sri Lankan batsmen will be much happier in their own conditions.

The problem of poorly attended Test matches in this country has been miraculously solved by the happy coincidence that it is still winter in England and that Sri Lanka is a wonderful place for a holiday. More than 5,000 England supporters have arrived to fill every hotel bed east, west and north of the lush and sunlit port which attracted the maritime empires of Portugal, Holland and Britain. The fervent hope is that they will have fun but behave themselves and that the British government's decision on Monday to ban the LTTE as a terrorist organisation will not, for the first time, make cricket a target for terrorism.

Saturday, 24 February

Judy's birthday and in a week she will be on her way here. By then all the players' wives will have returned home after their romantic stay at The Lighthouse, which seems much the best hotel in this area. Still, apart from the ants crawling everywhere in my room and the lukewarm 'hot' water, which hardly matters except when it comes to shaving in the mornings, our hotel is fine at under half the cost. Rather than sweltering in the stuffy little press box I had the luxury, this being the day of relaxation, of watching the Test on television from my room this morning, then going down to the Fort. I got to the other side of the high stone walls in time to see Marcus Trescothick reach his maiden Test hundred: a wonderful moment for him and for English cricket because he is going to get many, many more.

Dinner – at a very second-rate restaurant – with Tim de Lisle, who has been here for a few days, mixing a visit to the Test with fixing things for the new *Wisden* website. If anyone can make a success of it, he will, with his clear mind. He manages to be both imaginative and pragmatic.

Sunday, 25 February
England are in a pretty pickle in the first Test and it will need much more luck than they have had so far and probably another great rearguard innings by Michael Atherton to bale them out. All Trescothick's good work was undone today by good spin bowling, a dusty pitch, dodgy umpiring and brilliant catching.

Tuesday, 27 February
Back to Colombo after the tempestuous Test in Galle. Umpiring controversies have overshadowed the result, another innings victory for Sri Lanka. It has been an exhausting last two days on which I have written six different articles for *The Times*, having been woken by David Chappell at 3am on Monday morning to be told that Sir Donald Bradman had died. I had only finished my Test stuff at 12.30 and was in deep sleep for once when the phone rang. Last night I finished at about the same time after pieces on the match, the umpiring and another on the Don.

The next few days should be quieter and Cyril managed to get Mike Selvey and me back to Colombo in one piece, despite umpteen near-collisions with pedestrians, cyclists and the big, bullying, exhaust-belching buses. All the journalists in the John Snow group have been given executive rooms this time at the Taj Sumudra and they are of a different standard altogether from anything on the tour so far. I can plug this machine into a square-pinned plug; the lighting is good enough for me to see what I am doing; I can have a bath; and the bed is big. No feather pillows or mosquito nets, mind you. My only dilemma now is whether to open the windows tonight: this morning, actually: it's past two o'clock after dinner at The Gallery and an animated but good-natured argument with Mike Atherton in the bar about what he believes to be the worthlessness of county cricket. I see his point, of course, but he views it all from far too narrow a perspective.

Earlier Duncan Fletcher had come up for a chat about my criticism of England's batting. He thinks sweeping and cutting are the only feasible strokes against Muralitharan. (I had said that the batsmen were a little too obsessed with sweeping.) He was very convincing about the value of the sweep if it is played properly; and about the technique of pressing half-forward as the first movement for any batsman, the better to go either right forward or back when length and line have been assessed in mid-flight.

Wednesday, 28 February

Jason Brown, the ghost of England's team in Sri Lanka, will finally make his first appearance for a full England side in the re-arranged one-day match against a Sri Lankan Academy XI at Kurunegala today. Far from being bitter about not being given any chance so far, Brown is still engagingly starry-eyed about the prospect of playing any sort of game for his country.

'It's fantastic just to play a game,' was his reaction yesterday. 'My chance came last season in a one-day game at Northampton so it doesn't bother me that it's only a one-dayer. I just want to get involved. It's all happened so quickly for me, I know I'm just on the first rung of the ladder.'

Brown, who has still played only twenty-six first-class games, can only have been encouraged, having done all his bowling here in the nets so far, that Carl Hooper was so impressed with him during England A's first match against Guyana on his way to taking ten wickets at 26 – at an economy rate of only just over two runs an over – in the Caribbean. His performance will be closely watched today, although it is very unlikely that he could do enough in a maximum of ten overs to persuade the tour selectors to consider him seriously for the Kandy Test. Nor will the opposition be in any way easy meat: several players on the fringe of the Test side are being captained by the experienced Romesh Kaluwitharana.

The decision to play a limited-overs match instead of the scheduled three-day game at Kurunegala is a pointer to the way future cricket tours will be played, not least by visiting teams to England. There will be fewer first-class matches and less time spent in each country, but tours will be more frequent, with a greater number of back-to-back Tests.

The first and most important casualty of the brave new world, despite frequent assurances to the contrary, will be the next Ashes series in Australia. The ECB, as their chief executive, Tim Lamb, said during the match at Galle, has suggested four Tests rather than five to the Australian Board in view of the exceptional nature of the 2002/03 programme. England's tour of Australia will be sandwiched between an ICC tournament in Bermuda in October and the World Cup in South Africa in February and March.

A far better choice, not least because television screens the world over will be swamped by one-day cricket, would be to reduce the scale of the annual triangular one-day international tournament. Lamb said that this had also been suggested but, sadly, he hinted that a fifth Test, rather than any of the one-day games during a season which will be replete with them, will be the one to be sacrificed.

Nasser Hussain has expressed his unease at the probable loss of a Test but it remains to be seen whether the Australian Cricket Board, with sponsors to please, will be prepared to reduce the triangular tournament of fourteen or fifteen matches that seems to have become an immovable annual feast, probably now written into the national constitution. On the other hand the Australian players will be no less keen than England's not to play too much before the World Cup. They have exactly the same commitments throughout that winter.

Lamb stressed that even if there were to be only four Tests, as there were in 1975, the year of the first World Cup in England when the Ashes were not at stake, it would not be a precedent but 'only because of the exceptional circumstances'. The question to ask, however, is how often those exceptional circumstances might arise in future? Even if England and Australia do manage to hang on to five Tests, future England series in South Africa and the West Indies, to name but two, are likely to be reduced to four or even to three Tests.

It is an inevitable consequence of the new five-year international programme that county cricket will find it even harder to maintain a fully professional circuit with eighteen clubs. For one thing they will find it increasingly difficult to recruit overseas players: both Sri Lanka and Zimbabwe now intend playing home Tests regularly during the British summer while the West Indies increasingly play deep into May, so the leading cricketers of six nations will be taken out of the market for overseas players for portions of every season.

Apart from a shortage of established international cricketers, county cricket will have to do without most of the England team for the majority of their games. Because of the commitment to seven home Tests and ten internationals every season, there is little hope of centrally contracted men being available for the decisive matches in early September. In addition to World Cups every four years, ICC tournaments, to which all Test countries are also committed, will take place in October every two years.

Central contracts were overdue and it is right that priority should be given unequivocally to the interests of the England team: they generate the income needed to fund not just county cricket but the recreational game too. No less important, by television exposure, preferably on terrestrial television where audiences are at least four times greater, they provide the essential inspiration for each new generation of young enthusiasts. But the issue over which the ECB should have taken a stand, an immovable one, was the sanctity of county cricket in the first and last months of each season.

By failing to draw a line in the sand, our administrators have provided the straw that will now gradually break the camel's back. To put it more dramatically, they have probably signed the death warrant of the county game as it now exists, and especially of the competition that has been the bedrock of professional cricket in England and Wales for 120 years and the envy of other countries. No one doubts their responsibilities to the global game, but the ECB's top officials have repeatedly stressed that they also want to protect the County Championship. For all Lamb's assurances last week that 'we must not ride roughshod over the interests of the counties' and that 'we have to get the balance right', they have, and they haven't.

Wednesday, 7 March

An exhilarating day's cricket to open the Kandy Test. We have a nice open press box with an excellent view but it is also cramped, with a trestle-table for the computer but no room to stretch the legs. Still, there cannot be a more delightful view from any Test ground, unless it is Adelaide. Here there is a peak shaped a bit like the Matterhorn as we look out to the right, viewed over the vivid orange blossom of what in Australia they would call a Ponciana; elsewhere a Flamboyant. All round the ground, owned by Trinity College, other wooded hilltops jut up into the hazy grey-blue of the sky. On the left, above a small stand with a green roof that might have been designed by the same person responsible for the Ladies' Stand at Sydney, is a steep slope with coconut palms jutting above a whole variety of other trees.

The ground itself is flat and dry with a pitch that has enough life in it to give everyone a chance. England took four wickets with the new ball, then had an afternoon chasing a series of beautiful strokes by the 23-year-old Mahela Jayawardena, who made his fifth Test hundred in just under three hours. But for once the second new ball delivered all it promised and England hustled through the last five wickets in five overs.

Saturday, 10 March

A day of terrible anti-climax for England who seemed to have a highly controversial match virtually wrapped up last night. They had been two exhausting days for me, all the rows about dreadful umpiring decisions requiring me to do two pieces again tonight. It is hard on such occasions to do the job full justice and yet to try to please Judy, who is understanding but naturally disappointed when after a day on her own I have to work all night as well. We did manage to have a rather rushed dinner last night at The Citadel, also on the Mahwele River, where there is a restaurant much better than any others so far encountered at Kandy. I have booked again tonight and at least we can have a leisurely evening together even though I had to be at the Test today to see England labour to take the last four Sri Lankan wickets and then to lose four themselves. Nasser Hussain first strained a groin muscle and was then the victim of yet another erroneous decision. So much now hangs on what happens tomorrow morning because if England lose this Test and the series it would be heartbreaking for them. They had Sri Lanka at 80 for 4 in the first innings and dropped a catch; then at 81 for 4 in the second when Alec Stewart missed a stumping.

Sunday, 11 March

Immense relief for England and all who sail with her. It was tense all the way. They needed 70 with six wickets left and no one quite knew, after so many umpiring mistakes, what part B. C. Cooray and Rudi Koertzen would play. The South African could be relied upon not to panic but Cooray, a tubby little man of fifty-nine in his last Test before retirement, was under increasing pressure from the build-up of his earlier errors. This morning he gave Stewart out to a ball that pitched only just outside leg stump, but the batsman should have been given the benefit of the doubt. Hick was then dropped before he had scored and made 16 with some good driving before playing too ambitious a shot against Jayasuriya and departing, sixth out, with 41 still needed.

Robert Croft played his second fine innings of the match in company with Craig White, who has been the missing piece in the jigsaw since the middle of last summer. Croft was lbw with 19 still needed, however, and it was not until seven overs after lunch that White hit the winning runs.

From a writing point of view it was a good time of the day for the game to finish. I again had two long pieces to write, naturally, but there was time for a quick swim and for a short but relaxing trip by motorboat down the wide Mahewale with Judy, some of the MCC group, including the Hardmans, parents of my ex-*Telegraph* colleague, Robert, who has just gone to the *Daily Mail* on a generous salary. Richard and Charmaine Hutton were also on board with one of their holiday party, an attractive and interesting young botanist called Leona, who works in Brazil and loves her cricket. We passed various groups of smiling locals, washing either their clothes or their glistening bodies in the muddy water. Several herons too, plus a glorious kingfisher and a tern, flying along the overhanging trees with wonderful speed and sudden, sinuous switches of direction.

I managed to finish my work in time for a late dinner with the Huttons but I was very tired by the time I put the phone down for the last time.

Monday, 12 March

The reward for England of victory at Asgirya yesterday was considerable; the consequences had they been beaten would have been enormous. As they did after the innings defeat at Edgbaston last June they showed resilience and crucial tenacity in the lower half of the order to win the following match very narrowly indeed. At Lord's it was by one wicket; here in Kandy by three. They travelled to Colombo by bus yesterday evening in high spirits, albeit with some visible scars of victory. Nasser Hussain's are the worst: a badly cut knee, a sore back and a strained groin. He hopes to play in the deciding Test starting at the SSC ground on Thursday, but may then have to miss some or all of the three one-day internationals. Alec Stewart might again be his deputy if necessary.

Hussain said after England had squeezed home to the intense relief of their thousands of supporters that it was an exciting and excellent victory, but added: 'We still need to work on various things. I thought some of our bowling in the second innings was a bit excitable and we can learn from the way Chaminda Vaas bowled on these sort of wickets. We are still learning.'

Undoubtedly there is still ground to be made up before the Australians arrive but it is a true measure of England's improvement that this was the fourth time during the Hussain/Fletcher era that they have won a tight finish in the fourth innings: at Centurion under peculiar circumstances against South Africa in their first series in charge; at Lord's last summer against the West Indies in the classic encounter that Hussain missed because of a broken bone; in Karachi before Christmas; and now in Kandy where Sri Lanka came so close to producing a *bouleversement*.

Sri Lanka themselves have now lost successive Tests on this

ground by seven runs and three wickets. Had they bowled England out yesterday for fewer than 161 they would have won the series before this week's third Test, with the result, amongst other things, that they would have been placed higher in the World Championship table when it becomes official. There is, in fact, very little between these two teams in quality, but if England should win the series they would be, for what it is worth, third in the table, behind only South Africa and what they call in canine circles the supreme champion, Australia.

The luck in this game was capricious from the start, but it is nonetheless true in general terms that strong sides win games like these. They somehow find a way. Only thirteen England victories in their history have been won by three wickets or fewer, and three of them have come in the last fourteen months. This may not be an outstanding side yet, but it is one with certain essentials, not least a good captain (Hussain's hundred was a relief to all); a strong pair of opening batsmen (notwithstanding Michael Atherton's current problem against Chaminda Vaas); a formidable pair of opening bowlers in Darren Gough and, at least in most conditions, Andrew Caddick; and two genuine all-rounders in Alec Stewart and Craig White.

Still more significantly, the walk-on players are doing their bit. Ashley Giles may have had by far his worst game of the winter, but he held on at the end; and Robert Croft, not Darren Gough, would have been my man of the match. He took important wickets and batted valuably in both innings. His personal contribution is less the point, however, than that the team is finding someone to do the job more often than not. Ian Salisbury's batting performances in Pakistan were a part of the same development.

What can be said in summary of this game from an English viewpoint is not that it was a great victory but that it was a fine example of hanging on under pressure. Sadly it will be remembered every bit as much for being a game riven by controversy and tarnished by the acrimony between the two teams. In their various articles in Sunday newspapers, Hussain, Atherton and Stewart all tended to lay the blame less on the players than the umpires, Atherton making the case the most convincingly that bad decisions were at the heart of the problem. He added, in a thoughtful piece in the *Sunday Telegraph*: 'Ultimately it is the players' game . . . their responsibility to clean up the game. Each plays to his own set of principles but dissent, abusing umpires and clear cheating such as scooping up a catch on the half-volley have no place in the game.'

Hussain spoke both before and after this match – as he often has before – of playing 'hard but fair' in the aggressive 'Australian' way. He is right, of course, that it is the only way that any side will compete with Australia. It was the Australians who started both the sledging and the television slow-motion replays, although the frenzied appealing had its genesis on the subcontinent, and long before most people realise. The anarchy so passionately condemned here was already evident at times during the first series I reported in India just on twenty-five years ago. All professional sport is played in the same ruthless way these days, stretching rules to their limit. Moreover, cricketers only rarely set out to cheat each other, which is not to say that they do not appeal for everything remotely likely to be given out.

I wrote the other day that, given the sophisticated technology, there seemed no alternative but to use it to assist the umpires rather than to embarrass them. There is, of course, a diametrically opposing possibility, namely for cricket boards, when they agree contracts with television companies, to do so on the written understanding that slow-motion replays should only be shown to help umpires and viewers with line decisions (boundaries, stumpings and run-outs) as was originally envisaged. The bat/pad and lbw decisions would be far less contentious if they were permitted to show them only at normal speed. But it is too late: the television producers have seen the power that their technology wields and the excitement it creates and they cannot realistically be expected to relinquish it now. As with Frankenstein, the monster is out of control.

Wednesday, 14 March
Back at sea level in the soupy heat of Colombo after their exciting foray into the Kandyan hill country, the England team were like well-filled lions yesterday, not without wounds to lick but satisfied with a job well done. This morning they return to the nets,

ready to rouse themselves again for the decisive Test starting at the Sinhalese Sports Club on Thursday. The two teams were supposed to come together socially last night on the lawn in front of their hotel, but the Sri Lankan team were conspicuous by their absence and any social contact will have to wait until a celebration party tonight to honour Muttiah Muralitharan's 300 Test wickets. To their credit several of the England team intend to be there.

If that does not help to restore normal relations, the proposed meeting between the captains before the match to sort out their differences surely will. The much-exercised match referee, Hanumant Singh, said last night that he would like to sit in on the meeting. There was also a proposal yesterday that one possible source of irritation, the unfortunate B. C. Cooray, should be removed from the scene but it has been rejected and he will remain the third umpire for the final Test. Such has been the reaction to the errors he made in good faith and in difficult circumstances that although there was no truth in the rumour that his house in Colombo had been vandalised, police have been keeping an extra guard on both himself and his property in the last two days. It should not be forgotten, however, that Cooray got a great deal right as well as an unacceptable number of decisions wrong in Kandy. His mantle passes on Thursday to Asoka de Silva who is already being referred to, strictly in jest, as 'A shocker, de Silva'. In fact, although he has stood in only one relatively straightforward Test at Galle, when Pakistan defeated Sri Lanka last year, he starts with the great advantage of having played Test cricket as a leg-spinner himself.

Anyone who has played at that level has a head-start because the players feel that, metaphorically, he talks the same language. In England the Association of Cricket Umpires and Scorers, who do an essential job for the recreational game, have been lobbying for some time for more of their own fully trained officials to have the chance to become professionals. The ECB has now accepted that every new first-class umpire should have passed exams on the theory of the laws before they put them into practice. The combination of well-prepared and well-paid former professional cricketers is the one most likely to produce effective and respected arbiters.

If good preparation is one of three main reasons for the upturn in England's fortunes in the last twelve months the others are continuity of personnel and the way in which Duncan Fletcher and Nasser Hussain have persuaded each individual involved in the team not only that he should feel part of the wider effort but also that he should take responsibility for his own actions on and off the field. This, Fletcher feels, is the reason that they have prevailed in tight corners like the ones they found themselves in during phases of both the Sri Lankan innings at Kandy and also in the tense struggle to get 161 to win on a worn pitch.

'They really believe that they can win games in tight situations,' Fletcher said yesterday. 'The night before that last day there were some nerves, obviously, but they were quite relaxed. In games like that it's a question of which sides break under pressure. Had it been Sri Lanka chasing 161 I think there is a very good chance we would have bowled them out. Craig White knew he had a job to do at the death because that's what we stress all the time. Each guy who finds himself in the middle has to take responsibility for winning the game. It's too easy to say it's someone else's responsibility. Gough, for example, knew it was his responsibility to make the breakthrough. You could see it in him that he knew he had to do it. If you give individuals responsibility they have got to be idiots if they throw it away.'

Where, I wonder, does that leave Graeme Hick, after another disappointing batting performance and Test scores this winter amounting to 126 runs in ten innings at an average of 12? The other side of the 'continuity of selection' coin is that alternative players do not get sufficient practice. Michael Vaughan has not batted in the middle since the game in Matara on 17 February, when he missed his chance to force his way back into the Test side, but Fletcher gave perhaps half a hint that the switch will finally be made on Thursday: 'Most times you'd say let's not change a winning team but we'll sit down and analyse the next game and try to pick a team to win it, with one eye on the future to some degree.'

Vaughan is certainly part of the long-term future. Whether Hick is will depend to an extent on the first of several discussions today between Fletcher, Hussain and David Graveney about the England

contracts for the coming summer. Fletcher favours fifteen contracted players this season provided there are a sufficient number
of players who justify the favoured status. Tomorrow sees the
arrival of the one-day specialists, Alleyne, Ealham, Flintoff, Knight
and Mullally, who will prepare separately for a week for the internationals to come. To a man the new arrivals will be eager to
pick up the aura of understated confidence now radiating from
the Test party.

Saturday, 17 March

Amazing! Another Test series won. Through good bowling, some
frenetic batting and a pitch made arid as a desert by the sun at
the hottest time of the year in Colombo, twenty-two wickets fell
on the third day of what was supposed to be a five-day match.
Graham Thorpe was England's hero. It is salutary to see how his
life has improved since he decided to take last winter off and put
his wife and family before his career. He is enjoying his cricket
more and has batted brilliantly against the spinners all winter. I
wonder if he is good enough to be equally influential this summer
against McGrath, Gillespie and Lee? Unless he is, England will
not get enough runs.

Wednesday, 21 March

With respect to the cricketers, three of whom, Andrew Caddick,
Graeme Hick and Michael Vaughan, warmed up respectively with
a hat-trick, a century and a rapid 97 in Colombo yesterday, the
star of the show in the first one-day international tomorrow will
probably be the extraordinary new ground on which the match
is to be staged. The speed of its creation, in six months from planning permission by government decree to the bowling of the first
ball in a major match, is enough to make Hampshire committee
men contemplate an immediate journey to Nirvana.

While the new Rose Bowl at Southampton has been battling
with soaking weather and the constraints that follow from being
heavily in debt as it prepares for first-class cricket next month,
with international cricket as yet no more than a dream, the Rangiri
Dambulla Stadium has been built from dense jungle where

elephants were roaming last September. It is a huge ground, 200 yards from side to side and bigger than any of the vast Australian grounds. On one side is a huge natural lake; on the other the Buddhist rock temple that, together with the old rock fortress of Sigiriya a few miles away, has long been one of the essential places for serious tourists to tick off their list.

The impetus to tourism has been the main subtext of this cricket tour and defeat in the Test series has been but a minor blip in the Grand Scheme. The vision of Thilanga Sumithipala, the ambitious and well-connected but not universally loved president of the Board of Control for Cricket in Sri Lanka (BCCSL), is that the new ground will be followed within two years by another at Kandy and they will bring not only regular international cricket but, in time, more visitors and new hotels to the scenically magnificent central part of Sri Lanka. New roads will be the next imperative, but all concerned and especially the Minister for Sport and Tourism, Lakshman Kiriella, have learned very quickly what a wonderful means of attracting investment cricket can be on an island where almost everyone is passionate about the game.

'Money spent on sport gets a far better return for tourism than money spent on advertisements in international magazines,' according to Kiriella, whose Prime Minister, Ratnasiri Wickramanayacke, is expected to be at an elaborate opening ceremony starting at 7.45 tomorrow morning amidst the tight security that is inevitable in a country still plagued by civil war in the north.

The game itself is the harder to predict for the fact that the grass was sown less than six months ago from ground that was levelled by excavators on a site that was originally accessible only by boat from the adjoining lake. It has so far staged only a 25-overs match, played three weeks ago in front of the former West Indies Test batsman, Cammie Smith, who was observing on behalf of the ICC. Most of the crowd will have to be accommodated on concrete steps where stands will eventually offer them cover from the sun. It will be an uncomfortable day for some and a majority of the English visitors have opted out of two three-hour coach journeys each way from Colombo.

Friday, 23 March

Rangiri Dambulla Stadium (England won toss): Sri Lanka beat England by 5 wickets with nine overs and one ball in hand.

When England lost the first Test in Galle a month ago, Nasser Hussain quite rightly expressed dismay about the 'peripheral' events. When they lost the first one-day international after a poor batting performance yesterday, the peripherals almost *were* the main event. What mattered most to Sri Lankans was that international cricket was being played for the first time in an area where the game had hitherto been confined to rough clearings in the jungle.

An estimated 25,000 people came, drums drummed and trumpets blared all day, the pitch played well enough for a virgin strip, nothing fell down and there was only one quite short-lived riot when police removed an errant spectator and were pelted with bottles and cans. With the lake behind them and pointed hills beyond, two stately Indian elephants grazed all day in the shade of a coconut palm, apparently quite oblivious to the un-accustomed cacophony.

A match which never ignited on the inevitably slow pitch was won comfortably by Sri Lanka, but not quite as easily as they would have hoped, having bowled England out for a most dis-appointing 143 that owed almost everything to Graham Thorpe's 62 not out. Sanath Jayasuriya gave his side the rollicking start they expect from him and in the circumstances England's fast bowlers did very well to take four wickets for 29 in the nine overs that followed his blazing start.

The two coolest heads in the Sri Lankan side, however, belong to Marvan Atapattu and Russell Arnold, who combined in the fifth-wicket partnership which gave Sri Lanka deserved reward for the skill with which Muttiah Muralitharan had unravelled England's middle order. By the time that Atapattu was deceived by Craig White's slower ball, only 16 more runs were needed.

Politicians were almost falling over each other during the opening ceremony at breakfast time. There is much kudos to be gained when a project such as this begins to reach fruition in a relatively remote area, although not until there are better roads will the necessary infrastructure be complete. Whether this ground becomes a genuine cricketing centre rather than an elephant of the white kind will depend, of course, on how much it is used for local cricket. Although floodlights are apparently planned – heaven knows why if they can fill the place by daytime – it is not thought feasible to hold Test matches here until transport is improved because there would be insufficient local support. It is, therefore, something of a leap of faith to expect the ground automatically to become 'the centre of provincial cricket in the centre, north and east of the island' as the BCCSL hope. The doubts about it are that this area of historic rock caves and temples does not, like most towns in Sri Lanka, have any tradition of school or club cricket.

Monday, 26 March

Forget the forthcoming Ashes series for a moment. Here is a really tough challenge to Duncan Fletcher and colleagues: England to win a World Cup for the first time in 2002/03. If it were being held on pitches like those at Lahore, or Nairobi, or any of the handful of grounds in Colombo like the SSC where England play the final fixture of their tour of Sri Lanka today, it would be an impossible task. On grassier pitches in South Africa it certainly is not, but some decisions have got to be taken quickly about a Grand Plan. The great dilemma is that the best international sides play more matches (even now) than England and therefore have more experience; but also that youth, daring and fleetness of foot are all desirable qualities too.

They may be irreconcilable needs but if there is to be a policy, and there has to be, it should err on the side of youth. There is sufficient talent in county cricket to produce a side purpose-built for South African conditions, but, as usual, picking the right talent will be the hardest part. To beat Sri Lanka in Sri Lanka, as England must try to do today if they are to finish their tour on the high note that would be more appropriate to their deeds throughout the winter, you would not in an ideal world start with an attack comprising four fast bowlers and only one spinner.

Since England won their only one-day match of the winter, when Andrew Flintoff led a batting assault on a belter of a wicket, the batting has flopped. Of course Fletcher has a point when he says that they will not get better without experiencing high-pressure games at the highest level, but if Graeme Hick, for example, could not think on his feet sufficiently well, after playing in 117 previous games, in the charged atmosphere at the Premadasa Stadium on Sunday night, he has to be replaced by someone who might. That said, he tends to be the man who gets blamed when things go wrong, partly perhaps because of the bemused air he seems to have when a camera closes in on him.

Hick has actually got a good record by the relatively low standards of the regular English batsmen, with five hundreds, an average of 37.80 bettered only by Thorpe and Nick Knight, and a better rate of runs per hundred balls (75) than either of them. He is not the abject failure sometimes portrayed and he is as fit as anyone, but he is not as good as he was and the time has come for him to move on in one-day cricket as he has in Tests.

The Sri Lankans have shown how it should be done. Essentially they play aggressive but orthodox cricket where the English batsmen more frequently try the unorthodox – charges down the pitch, reverse sweeps or attempted hits over the infield from inside the line of the ball. Occasionally on very good pitches it comes off, but there too often seems to be neither a team plan nor the ability, as both Thorpe and Fletcher have put it in the last two days, to 'think on your feet'. A cool head under pressure is one essential quality the selectors will have to look for when they reshape the side this season.

Tuesday, 27 March

Third One-Day International, SSC Ground (Sri Lanka won toss): Sri Lanka beat England by 10 wickets.

The discrepancy between England's Test and one-day performances has widened disconcertingly. In 324 one-day internationals before Sri Lanka outplayed them again yesterday they had never been beaten by ten wickets. It is only the fifteenth time it has happened to anyone.

If Agatha Christie had been writing the story of the game she would have called it *Slaughter in the Sun*, but it was a match completely devoid of mystery. Sri Lanka's bowlers stifled the batsmen in the early overs and contained them expertly in the later ones before an inspired Romesh Kaluwitharana and the cultured Marvan Atapattu, captain for the day, pulverised five inadequate bowlers. There were 16.1 overs still in hand when hands were shaken for the last time, the tension and bitterness of the Test series forgotten.

To the deafening accompaniment of two strident brass bands, and in a temperature pushing 120 degrees Fahrenheit, Kaluwitharana, the little swashbuckler, hit twenty fours in an innings that will confirm his right to a place in the one-day side and may well encourage a return to the Test team too. He needed only 112 balls to reach his hundred with a leg-glance off Darren Gough that symbolised Sri Lanka's complete supremacy. England's champion bowler, like most of the team, was jaded and yearning for home. As for the new arrivals, the inability of Nick Knight and Mark Ealham to make any significant difference to the performance showed that the selections for the first two games had been irrelevant to the broader picture.

Graham Thorpe said at the end of a chastening first experience of leading his country: 'We need to play in these countries a lot more before we are able to give them a serious game of one-day cricket.' The countries he was referring too, no doubt, were Pakistan, who beat England 2–1 at the start of the winter; Sri Lanka, who have thrashed them 3–0 in this series; and India, who will be warm favourites to maintain the trend of England one-day defeats overseas – fifteen in seventeen matches now – when what must inevitably be a reshaped England side contests the limited-overs section of the tour in the middle of next winter.

Wednesday, 28 March
Education, education, education. In some countries they pay lip-service to it; in Sri Lanka they provide it, beyond the war zone at least. The fruits are visible in many aspects of life in this 'land like no other' but in nothing so obviously as their cricket. One of the enduring memories of England's intense seven-week tour of the island will be of the teams of schoolboys, all in smart white shirts, shorts, caps, socks and shoes, playing tennis-ball cricket in the intervals of all the big games to an altogether more exalted standard than the Kwik cricketers of England and Wales.

Sri Lanka may have lost the Test series, to the great credit and encouragement of a determined, tough and improving England team, but the strength and competitive structure of schoolboy cricket, the abundant natural talent and the technical excellence of the miniature batsmen in particular, guarantees them a prosperous cricketing future. England would give much, as the Australian shadow draws nearer and the age of their established batsmen begins to dawn on the selectors, for two batsmen in their early twenties as gifted and accomplished as Kumar Sangakkara and, especially, Mahela Jayawardena. Much, too, for the wide choice of young spin bowlers open to the Sri Lankan selectors.

None of them will equal the feats of Muttiah Muralitharan, for the obvious reason that a cricketing genius seldom appears more than once in a generation, but only in fast bowling do the Sri Lankans lack depth in quality and experience. Even there, four young ones, Ruchira Perera, Akalanka Ganegama and a brace of Fernandos, Dinusha and Dilhara, have all gone into the notebook as possible successors to the excellent Chaminda Vaas.

England did not play the canny Vaas well, as Michael Atherton would be the first to concede, but the key to their admirable comeback from heavy defeat in Galle was the fact that they largely nullified the potency of Muralitharan. He had more success in the one-day games, when time was limited and the pad therefore of no use, but it was the intelligent way in which England frustrated him, getting the pad outside the off stump, sweeping whenever they could and daring the umpires to be certain of the degree of turn, that enabled sufficient runs to be gleaned.

In Pakistan the same shrewd, patient approach had paved the way for the dramatic finale in Karachi and the twilight seizure of an even series. Here the tense, fascinating, dramatic match in Kandy was the high point of the tour, a game played on a beautifully situated ground in glorious weather that everyone present will never forget and that cheered every sports-lover in the nation in the depth of a singularly unhappy and unlucky winter. It was not only the match that turned the series after Sri Lanka's resounding innings victory in Galle, but the one which confirmed England's character and teamwork; their ability to win tight games and to find a man for each difficult situation.

Enough has been written for now about Nasser Hussain's century, Graham Thorpe's brilliant batting, Darren Gough's fast, crafty and lion-hearted bowling and the less eye-catching performances which finally settled the last two Tests after Sri Lanka's own spirited recovery in the second innings at Kandy. Impatient batting under pressure sealed their fate in the three-day Test in Colombo that followed, but it was aggressive bowling and fielding by England that hounded them into mistakes.

The last ten days of the tour could hardly have provided a greater contrast. In one-day cricket, as the last three games so clearly demonstrated, England have made no progress since the mercurial period in which David Lloyd, now confining his enthusiasm to the commentary box, introduced some life and new ideas but no consistency and no answer to the continuing lack of authority in the batting. After the second defeat under the floodlights last Sunday night, Fletcher reminded his players to think of every 50-over innings as an exercise in facing 300 balls. 'After every one of those 300 balls there is a new situation which the batsmen in the middle have got to analyse,' he said.

The ability to do so, the coach believes, comes only from having had the experience of playing at this level in different conditions and that, he feels, can only come when a team plays together often. His conclusion is that England will have to play even more one-day internationals, a point he illustrates by saying that Pakistan were involved in twelve games in the period between playing England late last year and the brief series of three matches in Sri Lanka. But one look at the fixtures ahead shows that England could not fit in many more games than they now do, nor, in the wider interests of the game, would it be prudent for them to do so, especially if the team is to continue to be comprised mainly of players already in the Test side.

Of the one-day squad in Sri Lanka, only Flintoff, Trescothick, Michael Vaughan and Ashley Giles (just) will be under thirty at the start of the next World Cup. There has to be some new blood, but England have to bear in mind that the seeding for the tournament will take into account all the results in one-day internationals between the last World Cup and next September. There is, therefore, a risk about attempting too much experiment.

Fletcher has a half-open mind, but is clearly against throwing in a whole lot of young players together. If he can persuade the Gloucestershire coach, John Bracewell, to forget his Kiwi patriotism for a day, he could do worse than to spend an afternoon talking to him about the art of winning one-day games, although Mark Alleyne will already have passed on what he knows.

Most of the places in the Test side are, of course, taken. Graeme Hick and Ian Salisbury have fallen by the wayside but Dominic Cork and Matthew Hoggard will be eager to become involved in the battles ahead against Pakistan and Australia. Most of the others are in need of a good rest and they thoroughly deserve it.

Three

Banana Skin

Only one thing could dampen the general enthusiasm in Britain for the imminent series against Australia: a defeat against Pakistan in the tricky little series that preceded the main event. Not that Pakistan should have been relegated to the status of a warm-up act. With one of the great opening bowling partnerships of history in Wasim Akram and Waqar Younis, an outstanding young off-spinner in Saqlain Mushtaq, a leg-spinner of high class in Mushtaq Ahmed, two masterly batsmen in Inzamam-ul-Haq and Saeed Anwar and several fine players on a swift ascending curve in Yousuf Youhana, Younis Khan, Abdur Razzaq and Azhar Mahmood, they had the potential to upset England.

To an even greater extent than Zimbabwe the previous year, however, they went into the first of their two Tests, at Lord's in the middle of May, badly under-prepared. Arriving only two weeks before, they had the advantage of a shrewd, personable and intelligent manager in Yawar Saeed, who had played for Somerset and had used his experience of England and the English to guide the previous touring team through a potentially difficult visit in 1996.

Following a tour in 1992 when they had been successful on the field but slated in some sections of the press for alleged tampering with the ball, Pakistan's visit four years later was a playing and diplomatic success. Wasim Akram, the captain, handled all activities, not least the team's relations with the press, with an easy charm and led a bowling attack that was too skilful and varied for England. Since then he had been one of the many Pakistan players investigated for match-fixing and Justice Mohammad Qayuum had recommended, amongst other things, that he should not lead Pakistan again.

No less debilitating to Pakistan's chances, Wasim had fallen out with his great opening partner, Waqar Younis, who had said of him: 'He is a great cricketer and I respect him as a great cricketer but I cannot call him a great human being.' Whatever the truth of that, and despite the fact that Wasim looked not a day older than the superb athlete who had led the attack so well on his two previous visits, he had now gone nineteen Tests without having one of the five-wicket analyses that were once almost habitual.

Waqar had even suggested that Wasim would not be in his team this time because of rivalry from Shoaib Akhtar and, a bowler new to England, the slim and whippy Mohammad Sami. Shoaib was back in contention after a miserable two years during which insult had been added to various injuries by the fact that he had been banned from international cricket because of a suspect action. His arrival in England, delayed by a stomach complaint, followed rehabilitation at Perth in Western Australia where he was supposed to have been cleared for action by the discovery by physiologists that he has 'hypermobility in the shoulder and elbow'.

The Shoaib who eventually started the tour at Derby looked overweight and his remodelled action rather strained and unnatural. His colleagues had gained a facile victory against the British Universities at Trent Bridge, with Wasim, Waqar, Sami and Mushtaq Ahmed all taking easy wickets. When it came to selection for Lord's, Sami had been ruled out by injury and, because of the recent dampness of the weather, Shoaib was preferred to Saqlain. It meant that both sides would play without a spinner, an immediate contrast to the winter just passed.

England welcomed Dominic Cork back to their dressing-room and in the absence of White, Giles and Hoggard, all injured, they gave a first cap to Ryan Sidebottom, making him the sixth fast or fast-medium bowler on Yorkshire's staff to have won a Test cap in recent years. Sadly, it rained throughout the scheduled opening day but on the second England made a reassuring start to the long season of Test cricket.

Friday, 18 May
First Test, Lord's (second day of five; Pakistan won toss): England, with 6 first-innings wickets in hand, have scored 254.

Taking three of only four wickets by dismissing well-set batsmen attempting attacking strokes was certainly not what Pakistan had in mind when they put England in on a grey morning yesterday. The fall of the commanding Graham Thorpe four overs from the end of the day to some extent restored the equilibrium but Nasser Hussain, whose steadfast four-and-a-quarter-hour innings was his first fifty in a home Test for almost two years, would cheerfully have settled for his team's close-of-play position when he lost the toss for the eleventh time in his last twelve Tests.

It proved to be no serious handicap. No one should blame Waqar Younis for wanting to bowl first, especially after leaving out both his specialist spinners in the expectation of good conditions for seam and swing bowling, but the decision to omit Saqlain Mushtaq for Shoaib Akhtar was a serious case of wishful thinking on the part of Pakistan's strategists. Despite a spirited second spell during which he briefly began to look more like the formidable fast bowler of two seasons ago, Shoaib limped off with an injury to his left foot after bowling only thirteen overs.

Had he won the toss the notoriously unlucky Hussain would no doubt have taken the same decision as Waqar but a pale pitch marked by small crowns of green grass had remained firm under its covers during the rain on Thursday and it played blamelessly. Worse, from the point of view of a Pakistan attack of five fast or fast-medium bowlers augmented by an inexperienced leg-spinner who was hit for 26 in his only over when he last played in Test cricket, there was relatively little swing even from acknowledged masters of the art.

England have also gone into the match without a specialist spinner but they have no one of Saqlain's class available and, in Michael Vaughan, a better occasional spinner than Younis Khan. Although Vaughan was one of the four batsmen to get out when going well, in his own case rather unfortunately to a thin leg-glance, the reshaped batting order worked well for England. The new number three played beautifully, Hussain with increasing freedom after the stickiest of starts and Thorpe, a place too low though he might be, with the same cool authority and sure judgement that he had displayed throughout the winter. He was hurrying towards his first Test hundred at Lord's when he aimed an overhead hook at a bouncer from Waqar despite knowing there were two men back on the leg-side boundary.

It was by far the best moment in a disappointing day for the Pakistan captain, whose face was to some extent saved by good performances from his two young all-rounders, Azhar Mahmood and Abdur Razzaq. Waqar and Wasim Akram will need a swift breakthrough this morning with the second new ball, taken ten overs from the close, if England, with Hussain in residence and two specialist batsmen still to come, are not to give their own fast bowlers a sizeable total from which to launch their attack on batsmen seriously short of preparation in English conditions.

In a way, however, the story of this first day of actual play was that these apparently typical English conditions were far less hazardous to batsmen than they looked likely to be. Only Michael Atherton, bowled when not fully forward to a good-length ball that moved late, was out playing defensively and the five specialists who got to the crease all got past 30 before Ryan Sidebottom played fifteen balls as the volunteer nightwatchman on his first day as a Test cricketer. He will have to bowl sensationally well to earn a regular place just yet but the sight of his new England helmet perched precariously on his mop of ginger curls was the first of many images which will no doubt delight cartoonists in years to come.

Marcus Trescothick, the first of England's new generation to establish himself, had few anxious moments as he and Atherton put on 60 in the first hour, scoring mainly in front of the wicket as the opening bowlers rightly pitched the ball up in search of swing. He had hit three fours when, perhaps a mite over-confident, he drove at a wide-ish ball and thick-edged it low to third slip. While Atherton bedded down it was Vaughan who then played the memorable strokes of the morning, an off-drive off Razzaq, a force off the back foot against Wasim and a pull for six off Khan's exploratory first over.

The fall of Vaughan and Atherton in the space of six overs after lunch left Hussain and Thorpe with plenty to do. Hussain played with exaggerated caution but it was calculated too. After fifty-seven minutes with his score stuck on 1 he caressed a drive through extra cover and thereafter batted with a poise to match his determination, needing luck only when an inswinger from Razzaq thudded into his front pad in line with middle stump. As for Thorpe, once he had been beaten by his second ball, there were few moments of doubt and eleven crisp boundaries in a delightful innings, however much he will regret its impetuous end.

There was a more optimistic interpretation of Craig White's back injury at the end of the day from the physiotherapist, Dean Conway. He suggested that although he is unlikely to be risked for the second Test at Old Trafford starting a week next Thursday, White has every chance of playing a full part as an all-rounder against Australia.

Monday, 21 May
Lord's (fourth day of five): England beat Pakistan by an innings and 9 runs.
The winning habit that eluded England so long seems now to have been learned so well that not even a day and sixteen more overs lost to the weather can stop it. Confident, assertive and, above all, playing excellent all-round cricket, they won their hundredth Test match at Lord's, beating Pakistan just as the light was fading on only the third day of actual play.

Positive batting and brilliant catching, with Graham Thorpe prominent in both cases, was supported by another command performance on the most famous cricket stage of all by Darren Gough and Andrew Caddick. The combination of Bob Willis and Ian Botham could be formidable too but this, surely, has become the best England opening pair since Statham and Trueman were in their pomp in the 1950s, and one has to go back to that era of brief world domination to find an England team that last won three Tests in succession at Lord's.

After the unexpected double success in the winter this was exactly the start England had hoped for. Pakistan played a long way below their potential, but they should be better acclimatised for the second Test at Old Trafford. England must play it without

Nasser Hussain, whose right thumb, broken by a bouncer from Shoaib Akhtar just before he was out on Saturday morning, will prevent him from playing for at least three weeks.

Alec Stewart will resume the captaincy at Manchester as seamlessly as he did here, no doubt. Gough's 200th Test wicket was also Stewart's 200th catch for England, either with the gloves or without them, and his sparkling 44 off fifty-four balls on Saturday was an ideal innings at a time when quick runs were needed. The selectors must decide also whether to ask him to lead again at the start of the one-day international series with Pakistan and Australia, for which the consistently unfortunate Hussain is unlikely to be fit. Stewart declined the job in the heat of Sri Lanka but he will no doubt be asked again.

By contrast the inclination of the selectors will be to choose a young batsman to cover for Hussain at Old Trafford, where Hoggard will also hope to get into the team again ahead of Sidebottom. Ian Ward's mature performance here emphasised the value of promoting those who have done well on A tours but Sidebottom, younger and more inexperienced, has some way still to go. He was far from overawed and bowled an excellent six-over spell yesterday in which he was unlucky not to claim an lbw, but there was only occasional sign of the late inswinger for which all good left-arm-over bowlers strive.

Dominic Cork, who took his first first-class wicket of the season in this match, is still not at full effectiveness. In Craig White's absence he played a valuable all-round role but it was Caddick and Gough who won the match. Though they took their wickets largely in individual bursts, they claimed sixteen wickets out of a possible twenty in the space of little more than twenty-four hours. Added to the twenty-five they garnered between them in the Lord's Tests against Zimbabwe and the West Indies last season, they have now claimed forty-one out of the sixty wickets taken by England in three successive victories on the old ground.

It was Caddick's turn to claim a man-of-the-match award. His now inseparable partner took the five wickets that went up on the dressing-room honours board but on this ground in particular and in English conditions generally it is Caddick who puts the fear of God into any batsman not utterly in command of his mind and technique. Hitting the pitch hard from a height of around eight feet, varying his length and getting steep lift together with the away movement that the Lord's slope assists when bowlers of his type operate from the Nursery End, he was the chief agent in Pakistan's destruction in both innings, taking three of the first four wickets on Saturday and two of the first three in the second innings yesterday.

Pakistan had resumed at 115 for 4 after the excellent partnership between Yousuf Youhana and Younis Khan that had steadied the innings on Saturday. Playing his first Test innings in England, Younis again hit the ball with a pleasing flourish in warmer weather yesterday morning but he lost Youhana in the third over when Gough beat him with a dead straight ball before he had got fully forward.

Azhar Mahmood kept the resistance going until falling to one of the occasional balls that lifted uncomfortably off a generally excellent pitch. Marcus Trescothick held the catch running back from second slip, off the shoulder of the bat, whereupon Cork chipped in by bowling Younis Khan off his pads before Gough strode to lunch in the middle of an over with his 200th wicket claimed through a leg-side catch.

'Dazzler', as his newly published autobiography is simply called, wasted no time when he completed his over after the interval. Waqar Younis was brilliantly caught at third slip by Thorpe, diving left, whereupon Gough unerringly castled Shoaib Akhtar to make it three wickets in four balls. The hat-trick was averted by Saeed Anwar ten minutes later but two more catches by Thorpe at third slip, this time off Caddick, set the ball rolling again.

First he dived far to his right and caught Salim Elahi's outside edge low and one-handed, then he clasped on to another edge from Saeed Anwar, two-handed to his right. When Inzamam also fell to a good catch, low, left-handed by the wicket-keeper, and Younis Khan was given out leg-before off an inside edge, it became only a matter of whether or not England could finish the game before the light went and the overs ran out. Abdur Razzaq, justifying his number-three position, made a stout fifty and Azhar Mahmood again showed his ability but Caddick and Gough would not be denied their day off.

Wednesday, 30 May

No matter what time of the year they schedule the Old Trafford Test match, it always seems to coincide with a break in the weather. The further north I drove on the day before the second Test of the summer, the bigger the build-up of clouds. I left Sussex at 6am in Mediterranean warmth and arrived in Manchester with rain in the air, although for once the England players were able to have their nets outdoors. Pakistan had practised assiduously since their defeat at Lord's by thrashing Leicestershire and, at the suggestion of their enlightened English coach, Richard Pybus, they spent the day instead at a fun-fair in Blackpool.

The pitch looks full of runs. Its surface is cracked, as they usually are here, but it is very hard and has a more even covering of thin grass than it sometimes does. Lancashire have tried to market the match in the local Pakistani communities but tickets have not sold well in advance and there is a worry that there might be a legacy of the recent fighting in the streets of Oldham between gangs of white and Asian youths. Except perhaps on Saturday, when the beer-drinking football supporters from over the road sometimes make their presence noisily apparent at Old Trafford Test matches, I doubt if there will be anything to worry about. On the field it could be different if England are not at their sharpest. It is not just in the World Cup in Australia that Pakistan have fulfilled the wounded-tiger prophesy: they tend to be at their worst after a victory and their best after a defeat.

Thursday, 31 May

Inzamam-ul-Haq played another glorious innings today. At Lord's on Pakistan's last tour his century on the opening day was the prelude to victory; in Karachi earlier this year it was not, but today he played so well that he has given his bowlers every chance to level the series. Coming in at 39 for 2, he scored 114 off 153 balls with eighteen fours and a six, the latter pulled into the pavilion off Michael Vaughan whom he immediately and deliberately removed from the attack.

His renowned indolence does not apply to his batting, because his eyes are so good and his feet invariably quick enough to get him into position for every stroke. Most of his runs today came through the on-side as he took a firm step across to the off stump or outside and continuously stroked the ball into gaps on the other side of the wicket.

England took eight wickets but had a bad day, leavened only by Matthew Hoggard's three wickets, his first in Tests coming when Inzamam slashed him hard to point. Old Trafford is a ground where fielders sometimes lose sight of the ball and Nick Knight, replacement for the injured Hussain, dropped slip catches at the beginning and end of the day. Atherton also muffed one when the first ball was new. The bowling was also a bit ragged, hindered by a strong wind from the north. Cork bowled steadily into it for long spells but did not swing the ball, as into-the-wind specialists like Chris Old or Ian Botham used to do. Pakistan are 370 for 8, helped by a series of perfectly timed strokes towards the close by the wicket-keeper, Rashid Latif, who has more than justified his selection ahead of Moin Khan.

I dined this evening in the excellent restaurant of the Stanneylands hotel near Wilmslow with my brother David for company. Having spent some of his formative years in Birkenhead and the Wirral, a period I was too young to remember, he has always supported Lancashire, Tranmere Rovers and Liverpool. This, however, was the first time that he had been to a Test at Old Trafford. He was lucky to see such an action-packed day. We all were, but the momentum never ceased.

Friday, 1 June
Second Test, Old Trafford (second day of five): England are 199 runs behind Pakistan with 8 first-innings wickets in hand.

New England need no spin-doctors to advertise their virtues. Struggling at 15 for 2 in reply to Pakistan's 403, Graham Thorpe's response was to carve his third ball for six over third man with the violence of an avenging crusader. With Michael Vaughan playing in the same counter-attacking vein England had seized back the initiative with real panache by the time that the long-anticipated rain arrived for the second time to rob the day of 18.4 overs of the final session.

Not since 1997 has an Old Trafford Test produced a win for either side. If rain has played its part in draws involving South

Africa, New Zealand and the West Indies in the years since, so too has the pitch. This one is the best of them all. Firm and true, it is a proverbial belter on which the batsmen of both sides have so far given the crowds who have braved the cold weather wonderful value for money. Ninety overs on the first day produced fifty-one fours and two sixes; yesterday, after Saqlain Mushtaq had contributed a six pulled high over long-on off a disgruntled Andrew Caddick during the merry little tail-end flurry that started the day, England hit twenty-three fours themselves in addition to Thorpe's defiant opening scoring stroke.

If there was a something that made the alliance between Thorpe and Vaughan, worth 189 so far, even more impressive than the one between Inzamam-ul-Haq and Younis Khan the previous afternoon, it was less the striking of fours than the running between the wickets. Not only did they take short singles with instant decisiveness but they stole second runs that ought not to have been taken, exposing Waqar Younis and one or two of the other Pakistani fielders, and irritating the bowlers.

It was rousing cricket by England and a demonstration, perhaps, that they are capable of carrying out their stated intention of playing equally positive cricket against Australia. Had they switched on their television in the dressing-room at Worcester yesterday, some of the newly arrived touring team might have looked at the events of the first half-hour here and concluded that nothing has really changed. Within minutes of the start Nick Knight, fine catcher that he is, had muffed a second apparently straightforward chance at slip off Rashid Latif's outside edge in Darren Gough's first over.

Rashid stayed to play a few more sweetly timed strokes through the off-side, surpassing his previous highest score before Marcus Trescothick ran him out from backward point with a deft left-handed pick-up and accurate right-handed throw. Gough got the third wicket he deserved when Waqar Younis stepped in front of his stumps, but Pakistan had given themselves every chance to win the game by scoring as fast as they did. It is rare indeed for a team to make 400 well before lunch on the second day. Pakistan managed it in 95 overs.

The other side of the coin is that it has opened up the possibility of something almost equally unusual: a team scoring 400-plus in the first innings and losing. Pakistani memories would have to be very short not to recall that it happened only five months ago in Karachi when their first-innings total of 405, completed 14 overs into the second afternoon after another century by Inzamam, looked like the safest of insurance policies against defeat. Thoughts of any swift repetition of history here seemed far-fetched in the extreme when Waqar and Wasim Akram brushed away Trescothick and Michael Atherton in the first eight overs of England's reply yesterday. Waqar gave himself the advantage of the wind but it was Wasim who immediately looked threatening. His first ball, predictably enough, swung into Atherton's front pad as he played no shot. It was certainly missing the off stump but after an assured start against Waqar, Trescothick was not so lucky when he, too, was opposed by pacey, swinging left-arm-over. Almost at once, in the seventh over, he was defeated by a ball that left him late and curved past his outside edge to trim the bails.

An over later Atherton went too, playing forward and edging Waqar low to Rashid Latif. There was a time when the departure of Atherton made English hearts sink but he is now just a part of a confident group of batsmen rather than the team's head and right arm. Equally to the point, he badly needs a decent second-innings score here, or at least some good runs for Lancashire, before he faces his old conqueror, Glenn McGrath. Australia's modern Spofforth has already started the attempt to undermine his old adversary by words, and no one doubts that he is capable of following them up with deeds unless Atherton is at his very best. So far in three first-class matches this season he has managed only 88 runs at an average of 22.

McGrath, however, was out of date when he said that Atherton's remains the key England wicket. It is actually Thorpe, in the prime of his career, who sets the tone and pace of the side's batting. Cutting, hooking and cover-driving with crisp assurance, he carried confidently on from Lord's, Colombo and Kandy and although he could not use the pace of the ball or the wonderful even bounce of the pitch quite so effectively against Saqlain Mushtaq, he was quick to sweep him or place the ball into gaps.

It says a great deal that Vaughan lost nothing by comparison.

Such has been his form for Yorkshire in the last few weeks that it would have been a genuine surprise if he had not made the most of a pitch as good as this one. Forcing off the back foot at the top of the bounce and driving through extra-cover with classical grace he has a chance this morning to make the maiden Test hundred that would establish him beyond any doubt. His fifty came from seventy-nine balls, only eight more than Thorpe's, with nine fours, and it was only the first break for rain, several fielders on the boundary and the steadiness and variety of Saqlain's slow bowling that checked the momentum of an outstanding partnership in the final phase.

Monday, 4 June
Old Trafford (fifth day of five): Pakistan beat England by 108 runs.
There will have to be a notice printed on tickets for Test matches in future, warning of the dangers to those of a nervous disposition. Time and again in recent memory the greatest game has reached a boiling climax. That on this occasion there was no happy ending for England should blind no one to the fact that it was a great match and, in the end, a memorable triumph for Pakistan.

Taking England's last eight wickets for 60 runs in 21.5 overs, they had six overs and a ball in hand when one of their young substitute fielders, Imran Nazir, leapt to take a brilliant catch at cover point to end a defiant little innings by Darren Gough. It levelled the two-match series, stretched Pakistan's run of unbeaten series in England to nineteen years and gave them a chance of settling down for a while under the captaincy of Waqar Younis, who would no doubt have been disposable had events unfolded differently. Whether he should remain as captain after being exposed by television for a gross breach of Law 42 on fair and unfair play is, sadly, another matter.

Those who watched the game on television, as so often, were given a different perspective. The mean eye of the camera exposed several umpiring mistakes, including four England wickets taken from no-balls that went unspotted in the excitement. Worse, perhaps, viewers of Channel 4's highlights in the early evening were given the clearest possible evidence that Waqar gouged the leather out of one side of the ball with his fingernail to encourage reverse swing shortly before Michael Atherton was bowled by a late inswinger towards the end of the morning session.

England did not complain and the referee, Brian Hastings from New Zealand, took no action. It is depressing that bowlers still think they can tamper with the ball despite cameras watching almost every move they make. I have no doubt that Pakistan are not the only culprits but they make better use of the advantage they gain by means that the law proclaims to be nefarious. Waqar bowled superbly and captained shrewdly, but he knew what he was doing and he should have been suspended, especially in view of the fact that he has already been punished for the same offence by a braver referee.

For England this match was like a cold bath. The batsmen wilted amidst the unbearable excitement of the last two hours against probing spin from Saqlain Mushtaq and furious pace and swing from Waqar Younis and Wasim Akram. Bowling all but three of the overs delivered yesterday from the Warwick Road End, Saqlain had to wait until his forty-first over to get a wicket but once the cat was amongst the pigeons the feathers flew everywhere: in his last six overs he took four wickets for five.

Marcus Trescothick's fine century, his first at home and the third in the match by an England batsman, receded rapidly in significance as England collapsed for the second time. More than ever the crucial wicket was Thorpe's. From the moment that Pakistan's captain sent his off-stump cartwheeling, England were exposed. They have plenty of time between now and the first Test against Australia in just over four weeks' time to chew over their shortcomings here. It is ironic that after years of inadequacy they should have lost this match in essence not because of a lack of self-belief but an excess of it. In a nutshell they paid for their over-confident cricket on Saturday when they imploded for the first time after Thorpe had run himself out.

They tried a little too hard, perhaps, to emulate the current Australian team, who believe that they can win from almost any position. The pragmatic approach by a side one-up in a two-match series, faced with an opposition total of 403 on a pitch that was going to last five days, would have been to bat and bat, making the game safe before they even considered the possibility of winning it. To have taken the bolder course was admirable in one way but coach, captain and all concerned have been given a timely reminder that they are not as good as they had begun to believe they were.

Atherton and Trescothick continued to bat with great skill through the morning against cautious field-placings and accurate bowling by Wasim, Waqar and Saqlain, but Pakistan's tactics proved dead right. By reducing the number of boundaries they steadily decreased the outside possibility of a successful assault on the target of 370. It was still just about in England's sights when Atherton was bowled by a typical Waqar inswinger three overs before lunch.

Vaughan had a torrid time as Waqar expertly varied more late in-dippers with balls that whistled past on the outside. Finally it was Abdur Razzaq who found his outside edge after 89 minutes and 62 balls of struggle, and by tea England had managed only 45 more runs from 29 overs as Saqlain successfully bottled up Trescothick by bowling over the wicket into the rough outside his leg stump.

Again, the end justified the means. Only 32 overs remained but the dam was spectacularly breached when the new ball was taken. Thorpe was beaten by a ball that left him late, Trescothick by a bouncer that took his glove to give Rashid Latif a diving leg-side catch before, amidst frenzied appealing, England lost four wickets for a single run in thirteen balls and, with them, the match.

Knight, Ward and Caddick were out to what replays proved were no-balls, bad lapses all by umpires under pressure but under-standable ones too. Apparently both umpires were warned by Hastings that no-balls were being missed but in the heat of the middle they were more concerned by what was happening at the business end. Knight, dubiously, and Caddick were both out first ball and Ward played a poor shot in his anxiety to take back the initiative and scatter some of the close fielders that were now surrounding the batsmen.

Cork and Gough lasted eleven overs after that but Cork went leg-before with seven overs still left and Gough's cover drive was taken inches from the ground only two balls later. No wonder most of the Pakistan team took to the outfield again when the crowd had dispersed to pray in gratitude for their deliverance.

The spectators themselves will never forget the extraordinary finish.

The overall attendance for the game was 65,000. It maintained Old Trafford's position as the best-supported Test ground outside London based on aggregate crowds over the last five years. Some Lancashire folk suspect that there are ECB officials who believe that Manchester should occasionally have a year without staging a Test. They need not worry so long as Peter Marron and his staff continue to produce pitches as excellent as this one.

Tuesday, 5 June
'Shep will be devastated,' said David Graveney yesterday about one of the game's best umpires and best-loved characters. It is how everyone who loves cricket will have felt about the embarrassing pictures that accompanied reports of the last day of a dramatic and constantly entertaining match, showing Pakistan's captain tampering with the ball behind David Shepherd's broad back and three England batsmen being given out to no-balls delivered by Saqlain Mushtaq under his normally sharp eyes.

Graveney's reaction, speaking on BBC Radio Four, was that of a decent man, steeped all his life in cricket. I must say honestly that it was my instinctive reaction too. It sounds like sour grapes, after a victory brought about mainly by brilliant bowling from three distinguished members of one of the most likeable (with all their accompanying peccadilloes), talented and entertaining sides in world cricket, to mention cheating by a great cricketer; and it feels like kicking a man when he is down to dwell on incompetence by an outstanding umpire and a delightful man under extreme pressure. Heaven knows that a robot would have found it hard to get everything right and to spot all that was going on in the frenzied finish to the match.

Alas, that is not the real point, which is that television cameras see practically everything, and so, therefore, do television viewers, who make up a bigger and, these days, better-informed group of people than anyone on the ground. Let us be candid about this: in this case television exposed mistakes that decided the outcome of the game. That is not to say that the mistakes, as usual, did not affect both sides at different times of the match. Generally, moreover, David Shepherd and Eddie Nicholls got most things right. It was Nicholls' good fortune on the last day to be at the fast bowlers' end where there were no bat/pad and few lbw decisions to make.

All sentiment apart, however, it is not good enough for administrators to sweep the latest controversies under the carpet as the ICC did yesterday. 'Brian Hastings, the referee, has decided to take no action,' a spokesman said. Hastings, the former New Zealand batsman, was aware of the no-balls, of course. The ICC spokesman added that he was not sure whether Hastings, who was due to meet the operations manager, Clive Hitchcock, at Lord's yesterday, had seen Channel 4's pictures of Waqar gouging the side of the ball with his fingernails, but he had already decided that no further action would be taken. It was obviously relevant that the umpires had inspected the ball periodically, as is their duty, and had not noticed any unnatural change in its condition. There are, however, plenty of precedents for the use of television evidence by referees. Either referees are going to enforce the spirit of the laws, the laws themselves and the ICC's own code of conduct, or they are not. If they are not going to act we might as well scrap the whole expensive system.

Television viewers know, if Hastings does not, that Waqar acted in direct contravention of Law 42. It appears to make no difference that this is an offence for which he has already been punished. He was suspended for a one-day international last year after being found guilty of changing the condition of the ball in a match between Pakistan and Sri Lanka. As captain, he is supposed to have responsibility for his side playing the game fairly, let alone for doing so himself.

I understand why England have no wish to follow this up but it was a pity that Graveney should have blamed 'the press' for writing about no-balls and ball-tampering when they should have been praising Pakistan for a deserved victory. Quite apart from the fact that this was the first point made by this and most other writers, can the chief executive of the Professional Cricketers' Association not see that it is television that creates and dictates the debate?

Television rules cricket. It pays for the whole professional circus

and it drives most of the changes. With ever-increasing sophisti-
cation it graphically displays the glories of the game. It also makes
fools of umpires, players and administrators.

The first lesson of this aspect of the Old Trafford Test is that
the third umpire should be the most experienced of the three.
He should be constantly in touch with his colleagues and, where
the technology is indisputably correct, empowered to guide them
to the right decision; even, provided it is done quickly, to correct
mistakes. Cricket has always been prey to human error, and some
cricketers have always pushed the laws to the limit but, like them
or hate them, television replays have changed our perspective for
ever.

Four

First Encounters

In rough waters after Old Trafford, the English ship now found itself trying to sail between the Scylla of Australia and the Charybdis of Pakistan. It was soon bouncing more or less helplessly from one set of rocks to the other, eventually to emerge with sails tattered and mast broken, urgently in need of a refit and a fresh crew.

The voyage was a necessity given the economics of contemporary cricket, but it did immediate damage to the morale of the game in England and raised security problems that gave the new Minister for Sport, Richard Caborn, appointed after Tony Blair's second triumphant election on 7 June, his first headaches in a job in which he seemed at first to be floundering as much as English one-day cricket.

Eight of the nine one-day internationals before the final of the NatWest Series on 23 June were played in fine weather and to full houses. There were more good matches than usual, notably those at Bristol, where Australia prevailed only in the final over against England; at Trent Bridge, where they suffered their only defeat of the tournament in the face of a major total by Pakistan; and at Lord's, where England missed their chance to win a game that reached a feverishly exciting climax.

At Bristol on an occasion particularly well-planned and executed by Gloucestershire's staff, there were notable stands first by Trescothick and Knight, and then by Owais Shah and the resurrected Ben Hollioake. One never quite felt, however, that England had scored enough, even with a total of 268 for 4, on a ground reduced in size to accommodate the extra spectators. By the time that Steve Waugh had hit the winning four with three balls in hand, twelve sixes had been struck, the most significant of them by Gloucestershire's very own mercenary, Ian Harvey, off the last ball of the 49th over. Ricky Ponting, who looked to be in the early stages of a prolific tour, added 102 to the 70 he had made against Pakistan in Cardiff the previous day.

England's next match, at Lord's on 12 June, was one of the best on a ground where expectations of limited-overs games are so seldom satisfied. Superb fast bowling by Waqar Younis and sharper fielding under pressure won the match for Pakistan in the end. For the England side there was considerable consolation not only in the fact that they had again pushed strong opponents so close but also in the performances of Shah and Trescothick, whose 137 was the second-highest innings in a one-day international at Lord's. Chasing 243 to win, perfectly feasible on a true pitch against a Pakistan attack possessing only one outstanding fast bowler, they had started dreadfully, losing three wickets for 26 in the first 11 overs.

Shah's run-out by Younis Khan for 60 after he had backed up too far started a second collapse in quite different circumstances, but they had still reached the final over needing only nine to win with two wickets in hand. Trescothick drove the first ball of Saqlain Mushtaq's over for two and the second ball was a wide but Somerset's young champion was out to the second legitimate ball of the over, trying to hit a six in the direction that he had already hit three and dying by the sword with which he had lived.

With only six runs needed Shahid Afridi coolly held on to the skier at square-leg that virtually settled the game despite the distraction of Shoaib Malik rushing in to claim the catch from his position backward of square. Shoaib collided heavily with his colleague, damaging a shoulder as he fell, but Afridi flung the ball skywards in triumph and Pakistan duly squeezed home when Andrew Caddick missed a swing at the final ball with three runs still needed.

Such thin margins decide games like this. Trescothick will no doubt realise that he need not have gone for so big a shot, having got the equation down to six runs off five balls. It was an example of the inexperience of pressurised situations which is still losing matches for England.

That was effectively the end of their interest in this tournament. Losing the toss in damp weather at Old Trafford against Australia they were hounded to a humiliating defeat under the floodlights by McGrath, Gillespie and Lee as Waugh posted a semi-circle of slips and gullies to ram home the point that his fast bowlers would dominate whenever conditions allowed. Three days later the batsmen were mauled again, this time by Waqar Younis, who took the first seven wickets at Headingley.

He followed this amazing performance by taking six more wickets in two spells to boost his side's morale before the rematch in the final, despite a typically dashing display of vengeful stroke-play by Gilchrist. He repeated it at Lord's, but, sadly for the occasion, not in circumstances that stretched him. On a beautiful day and good pitch they bowled out a strong Pakistan batting side for 152 and would have won by 10 wickets if they had not shown a trace of humanity by offering Mark Waugh's wicket in the form of a run-out.

Hesitation, the cause of this unaccustomed and strictly temporary fall from grace, is not customarily a fault of the best Australian cricketers. The one blot on an otherwise unblemished copybook was swiftly erased by Gilchrist's forward march to 76 not out and a performance of such rarefied virtuosity by Ricky Ponting that Pakistan's bowlers had a hint of what it must have been like running in against Bradman.

Gilchrist looked what he is, a batsman of the highest class, who gets right forward or back according to the length of the ball and hits it with the full face of the cleanest of blades. In his brief appearance on the sunlit stage, Ponting looked even better on his way to 35 off 23 balls, hitting a six and five fours. He included amongst them a cut, a trademark, quick-footed pull, a leg glance and three drives through the 'V', the last of them no more than an extended forward defensive which left mid-off sprawling as the ball seemed magically to gather pace past his right hand. It would be a surprise if the Australian strategists do not conclude that the time has come to promote Ponting to three in the Test order, thereby solving the problem of how they can fit the deserving Damien Martyn into the team.

Not, of course, that Gilchrist, Ponting and Waugh, who played sublimely off his legs in particular, had much to do after the bowlers had all performed so well. Pakistan were quite right to bat first on a dry, true pitch which lost pace as soon as the ball became softer, but the total of 250 needed to give Waqar Younis and Wasim Akram a chance on what might have been a farewell appearance from them both at Lord's was beyond them from the moment that Brett Lee, confirming his fitness and quality on the big occasion, took the first of his two wickets for 20 in eight fierce but controlled overs of fast bowling.

Both Lee and Jason Gillespie bowled balls recorded at over 90mph but it was Glenn McGrath, quite fast enough, who made the first incision, as he invariably does, finding the top corner of Salim Elahi's bat as he played forward to a ball that bounced too sharply for him. Saeed Anwar had his sights set on a big innings, so much so that he refused Yousuf Youhana's call to get off the mark with a single hit wide of mid-on, but, aware that a score of 47 was insufficient, he miscued a lofted drive to mid-off in the fifteenth over. After that only Abdur Razzaq looked likely to play an inspirational innings, only Inzamam-ul-Haq a substantial one. Abdur tried in vain to take on Lee's pace, pulling to mid-wicket from too high on the bat, while Shane Warne accounted for Inzamam with a straight ball.

Going well forward to it, Inzamam had read it as a leg-break but there was no evidence that it would have turned past the off-stump. On the other hand he clearly expected the benefit of the doubt. His extended portrayal of a man in a profound state of extreme grief, worthy of Sir Henry Irving at his most melodramatic, cost him half his match fee and a two-match suspension from the referee, Brian Hastings.

Warne claimed three wickets eventually in exchange for a few good blows from the later batsmen, none of whom could make much else out of the pace and control of the three big fast bowlers or the accuracy and clever pace-changes of Harvey on his annual mid-summer visit to the home of cricket. He was as effective for Australia as for Gloucestershire.

Australia's celebrations were marred when Michael Bevan, whose renowned expertise had hardly been required throughout the competition, was hit by a full beer-can thrown from the crowd on the outfield to his position on the middle balcony of the pavilion. Waugh, increasingly determined to get something done to keep the players away from stupid, mischievous or downright anarchic spectators, immediately walked his players back to the dressing-room, leaving sponsors, officials and television personnel embarrassed and annoyed.

After a meeting between the ECB and the England Management Advisory Committee it was agreed that a separate group of twenty-five players, shortlisted for the 2003 World Cup but not contracted, would be announced at some time in the next few weeks. England's more or less hopeless performances in the one-day game had vied for newspaper space with the other 'English' problem of the moment, the unruliness of British-domiciled Pakistanis who, in Birmingham, Leeds and Nottingham, had invaded the field in defiance of police, stewards, temporary plastic fencing (at Trent Bridge) and all entreaties.

Rioting crowds used not to be an English problem, in cricket anyway. Ray Robinson wrote a book entitled *The Wildest Tests* which included chapters on riots in Adelaide, Brisbane, Sydney, Karachi, Bombay, Hyderabad, Georgetown, Port of Spain, Kingston, and, more than once, Calcutta, but the best he could do to unearth an English example was a Test at The Oval in 1884 when the players went into lunch with Australia needing only eleven to win. A section of the crowd objected and held up play by taking to the field, apparently because they thought this was an attempt to extract more gate money from people coming in for the afternoon's play. The periodical *Cricket* recorded: 'For some time a certain section of the crowd remained in front of the pavilion, behaving in a very disorderly manner. When the bell rang for a renewal at half-past two, their attitude became still more hostile, and the middle of the ground was not only occupied but the stumps sent flying. Seeing the mob pull up the stumps, some of the Australians went out to explain that they left the field not to get more gate money but to save the caterers heavy loss. No charge would be made after lunch.'

1. 'England to win the Ashes?' The two captains, Nasser Hussain and Steve Waugh, share a joke before the first Test at Edgbaston.

2. At last! Darren Gough celebrates the wicket of Steve Waugh during the third day of the Edgbaston Test.

3. Marcus Trescothick glances Shane Warne during the fourth day in Birmingham.

4. One of the great teams: Australia in England, 2001. Back row, left to right: Pat Farhart (fitness trainer), Simon Katich, Brett Lee, Jason Gillespie, Damien Fleming, Damien Martyn, Justin Langer; middle row: Errol Alcott (chief physiotherapist), Michael Slater, Colin Miller, Matthew Hayden, Ashley Noffke, Wade Seccombe, Mike Walsh (scorer); front row: Ricky Ponting, Glenn McGrath, John Buchanan (coach), Steve Waugh, Adam Gilchrist, Steve Bernard (manager), Shane Warne, Mark Waugh.

5. Biter bit: Mike Atherton hooks Glenn McGrath for four at Lord's – but McGrath was too good in the end.

7. The Australians repeatedly claimed the series was tougher than it seemed. Andy Caddick bounces Mark Waugh at Lord's.

6. Cool command: Mark Waugh on the way to his flawless century at Lord's.

8. Pace like fire: Graham Thorpe hooks Brett Lee for four shortly before a broken hand put him out of the rest of the series.

9. You beauty! Lee celebrates bowling Mark Ramprakash at Lord's.

10. Man of the match Glenn McGrath leads Australia's lap of honour after winning the Lord's Test.

11. The most exposed job of all: umpires John Hampshire and Srini Venkataraghavan during the second day of the third Test at Trent Bridge.

12. The wizard in his pomp: Shane Warne claimed early in the series that his would be a supporting role, but he was a constant menace to England throughout. Here he celebrates another five-wicket haul at Trent Bridge.

13. A dejected England side after losing the Ashes. Left to right: Ramprakash, White, Ward, Tudor, Trescothick, Caddick, Stewart.

14. Ricky Ponting hastening Australia towards a bold declaration on the fourth day at Headingley.

15. Mark Butcher hooks Glenn McGrath during the critical spell after lunch on the fifth day at Leeds.

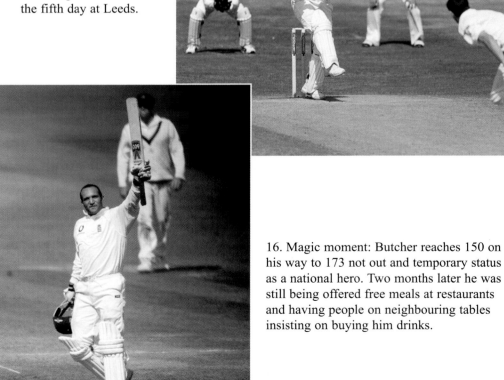

16. Magic moment: Butcher reaches 150 on his way to 173 not out and temporary status as a national hero. Two months later he was still being offered free meals at restaurants and having people on neighbouring tables insisting on buying him drinks.

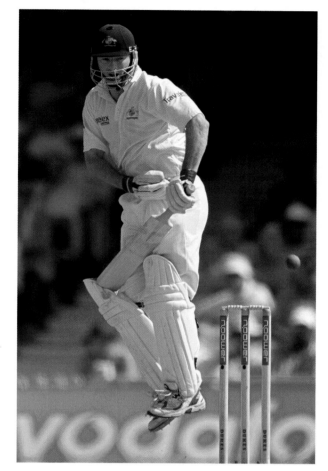

17. A wounded Waugh is better than none. Australia's flinty captain on his way to a century at The Oval, in a match he was supposed to have missed.

18. Watching it on to the bat: Mark Ramprakash approaches his hundred with a swept four off a tiring Shane Warne.

19. All good things must end. Michael Atherton walks to the Pavilion after his final Test innings, dismissed for 9 by, inevitably, McGrath.

20. Mission accomplished: Steve Waugh raises the Ashes replica after his team's triumph at The Oval.

The answer to the current spate of crowd invasions was harder to find than the causes, which had invariably been as much social as cricketing. The behaviour, generally speaking, had been over-exuberant rather than menacing, but as Waugh had pointed out, the steward who had been trampled and kicked at Leeds might be an injured player tomorrow – or worse.

The invaders had been mainly young Pakistanis, objecting in some cases to perceived racial and social injustices, in others simply behaving as they have seen others do on their television screens. Cricket grounds are places for them to vent their feelings; some simply to let off steam and say boo to the forces of established order; others merely to show off and have a good time. By making the spectators such a big part of their transmission of cricket, tele-vision producers since Channel Nine set the trend in Australia in the late 1970s must take some of the blame for the fact that crowds no longer seem to know their place.

If invasions in England were currently a problem confined to youthful and rebellious British Muslims, crowd yobbery generally had been more the preserve of the beer-swilling English. Dr Khalid Anis, a GP from Warrington, wrote to Lancashire and the ECB after the Old Trafford Test complaining of 'aggressive English sup-port, continuous abuse, foul language and chanting of "Oldham", an obvious incitement'.

The horn-blowing that is the latest fad of the Pakistani sup-porters (it is whistles and conches in the Caribbean) is a monot-onous irritation to many other spectators and, as a thousand e-mails attested, to radio listeners too, but it was the chanting refugees from the football terraces who long ago made it impossible to go to any big cricket match and to watch it in peace, picking up vibes from the middle, hearing bat on ball, absorbing the envi-ronment. That is a pleasure restricted now to aficionados of the County Championship.

Noise is a matter of taste and opinion; so, up to a point, is what some would call oafish behaviour, others youthful exuberance. But about the safety of players, umpires and stewards, not to mention other spectators, there can be only one opinion. It has to be guaranteed if the game is not to suffer serious degradation. If plastic fencing held up by stewards delayed the worst excesses of the young invaders at Trent Bridge, it was clearly not the whole answer. Nor could the ICC come up with anything more practical at its simultaneous AGM at Lord's, where the legacy and continuing threat of fixed matches was a much more pressing item on the agenda.

The ICC already had two formal rules on safety issues, stating that no spectator has any right to enter the field until the players and umpires have left it; and that no spectator has a right to throw any object at any player, umpire or fellow spectator. It is the duty of each country to take the corrective measures necessary. The ECB began pressing the government for authority to apply heavy fines to those who take the field before a match is over and the field cleared. That may stop isolated streakers, but not mass invasions by thousands of the kind that had been seen in the last fortnight.

Only solid, high fences could guarantee that. They are ugly, obstructive to the spectators' view of the game and, since the Safety of Sports Ground Act, no longer permitted in the UK. If, perish the thought, this sort of invasion were to become commonplace rather than a temporary phenomenon, a moat between the crowd and the field of play, such as the one that stopped the trouble at the Maracana football stadium in Rio de Janeiro, would be no less effective and aesthetically less objectionable. But it would reduce the playing area and might endanger the safety of fielders diving to stop boundaries.

For the time being, mounted police or roving Alsatians, or both, might curb the excesses at games wherein trouble could be anticipated in advance. Spectators have a distinct aversion to sharp teeth or flying hooves; but the longer-term and more attractive solution was to deal with the social problem to which some of the young Pakistanis had been objecting through the medium of their brilliant cricket team; and to educate them into a changed culture that encourages greater discipline and outlaws bad behaviour. The same goes for the excesses of the beer-swillers.

Five

Edgbaston: The Die is Cast

It was not just the stock of individuals that had fallen as England approached the opening Test against Australia. The whole carefully planned enterprise was in trouble. The captain, Nasser Hussain, had played for Essex against the touring team but not with any success, and he was short of match practice. Neither Craig White nor Ashley Giles was fully fit. Michael Vaughan was about to have a knee operation. Graham Thorpe was under orders to give his damaged calf muscle seven days of total rest. Mark Ramprakash, originally selected as his replacement, had strained a hamstring and, to his bitter disappointment, he too had withdrawn.

For the Australians, everything had gone right from the moment they had arrived. Australian sport was more buoyant than ever with Pat Rafter smoothly moving through the rounds towards another Wimbledon final and the Wallabies about to bounce back decisively in their home series against the British and Irish Lions.

Some, standing in the Long Room at Lord's as the Australian team had walked out to field in the recent one-day final, had described them as looking like boxers on their way to the ring for a world title fight. The same sort of intense focus would be applied to the next task.

Wednesday, 4 July
Less has changed about the prospects for the most eagerly awaited Test match in England for four years than seemed likely even twenty-four hours ago. Forced by injuries to shed the best batsman

in the country, Graham Thorpe, and one of only three other men to have scored a hundred in the last five Tests, Michael Vaughan, the home side will still go into the first game against Australia at Edgbaston this morning with at least seven and possibly eight of the ten men who battled their way though every Test in Sri Lanka.

Being realists, they must recognise that Australia remain the best side in the world and that Thorpe's absence in particular only enhances their favouritism for this potentially critical first match. Blissfully free of injuries, the majority of the Australian XI took to the golf course yesterday whilst Steve Waugh was accepting the ICC's new Test Championship trophy on their behalf. He has every reason to hope that his team will be even further ahead of the pack by the time that the Ashes have been won or lost for the sixty-first time since Ivo Bligh was presented with the urn by those admiring ladies from Victoria in 1883.

After a week of unavoidable prevarication, Robert Croft, one of the ten common to England's 2–1 success in Sri Lanka, was sent back to Wales yesterday. Matthew Hoggard, having lost form disappointingly since his stout performance against Pakistan at Old Trafford a month ago, returned no less disconsolately to Yorkshire, especially as he was promptly left out of his county side as well. It is hard to imagine Australia leaving out a bowler who has taken six wickets in his second Test match – let alone dropping him from a State side as well – but Yorkshire folk often think like Australians and they would say, no doubt, that it just goes to show the strength of county cricket.

Anyone wanting to put a more optimistic spin on England's situation would make something, too, of yesterday's more optimistic news that Craig White has pronounced himself fully fit and that Ashley Giles has shaken off a viral infection. Happy that his Achilles tendon weakness will not impair his return to the side on his home ground, Giles was named in Nasser Hussain's favoured XI after nets yesterday as the England captain endeavoured to give an impression of the same sort of decisiveness in the home dressing room as there is in Australia's. He confirmed that he was happy to have White as one of only three fast bowlers, potentially supported in swing bowling conditions by Mark Butcher or Marcus Trescothick.

CRAIG WHITE

Nice fellow, Chalky. Talented cricketer, too. Pity he didn't quite make it as a Test player. That was the general view until two things transformed his career in 2000. First came the injuries that prompted Duncan Fletcher and Nasser Hussain to track him down to New Zealand, where he was spending his winter, to reinforce England's one-day team in South Africa and Zimbabwe; then the greater use of radar to measure the speed of international bowlers. Everyone knew that White was capable of bowling inswinging yorkers at an explosive pace but no one took his bowling seriously enough until they realised from scientific evidence (however fallible) that he was on a level with the specialist fast bowlers.

Anxious to find someone to stiffen the England batting in the lower part of the order, Fletcher saw White as the answer to a prayer. Once he showed, during the one-day games against the West Indies, that he could also be a highly effective bowler from round the wicket against left-handers, he was inked in as a permanent member of the Test team too. His special art lies in reverse-swinging a worn cricket ball and cutting it away from left-handers – or in to right-handers – at speed.

Success was overdue for a modest, friendly man and a cricketer curiously diffident about his ability, considering that he had spent much of his youth in Australia. He went to the Australian Academy at Adelaide as a wicket-keeper who could also bowl off-breaks, but Yorkshire colleagues encouraged the ability to get the ball down quickly when he proved it in the Headingley nets.

White's confidence grew visibly as his influence in the team became stronger and stronger during the tours of Pakistan and Sri Lanka. A maiden first-class hundred before the first of the Tests in Pakistan proved that he could bat with real authority, taking the attack to good spin bowlers with quick feet and clean, strong strokes. When the Ashes series started he was the established all-rounder England had craved since Botham. What he himself craved most was success against Australia and the respect it would give him in the opposition camp. This was the opportunity of his life and he had said in Sri Lanka that he believed the challenge would raise his game.

If he had been as good as his word it might have been a very different series. But he could not get a meaningful run until they dropped him, where-upon he reeled off two huge centuries for Yorkshire; nor could he get a wicket that mattered. Only White himself knew how much he had been restricted by his back injury but his bowling depends on his elastic action. Untune that string and hark what discord follows.

Fully fit, this amiable man is a proper Test all-rounder. Fitness will deter-mine whether he gets another chance to prove it against Australia, but they will not believe he can truly play until he does so against them.

2001 v. Australia: 3 matches; 38 runs at 7.60; 1 wicket at 189

The sweltering heat in Birmingham yesterday promised an almighty thunderstorm, or at least thundery rain, some time during the next twenty-four hours, which bodes well for swing bowlers. Even with seventeen names whittled down finally to twelve, Hussain will have a tricky decision to make between Giles and Dominic Cork this morning. 'It's pretty much in my mind that we will need a spinner,' he said. 'It looks a good wicket. There are not too many cracks; it's not too damp and I don't think it will favour anyone in particular.'

The covers were on by early afternoon yesterday, despite no immediate threat of a storm. Both captains will wish to see how much of an old-fashioned covering of grass Steve Rouse takes off when he gives his strip, two away from the notorious pitch of recent years, a final trim this morning. If he leaves too much the Duke ball might dart about a bit and in these conditions it should certainly swing. That might yet mean that Cork keeps the place that three weeks ago he looked more likely to lose to Hoggard than to Giles.

Logically Hussain will play his spinner if he decides that he would like to bat first. Taking both an evenly grassed pitch and the uncertain weather into consideration, this is one Test toss he would not mind losing. Knowing his luck, that is sure to mean the end of his extraordinary run of eleven lost tosses out of twelve. It was in humid, cloudy weather four years ago that Gough, Caddick and Devon Malcolm bowled Australia out cheaply in ideal swing bowling conditions to set up the deceptive victory that followed.

If the weather is similar this morning, McGrath, Lee and Gillespie will be like greyhounds in the slips. It was a typical piece of calculated bravado for Australia to name their XI, and their batting order, three days before the game. Let it rain, let it thunder, they know what they want and how they propose to get it. As Waugh expressed it yesterday, without conceit, it will be by trusting their talent and applying themselves fully to the task in hand. In his words, by 'discipline in everything we do, on and off the field, and eliminating the bad session which can cost a Test match'.

The bookmakers William Hill are offering seven to one against an English win here, generous odds no matter how vulnerable the England batting appears. It was typical of cricket, and can only be good news for his own and England's future, that Owais Shah should have reacted to the selectors' preference for Usman Afzaal by playing another outstanding innings for Middlesex yesterday. Afzaal, who will bat at seven after Atherton, Trescothick, Butcher, Hussain, Ward and Stewart, is still a poor fielder (in contrast to Shah) but he will not lack confidence and he is a crisp stroke-player who plays closer to the body than Shah around the off-stump. With White back to add quality and resolve, and Giles or Cork at nine, there is the depth to the batting order on which Duncan Fletcher has always insisted.

USMAN AFZAAL

It said much for the ebullient 'Uzzy' that he played his natural game for England in his first three Tests despite knowing, as he must have done, that most of those watching him were wondering why he was in the side. He was picked on a hunch when the selectors had been expected, by most journalists at least, to opt for Owais Shah of Middlesex. They had both been on England 'A' tours and Shah got the first chance in the One-Day Internationals for which Afzaal had been overlooked because of his reputation as a mediocre fielder.

Self-confident to the point of irritating cockiness in the eyes of opponents, Afzaal was wise enough not to provoke the Australians. He hit some memorable strokes in his first six innings in Test cricket but the manner of his dismissals somehow stuck in the mind too. The impression was of a plucky boy trying to live amongst men. There is much natural ability on which to work and he can bowl tidy left-arm spin, originally his stronger suit, but the batting technique needs a great deal of work if it is to measure up to the demands in the long-term.

There is certainly a will, so there may be a way: he is as dedicated to his cricket as he is to his Muslim faith.

2001 v. Australia: 3 matches; 83 runs at 16.60; 1 wicket at 49

England now have to run the race that is set before them. Hussain believes that they can, and will. 'I just want all my team to earn Australian respect,' he said. 'If we do that and don't shy away and show them that we've got the character that we've worked on for eighteen months, then we can definitely beat them.'

To prove it, a less convincing-looking group of close fielders will need to hold all the chances and either Atherton or

Trescothick, or both, will need to establish a bridgehead against Australia's formidable fast bowlers before Shane Warne gets his chance to show that he can still be a match-winner, even if he is not quite the bowler he was. Atherton is one of four players on the two teams, with Stewart and the Waugh twins, to have played more than a hundred Tests. It is the first time that there have been more than three with over a hundred caps in the same game. All 20,000 seats have been sold for the first four days, another first. It is one indication of the excitement stirred by a series that promises so much.

Thursday, 5 July
First Test, Edgbaston (first day of five; Australia won toss): Australia, with 8 first-innings wickets in hand, are 161 runs behind England.
Steve Waugh cares far more about what happens on the field than what is said off it, but there was much busy scribbling in notebooks when he said on Wednesday: 'The first session of the first day of the first Test really is crucial.' It was an aphorism wise enough, it seemed, to be the birth of an adage, but it took no more than a day for its truth to questioned. The last session of the first day of the first Test at Edgbaston yesterday was every bit as significant.

Shane Warne started it with two wickets in five balls to claim five wickets in a Test innings for the seventeenth time and the fifth against his favourite opposition. Michael Slater, batting with the glittering brilliance of a diamond, finished it by racing to 76 not out in the first 22 overs of Australia's reply. But in the 79 balls that intervened, Alec Stewart and Andrew Caddick turned a patently unsatisfactory England total of 191 for 9 into one that gave their bowlers at least a sporting chance on a dry pitch. Their last-wicket partnership of 103 was battered out to roars of patriotic fervour by the crowd that resounded like a long echo of those that in the last few days have hailed the deeds of Tim Henman and the British Lions.

ANDREW CADDICK

Able but sometimes tactless, knowledgeable but still inclined to be gauche, good-hearted but often graceless, Andrew Caddick is a sheep in wolf's clothing. He can be curt; smiles do not come naturally but those who know him well, like him. He has gathered a wealth of experience between those prominent ears and he wants to help.

Caddick the bowler can be a wolf as vicious as any. In the mood, with, so to speak, the scent of food in the air, there is no stopping him. Hitting the pitch hard at just short of a length he can threaten a batsman's ribs with every ball. When it is swinging as well, as it was when he took his four wickets in an over against the West Indies at Headingley, he can become a Lindwall on stilts.

The weaker side of his bowling is well known. He has the respect of every batsman he confronts but some of the bolder have successfully nettled him by attacking him early in his spell, believing his spirits droop quicker than most. Increasingly, however, he can point to his figures. He has been at least an equal part of England's best opening partnership for years and physically he has never shirked a challenge. Since bowling through the pain of shin-splints in the Caribbean on his first England tour his long, lean frame has been put through the mill, but usually it has stood the strain, not least because of the excellence of his action.

If his captains want long spells, Caddick, like Barkis, is willing. It is on the days when they feel like asking him to keep going that batsmen have to fear. Once he hits that formidable rhythm he can bowl out all but the best sides in most conditions. Fifteen wickets at 50 each against Australia reflected not so much a loss of form as a batting side that was simply too good for him.

2001 v. Australia: 5 matches; 101 runs at 14.42; 15 wickets at 49.86

Nothing lifts the spirits of a team like a last-wicket stand and Caddick's 49 not out off 40 balls, the penalty for Australian bowlers trying to break his bones rather than his wicket, was almost a mirror image of the sort of treatment that Australian tail-enders have handed out to tiring English bowlers on hot days over the recent period of unbroken Australian domination: from Geoff Lawson at Lord's and Merv Hughes at Leeds in 1989 to Damien Fleming at the 'Gabba in the 1998.

Those innings (74, 71 and 71 not out) symbolised Australia's supremacy. This, the fourth-highest last-wicket partnership for England, only the fourteenth ever last-wicket hundred in Test cricket and the first for England against Australia since Tip Foster and Wilfred Rhodes put on 130 at Sydney in 1903/04, did no more than confirm that there is character in this team. Whether it will affect the result of the game is doubtful after the flying start given to Australia's first innings by Slater and Hayden. Already Australia have hit twenty-one fours and a six in exchange for the wickets of Hayden, the victim of an astounding left-handed catch by Craig White at mid-wicket off Ashley Giles, and Ricky Ponting, given out lbw to a no-ball from Darren Gough.

ASHLEY GILES

Success at Test cricket could not have come to a more deserving fellow than Ashley Giles. It was not just that he is one of life's sunny characters but also that he had battled with injury and bad luck to get a proper chance for England. Few had filled the baths or carried out the drinks more cheerfully than this perennial twelfth man. He was like a large and amiable teddy bear in the corner of the dressing-room.

He was not fit for the Edgbaston Test but he had been part of the long-term plan and everyone was as keen as Ashley himself that he should play. To Australian batsmen, however, the wicket-taking demon of Karachi and Colombo became no more than a generous-sized punch-bag.

2001 v. Australia: 1 match; 7 runs at 3.50; 1 wicket at 108

It would be too much to hope that the second day can match the frenetic pace of the first. By the end of a quite extraordinary third session in which 236 runs were scored from 43.3 overs at a rate of 6.84 an over, 427 runs had been exchanged for 12 wickets. In all, there were fifty-five fours and two sixes and, believe it or not, five possible catches missed. How, in all seriousness, can anyone prefer limited-overs cricket to this?

Today's events may depend to some extent on atmospheric conditions after the thunderstorm that seemed to be approaching fast as the bails were lifted at last on the spellbinding third session. Gough had a worthy appeal for lbw turned down when Slater was 71 but he will have to bowl with better control than he did in an over-excited first over from which Slater, Australia's D'Artagnan, cut, drove and sliced four fours. England must be relieved indeed that they included Giles in the final XI because the pitch is taking spin and its bounce is uneven, but if they are not to concede a first-innings lead of fatal proportions they must take half-chances like the one to Ian Ward, when Hayden carved his first ball from Caddick through the fieldsman's hands at cover point.

MICHAEL SLATER

When Alec Bedser first saw Michael Slater batting for New South Wales, shortly before his dazzling start for Australia in England in 1993, he recognised the first batsman he had seen with footwork as good as Don Bradman's. If Slater had possessed the greatest batsman's temperament, he might well have been as good a player.

He started with a fifty in his first Test at Manchester, the very city his father had left to emigrate to Australia. If only he had stayed, I wondered as this bright-eyed, eloquent, naturally charming young man came up to the BBC commentary box to talk with infectious enthusiasm about the game, would he have come through the English system as such a wonderful player? Would he have played for his country so young? Would his talent have been recognised so clearly?

The answer had to be no. Brought up in Wagga Wagga and taught a correct technique by a persevering coach who would make him hit a ball on a string straight down the line from which it had come, he may have English blood in his veins but is a true son of Australia. It was indeed with all the commitment of the relatively new Australian that he kissed the badge on his helmet when he reached his hundred in the Lord's Test.

How he has made England pay for his father's decision since that electrifying innings of 152. He famously inaugurated the series that followed in Australia by cutting the first ball of the series from Philip DeFreitas for four at the 'Gabba. He made 176. Four years later he lacerated Darren Gough and the rest of the England attack on the same Brisbane ground in the first Test of the series and back in England in 2001 he did it again in the critical opening game at Edgbaston. This time he had to be content with 77 but it was the way that he scored them, rattling away at a run a ball and stopping the England team in its tracks after a last-wicket stand that would normally have been the prelude to a cascade of wickets, that knocked the stuffing out of his opponents again.

Again it was Slater's destiny to set the pattern for Australia's domination. He and his mates had been shocked by the suddenness and fury of the England counter-attack, when Stewart and Caddick robbed them of the satisfaction of bowling them out really cheaply. Yet when Darren Gough bowled his first ball in Australia's reply short outside the off-stump Slater seemed to have time to weigh up the possibility of leaving it alone (as any English counterpart would certainly have done) before deciding that he really might as well go ahead, bring the bat down at the top of its bounce and send it skimming along the ground to the third-man boundary. Four from the first ball; an incredible eighteen from the first over; the England bubble burst cruelly soon. If the buccaneer from Wagga Wagga did nothing else of significance in the matches that followed, it would not really matter. He had made the point: sorry Goughie, you're a great trier, mate; but we're better than you boys.

Passionate, hot-blooded, impetuous and sensitive, he really can find some compassion in his heart for beaten opponents. His own failures weigh as heavily as his days of triumph raise him to heights of elation. A media career beckoned after the shock of being dropped for the last Test of the series, but he may not get quite the same kick from anything as he has from playing Test cricket. Heaven knows why Australia's selectors stopped picking him for one-day internationals. He has every stroke at his command and the format gives him leave to play them.

2001 v. England: 4 matches; 170 runs at 24.28

The day had not started at quite such a heady pace, although 106 for 2 from the 26 overs of a tense morning's cricket was a fair prologue. Hussain duly lost his twelfth toss in thirteen and England their twelfth in the last thirteen Tests with Australia, leaving Waugh to make the tricky choice between using good atmospheric conditions for swing bowling and risking the stamina of only four bowlers in hot conditions should things go wrong.

To some extent they did after Waugh had taken the aggressive course and risked having to bat last on a pitch that should be spinning sharply. When Waugh crept in to bowl his first over and the last before lunch England had sailed their way through the early shoals to the calmer waters of 106 for 1.

In all the excitement that followed it would be easy to under-estimate the sheer menace and excellence of Jason Gillespie's new-ball spell, not to mention his second after lunch, and the skill and determination with which Michael Atherton and Mark Butcher played after Marcus Trescothick had edged his second ball, Gillespie's first, low to first slip. The ball had straightened suffi-ciently for Trescothick to have to play at it and Warne's catch was taken unerringly by his left ankle.

He and Gillespie might have shared an immediate double had Adam Gilchrist, clearly nervous on his first appearance in an Ashes Test, not dived across his bows and missed a low, wide chance before Butcher had scored. But Butcher settled quickly, reminding McGrath of his ability with a hook played with a measured roll of the wrists and driving straight with the full width of his blade.

Atherton needed to be at his sharpest not only against McGrath, probing outside his off stump and occasionally aiming for his ribs, but also against Gillespie's late outswingers. But like Butcher he was true to England's plan to bat positively, and one pull for four off Brett Lee was played with all the relish of a latter-day Everton Weekes. All the more unfortunate for Lee that Atherton should then have cut him at head height past Slater in the gully and then edged the next ball into and out of Gilchrist's right hand.

He proceeded without further alarm to his first fifty in seventeen innings against Australia but either side of lunch England's comforting progress was rapidly reversed. Warne started it, of course. Waugh had missed a trick by not bringing him on earlier than the last over of the morning to exploit Butcher's uncertainty against the best spin bowling. Pressing forward to his second ball, his fine innings was ended by a catch at silly mid-off from pad and bat.

Atherton followed in the sixth over of an afternoon session utterly different from the other two. Caught at second slip off a ball that leapt after hitting ten fours, he was followed in a steady and increasingly melancholy procession by the middle order. Hussain padded up to a ball that bit back; Ward, having started well, not least against Warne, tried to force off the back foot with a bat at 45 degrees; Afzaal aimed loosely at a ball that spun back a long way out of the rough; and White was given out leg before, sweeping. What followed after tea was scarcely credible.

Friday, 6 July
Edgbaston (second day of five): Australia, with 6 first-innings wickets in hand, are 38 runs ahead of England.

If Billy Woodfull was the unbowlable, Steve Waugh is surely the unbreakable. Conditions were thoroughly inimical to batsmen when he walked to the wicket for the eighth ball of the second morning of the first Test yesterday. Thursday's hero, Michael Slater, had lost his off stump driving at Darren Gough's first ball, the light was gloomy, the air heavy with mist. If England had got him out quickly, the advantage would have moved their way. But he would not and did not let it happen, moving with all his renowned resolution and carefully honed craft to his ninth hundred in thirty-nine innings as Australia's captain.

In difficult batting conditions in a match of such significance, it was one of the finest of the twenty-six centuries he has now scored for his country. It was completely without chance, virtually without flaw or anxious moments, and Waugh himself rated it as 'among his best six'. To some extent England missed a chance in what looked like ideal conditions for swing bowling, but the ball did not move as they had hoped, the only slip catch offered was dropped, and essentially Waugh was too good for them, literally and faultlessly playing every ball on its merits.

By the time that he had shared a fourth-wicket partnership of 133 with his far less comfortable brother, Mark, and another of greater fluency later with an assured-looking Damien Martyn, the indomitable captain had taken Australia not only into the lead but also into a position from which they will almost certainly win the game. Only if England knock over the last six wickets with the second new ball, taken two balls before bad light and heavy rain closed in for the evening, can they hope to escape.

It is much more likely that they will be bowled out a second time for a total that will not put the Australians to the test in the kind of fourth-innings challenge they used not to relish in what might be called the pre-Waugh days. 'Anything over 120 to win in the fourth innings would be hard,' Waugh said last night, adding, 'but we're not planning to have one. I think the pitch will start to play a few more tricks.'

England's bowlers were disappointing yesterday and, naturally, very disappointed. Craig White proved his fitness with nine hostile overs before lunch and four more afterwards during which he gave Mark Waugh a torrid time, often striking his gloves, and demanded Steve's respect; but Andrew Caddick never found his most formidable rhythm, while Gough gradually spent his energy and his hope on Waugh's adamantine blade. Giles, though he got the turn that was expected, was defeated more often than not by the quick footwork of batsmen brought up to move boldly to the pitch of the ball. He might have had Mark Waugh stumped for 28 but the ball bounced too high for Stewart to gather it with Waugh a long way down the pitch. He had added only one more run when Trescothick did not react quickly enough to clutch a catch to his left at second slip from an edged cut off White from the second ball after lunch.

It is asking for the impossible, perhaps, for every half-chance to be taken but these are the moments on which series after series have turned towards Australia. Such is the balance of power, they can afford to make more mistakes than England.

Not that Steve Waugh looked like making any yesterday. He ducked the short balls, of which there was no shortage at all as the fast bowlers strove in vain to exploit such uneven bounce as there was; he met those that had to be defended with unyielding resolution and the straightest of bats; and those he knew he could punish he hit to his designated scoring areas with unerring placement and compact power, his body low to the ground and surging into the stroke like a tug butting through the waves. Exploiting a rapid and immaculate outfield he needed only 164 balls and a little less than four hours to reach his latest landmark, preceding the obligatory punch of the air with a clip off his hip to send a ball from Craig White skimming backward of square-leg for his thirteenth four.

Most of his other boundaries were hit, as usual, through extra cover or between mid-wicket and mid-on, his favourite areas. When he did get a ball to cut he never missed the chance, his bat coming hard down on top of the bounce. It was the innings of a pragmatist, a hard, clear-minded man and a technician of the highest quality.

STEVE WAUGH

At a private lunch given in the carpeted elegance of the Sydney Cricket Ground Trust one day in 1980, Alan Davidson, the broad-shouldered match-winner of Richie Benaud vintage, was asked about young players from New South Wales who might make it to the top. Not a man to lavish undue praise he mentioned only one: 'A boy called Steve Waugh hit a ball over extra cover into that Stand over there the other day,' he said. 'He's going to be something special.'

He did not mention his twin brother. Steve was the precocious one and at first it was his sheer talent as a batsman and medium-paced bowler, rather than the hardness and shrewdness for which he later became so famous, that Australians recognised as being the real thing. At a time when they did not stick by every young player they picked, they were very patient with the taciturn young all-rounder from Bankstown.

His lively and intelligent medium-paced bowling kept him in the side at first. It took him six Test innings to reach 20. He had only three fifties in his first twenty innings and played forty-one times before he made a century. He managed it at last against England at Headingley, an innings of such consummate class that everyone knew he would make many more Test hundreds. No one, though, could have predicted that it would be so many. He followed 177 not out at Headingley with 152 not out in the second Test at Lord's and it was one of the memories of the summer when Angus Fraser, in his first Test, finally pierced his defence at Edgbaston.

It has been since then a story of continuous growth, to the point where he has taken on the legendary status of his first captain, Allan Border, and somehow managed to build upon the lofty achievements under his predecessor, Mark Taylor. Many thought it would be beyond him, but Waugh has grown in stature as a captain to the point of becoming one of the statesmen of world cricket. Magnanimous in victory and defeat, he has acquired a wisdom that extends far beyond the game itself.

As a player too, responsibility brought even greater mastery of himself and his opponents. When Australia first won a World Cup, in Calcutta against England, it was Waugh's bowling in the closing overs of a close game that had much to do with it. When they won it again under his command in England in 1999 it became possible because he turned a lost cause into a winning one with a dominating century against South Africa at Leeds. 'You've just dropped the World Cup, mate,' he is supposed to have said to Herschelle Gibbs when he missed him early in that crucial innings. If he didn't say it, it is exactly the sort of thing he would have said. He is supremely self-confident rather than arrogant; aggressive rather than nasty; and as hardy as a thorn tree in the bush.

He is also bright; a respecter of cricket's traditions; interested in people and in the world around him. The natural cricketer has proved also to be a natural leader of men. In a world of international cricket that can easily become all-consuming, he learned perspective both from a happy marriage and a challenge one day on a tour of India to get involved with poor children in Calcutta. Not satisfied with giving some money and moving on, he has taken a close interest in the project ever since.

That is what makes him special, every bit as much as being able to hit a cricket ball over extra cover or, these days, over mid-wicket off the front foot and backward point off the back. Francis Drake's prayer might have been written for Steve Waugh: 'Teach us to remember that when Thou givest us to endeavour any great matter, it is not the beginning but the continuing of the same until it be thoroughly finished that yieldeth the true glory.' He is a man who sees things through to the end.

2001 v. England: 4 matches; 321 runs at 107; 2 hundreds

That much was proved by the strongly contrasting struggle endured by his twin brother. Normally Mark is the Waugh to whom batting looks natural, Steve for whom it looks a battle. Yesterday the roles were reversed and something nearer the truth revealed, namely that Mark, too, has plenty of his sibling's grit, just as Steve has every bit as much natural ability. It is sometimes forgotten that Steve was picked for Australia six years before his brother; and that whereas Mark started with a commanding century against England at Adelaide, Steve's first steps as a batsman in Test cricket were faltering. Until the inspiration of the Ashes began to mature his game in 1986–87, his first fourteen innings in Test cricket were 13, 5, 8, 0, 11, 74, 1, 1, 0, 12 not out, 2 not out, 39 not out, 6, and 0 again.

Yesterday afternoon Martyn gave every impression of another Australian batsman whose time has come. After Caddick had found the very outside of Mark Waugh's edge to end his 185-minute innings 16 overs before tea, Martyn hustled eagerly to the middle and was there almost before England's huddle of relief had started. He settled in calmly and began to reveal the breadth of his repertoire by taking 14 off an over from Giles with two late cuts and three more shots stroked with utter assurance through mid-wicket.

DAMIEN MARTYN

In 1994 I got into a lift at a hotel in Hobart with Damien Martyn and Justin Langer on the day that Martyn had made a brilliant hundred against the England touring team for 'An Australian XI'. The two young Australian batting prospects looked strikingly alike and it was only because Martyn was much the more confident during our brief conversation that I knew by his reputation who was whom. He was the captain of that side, a former captain of the national team at Under-19 level, and already had seven full Test caps in his bag, with three fifties to his name at that level.

Bobby Simpson, the coach, knew him to be an absolutely outstanding talent. In Australian sport, however, the team comes before the individual and talent has to be supported by performance, all the time. It was not until 1999 that Martyn got another chance at Test level; not until the first Test of the series in England that he finally earned a place on merit in the first team. On the way he had been forced to change his free and easy lifestyle, buckle down to hard work and, in the jargon of Aussie sport, 'renew his commitment to excellence'.

The results were awesome. From the first innings of the tour at Arundel he batted with a purity and command that could not be overcome by anyone. Absolutely in control of his own temperament, supremely sure of his natural ability and impeccable batting technique, fit and hungry for overdue success, he was the batsman of the tour. It did not matter who was bowling to him: Martyn made batting look easy. Goodness knows how many runs he will score in the next five years.

2001 v. England: 5 matches; 382 runs at 76.40; 2 hundreds

Saturday, 7 July

Until deciding to watch some of the third day on television for a change, I had no idea of the frustrations suffered, as well as the pleasures enjoyed, by those who watch their cricket on Channel 4. We have heard and read a great deal about what the game has gained since they took on the contract for Test cricket from the BBC two years ago. Rightly so in many respects: much of their approach has been innovative in the best sense, especially in the area of graphics and technical analysis. The *Roadshow* on Saturday mornings is wide-ranging and keeps a useful contact with the counties and the levels below.

Nursing toothache on another hot day in the comfort of Brockencote Hall at Chaddesley Corbett I was interested to monitor what life is like without access to the friendly voices of my colleagues on Radio Four on 198 longwave. I discovered that the television coverage on Saturday afternoons is as fractured as the BBC's used to be and just as infuriating. For the major part of the afternoon, whilst it was raining at Wimbledon, the fare seemed to be a few balls of Test cricket, a succession of races from Sandown and Haydock and, when we did go back to Edgbaston, far too many instances of Mark Nicholas uttering commercial television's favourite catchphrase: 'We'll take a break.'

I wonder, too, whether some of the commentators – so excellent in many ways – appreciate quite how much they sound like Harry Enfield's impersonation of the Alan Freeman-type disc jockey, with his selfless work for 'charidy'. It is not, apparently, 'batting' any more, but 'badding'. As for adverbs, forget them: the ball does not travel quickly, it goes 'quick'. It sounds more impressive when you are determined to be trendy. So, one or two of them seem to think, do American superfluities such as 'meeting with' and 'outside of'.

At least and at last there was no interruption as Mark Butcher enjoyed his surprise success with the ball before Adam Gilchrist peppered the crowd and the boundary boards like a left-handed Gilbert Jessop. It was great entertainment and both camerawork and commentary reflected it. What is more, the umpires decided the light was too bad just as the action was starting at Wimbledon.

In the end no one was satisfied except the Australians. Rafter reached the final but Henman's semi-final with Ivanisevic was interrupted again, without reaching a conclusion. Australia were all over the Lions in the second half at Melbourne and at Edgbaston they got Atherton out – McGrath, of course – having totalled 576. There can be only one result.

Sunday, 8 July
Edgbaston (fourth day of five): Australia won the first Test by an innings and 118 runs.

England's situation in the gloomy aftermath of Australia's admirable and irresistible innings victory in the first Test is as bleak as the one in which Ian Botham was relieved of the captaincy in 1981. Assuming the cracked bone on the top joint of Nasser Hussain's left hand keeps him out of next week's Lord's Test, the only solution is to do what Alec Bedser and his fellow selectors did then: to turn to an *éminence grise*.

Michael Atherton the captain was no Mike Brearley, but he is experienced, established, determined, close to retirement and sufficiently far removed now from his own resignation in 1998 to be asked to attempt, on a temporary basis, the kind of resurrection that occurred under Brearley. Where his Botham will come from is, of course, another matter.

Atherton turned down the idea of taking over from Hussain when he was injured in 1999, but much has changed since that injury, the first of Hussain's four broken bones since assuming the captaincy and the fifth in the last five years of his wretchedly unfortunate Test career. No feasible alternative as captain exists unless Graham Thorpe makes a more rapid recovery from his calf muscle injury than present indications suggest.

Thorpe is not expected to be fit for the Benson & Hedges Cup Final on Saturday. In any case, he was a reluctant caretaker for Hussain at the end of the tour of Sri Lanka when the appointed leader went home early with a variety of leg injuries and general exhaustion. He has played two Tests since, breaking a thumb at Lord's and a finger yesterday when Jason Gillespie's first ball of the day reared to strike his top hand.

Alec Stewart and Michael Trescothick will be considered when the selectors get together today or tomorrow to discuss the crisis.

Even the resilient Stewart, however, will want no extension of his bruising experience as a restored captain in the second Test against Pakistan at Old Trafford and the six one-day internationals that followed. He has sufficient on his plate as a batsman and wicket-keeper whose pugnacious first innings of 65 at Edgbaston was devalued by missed chances behind the stumps and a swift dismissal yesterday as Gillespie ripped away the middle order in a devastating spell of high-class fast bowling before leaving the final pickings to the maestro, Shane Warne, after lunch.

ALEC STEWART

Peter Pan was a myth, unfortunately for Alec Stewart. There comes a time when even the fittest and most dedicated have to move on from a career in professional sport. If 2001 proves to have been his last year as a Test crick-eter, at least it would mean retirement when he was still the best at his trade in England. Despite numerous finger injuries (the decision to bat with an extra guard on his right glove undoubtedly prolonged his career) he was still per-forming like a model professional.

All his career Stewart has enjoyed proving doubters wrong. Picked for his first tour as a reserve wicket-keeper, people said his keeping could not be taken seriously. Selected as a specialist batsman, they suspected paternal favour. When he began opening, they said he was better suited to batting lower down, as a natural stroke-player. When he dropped to the middle-order, they said he should be playing as a specialist opener. When he lost the England captaincy in 1999, he lost the Test wicket-keeping place too and, seeing him dropping catches and failing with the bat in his first Test back in the ranks at Edgbaston, people said (myself amongst them) that he seemed to have lost the super-sharpness of reaction necessary for continued success at the top. Wrong again. First he scored runs; then he regained the gloves in Test matches; then, when he lost them for one-day internationals, he reclaimed them for limited-overs matches too.

The challenge to his integrity by a self-confessed Indian match-fixer was different. He had to carry on knowing that speculation continued behind his back, about whether he had taken money to give basic cricketing information. It was based upon nothing more substantial than one man's word against another. Days before the start of the Ashes series, he was officially exoner-ated because it was clear that his accuser was not prepared to repeat his allegations against Stewart in any further judicial inquiries.

This final series against Australia offered one more chance to prove him-self. He had scored only one Test century against opponents he deeply admired. They had taught him, during several winters in Perth, to play the game hard, pushing himself, the laws and the opposition to the limit. But a batting average against them of only 27 was unworthy and he had never known what it was like to win the Ashes.

His success over a distinguished career came from a deep will to succeed.

When he went to watch an international at Wembley as a young boy he came home to tell his father that he was going to play for England. 'It's not as simple as that,' said Micky, trying to be realistic without deflating young Alec's enthusiasm. 'There were probably at least a thousand youngsters in the crowd today who have set their heart on playing for England but only one of them is going to make it.' There was barely a pause for father's words to sink in before Alec responded: 'It might be me.'

It was not, but only because cricket was the game at which he truly excelled, fuelled by a steely determination to get to the top and an unwavering self-belief. Once he knew his goal he followed it with dedication, eschewing temptations after marrying Lynn in 1991 and settling to as close a family life as the remorseless travels of a successful international cricketer will allow. He had been brought up in a warm, happy and naturally competitive sporting family by Micky, Surrey and England like himself and coach when Alec first joined the England team in 1990; and Sheila, herself a fine games-player.

Micky went on playing until he was forty. Two years younger when the series against Australia began, Alec had suffered a deflating series of defeats as caretaker captain after Hussain's broken finger against Pakistan at Lord's, but there was no proof of diminished skill nor, significantly, of any loss of that enthusiasm which drives him. In late June, asked, in effect, if he was contemplating retirement, he replied: 'There's nothing better than playing cricket for a living.'

2001 v. Australia: 5 matches; 283 runs at 35.37; 13 catches

Trescothick may well be Hussain's longer-term successor but to burden him with all that the job of captaining England against Australia entails, in only his second season as a Test player, would simply be foolish. His batting yesterday, a commanding display of solid defence and shrewd, powerful strokeplay, was one of only two performances that assuaged the misery of a comprehensive thrashing. Mark Butcher's was the other, as he added a second good innings to his four wickets with intelligent swing bowling on Saturday, but he, too, has enough on his plate in restoring his credibility as a Test player to want to be saddled a second time with the job of caretaker captain.

Unless there is better news after Hussain has seen a specialist today – he must be sick of the sight of the waiting rooms of orthopaedic surgeons – it boils down to Atherton, who himself must summon up the positive mental approach against Australia's fast bowlers that he visibly lacked in the second innings on Saturday. Without calculated aggression, England are going to lose the series for sure.

This, holding catches and a complete change of fortune, is the only hope of revival in the Lord's Test starting on Thursday week, but it is hard to see that happening. As Hussain said yesterday evening, 'It will take our best side playing its best cricket to beat Australia.' Far from that, England will certainly be without Michael Vaughan, almost certainly Hussain and probably both Thorpe and his first-choice replacement, Mark Ramprakash. Vaughan had an arthroscopy on his damaged left knee on Thursday and is not now expected to be available until the fourth Test at Headingley; Ramprakash is given only a 50–50 chance of playing in Surrey's final against Gloucestershire on Saturday because of his hamstring strain.

Already Australia's mighty team has exploited these misfortunes ruthlessly. Balanced observers knew that for England to beat them not only did the successful winter team have to remain fit and all possible chances be taken, but also that Australia had either to suffer injuries or play below their potential. The contrary reality at Edgbaston was a superb all-round performance by a full-strength Australia side playing at its formidable best, against a team two short of its strongest combination that bowled too inconsistently, missed eight possible catching and stumping chances (none of them easy, but all of them important) and, in the final Australian blitzkrieg yesterday, lost 7 wickets for 22 runs in 63 balls.

Given the recovery of the weather and dedicated work by Warwickshire's groundstaff (fifteen years ago, before the arrival of efficient water-sucking machines, yesterday's play would have been abandoned without a ball bowled after heavy overnight rain), England were going to lose anyway after Adam Gilchrist's magnificent 152 from 143 balls on Saturday. It is testament to his status that his relatively sedate progress to three figures actually made this the slowest of his three Test hundreds to date. His partnership with the accomplished Damien Martyn snuffed out all remaining England hope.

Butcher and Trescothick actually played exceptionally well in the first hour yesterday against an attack led initially by Warne and McGrath. Butcher drove Warne backward of point for four and clipped him wristily off the back foot through mid-wicket for another before Trescothick temporarily extinguished his threat by sweeping him well in front of the two men back on the leg-side boundary and striking a long-hop handsomely past cover.

Butcher hit successive fours off McGrath, a back-foot force followed by an on-drive, and Trescothick hooked him for six, but English fun ceased when Steve Waugh switched to his hungry young fast bowlers. In the twelfth over of the day Lee's virile pace produced a bounce that defeated Butcher, caught off the outside shoulder of his bat, and from the moment that Hussain was hit by Gillespie's first ball from the Pavilion End, England's innings lasted only 78 more balls.

Ian Ward was bowled off an inside edge for the second time in the game; Stewart was turned round by Gillespie and caught at second slip from a leading edge; Usman Afzaal beaten for pace; and Craig White by a ball that held its line. In splendid defiance, Trescothick hooked Gillespie for six, but this was fast bowling of far greater venom and consistency than Caddick or Gough could manage. Lunch intervened before Warne returned to have Trescothick caught at slip, Gough leg-before first ball to the deliberate straight one and Giles, too, caught at slip for his 384th Test wicket, putting him ahead of Botham.

Spectators were content to stay in their seats to watch Gilchrist win the man-of-the-match award on the big screen. The match has restored some of Edgbaston's lost prestige. Warwickshire's organisation was faultless and apart from his immaculate outfield, Steve Rouse produced a lively pitch with something in it for everyone. The high boundary count throughout the four days richly entertained capacity crowds, all of whom behaved well and enjoyed themselves, whatever their loyalty. All who have booked for the matches to come, however, must wonder how the Australian juggernaut can possibly be stopped.

The margin of Australia's victory, an innings and 118 runs, was precisely the same as England's in the corresponding match of 1997.

England 1st innings			R	M	B	4	6
MA Atherton	c ME Waugh	b Gillespie	57	146	107	10	0
ME Trescothick	c Warne	b Gillespie	0	5	2	0	0
MA Butcher	c Ponting	b Warne	38	111	71	4	0
*N Hussain	lbw	b McGrath	13	54	35	1	0
IJ Ward		b McGrath	23	50	39	2	0
+AJ Stewart	lbw	b McGrath	65	130	82	9	0
U Afzaal		b Warne	4	11	9	0	0
C White	lbw	b Warne	4	9	8	0	0
AF Giles	c Gilchrist	b Warne	7	16	13	1	0
D Gough	c Gillespie	b Warne	0	2	3	0	0
AR Caddick	not out		49	59	40	7	1
Extras	(b 10, lb 8, nb 16)		34				
Total	(all out, 65.3 overs, 289 mins)		294				

FoW: 1–2 (Trescothick, 1.1 ov), 2–106 (Butcher, 24.2 ov),
3–123 (Atherton, 31.3 ov), 4–136 (Hussain, 37.4 ov),
5–159 (Ward, 43.2 ov), 6–170 (Afzaal, 46.1 ov),
7–174 (White, 48.3 ov), 8–191 (Giles, 52.2 ov),
9–191 (Gough, 52.5 ov), 10–294 (Stewart, 65.3 ov).

Bowling	O	M	R	W	
McGrath	17.3	2	67	3	(3nb)
Gillespie	17	3	67	2	(4nb)
Lee	12	2	71	0	(7nb)
Warne	19	4	71	5	(2nb)

Australia 1st innings			R	M	B	4	6
MJ Slater		b Gough	77	111	82	13	0
ML Hayden	c White	b Giles	35	71	41	6	1
RT Ponting	lbw	b Gough	11	23	13	2	0
ME Waugh	c Stewart	b Caddick	49	153	143	7	0
*SR Waugh	lbw	b Gough	105	245	181	13	0
DR Martyn	c Trescothick	b Butcher	105	222	165	15	0
+AC Gilchrist	c Caddick	b White	152	205	143	20	5
SK Warne	c Atherton	b Butcher	8	11	10	2	0
B Lee	c Atherton	b Butcher	0	6	1	0	0
JN Gillespie	lbw	b Butcher	0	2	3	0	0
GD McGrath	not out		1	36	19	0	0
Extras	(b 3, lb 7, nb 23)		33				
Total	(all out, 129.4 overs, 545 mins)		576				

FoW: 1–98 (Hayden, 14.6 ov), 2–130 (Ponting, 19.4 ov),
3–134 (Slater, 23.1 ov), 4–267 (ME Waugh, 63.6 ov),
5–336 (SR Waugh, 83.2 ov), 6–496 (Martyn, 117.3 ov),
7–511 (Warne, 119.6 ov), 8–513 (Lee, 121.1 ov),
9–513 (Gillespie, 121.4 ov), 10–576 (Gilchrist, 129.4 ov).

Bowling

	O	M	R	W	
Gough	33	6	152	3	(10nb)
Caddick	36	0	163	1	(12nb)
White	26.4	5	101	1	(1nb)
Giles	25	0	108	1	
Butcher	9	3	42	4	

England 2nd innings			R	M	B	4	6
MA Atherton	c ME Waugh	b McGrath	4	34	9	1	0
ME Trescothick	c ME Waugh	b Warne	76	208	113	11	2
MA Butcher	c Gilchrist	b Lee	41	95	73	5	0
*N Hussain	retired hurt		9	26	20	1	0
IJ Ward		b Lee	3	12	3	0	0
+AJ Stewart	c Warne	b Gillespie	5	6	6	1	0
U Afzaal	lbw	b Gillespie	2	10	6	0	0
C White		b Gillespie	0	8	6	0	0
AF Giles	c ME Waugh	b Warne	0	22	12	0	0
D Gough	lbw	b Warne	0	1	1	0	0
AR Caddick	not out	6	14	15	1	0	
Extras	(b 1, lb 5, nb 12)		18				
Total	(all out, 42.1 overs, 218 mins)		164				

FoW: 1–4 (Atherton, 2.3 ov), 2–99 (Butcher, 24.2 ov),
3–142 (Ward, 32.1 ov), 4–148 (Stewart, 33.1 ov),
5–150 (Afzaal, 35.3 ov), 6–154 (White, 37.3 ov),
7–155 (Trescothick, 38.1 ov), 8–155 (Gough, 38.2 ov),
9–164 (Giles, 42.1 ov).

Bowling

	O	M	R	W	
McGrath	13	5	34	1	(5nb)
Gillespie	11	2	52	3	(4nb)
Warne	10.1	4	29	3	(1nb)
ME Waugh	1	0	6	0	
Lee	7	0	37	2	(2nb)

Australia won by an innings and 118 runs.

Six

Cakes and Butter Fingers

One script said: England to steal a march at Edgbaston; everybody fit; catches being plucked from the air like ripe raspberries; Australia faltering; Lee feeling his elbow; Gillespie his back; Buchanan out of tune with Waugh; Hussain riding high but telling everyone not to count chickens . . .

The real one said: Australia sailing through the tour like a liner amongst rowing boats; everyone fit; everyone in form; feet on the ground but not a negative thought in a single head; one in the bag and the luckiest Australian ground of all approaching fast; wives and children on tour in a sunny English summer; plenty of supporters here for the Lord's Test; England in disarray; captain injured; batting order uncertain; more hope than confidence; fair dinkum, fellows, we've got 'em on the run . . .

Wednesday, 18 July
England have won their last three Tests at Lord's, and they have not lost to Australia here this century. Michael Atherton has a sense of humour, so he might remind the team he has borrowed from Nasser Hussain of these two indisputable facts before he goes out to toss – is it too much to hope in his England cap and blazer? – with Steve Waugh before the start of the second Test at Lord's this morning.

If it is actually too early for gallows humour, it is still hard to avoid the feeling that it is now or never for England. There are those who believe that their best strategy is to hang on to Australia by drawing the next two Tests and stealing the series on 'result' pitches at Headingley and The Oval, but it is an argument that holds little water when it is remembered that Australia have won seventeen, lost two and drawn none of their last nineteen Test matches. Even England have not drawn for six games. Nor has there been a draw in five matches at Lord's since rain saved England here against Australia in 1997.

It could happen again if the weather so dictates but even with showers expected at various times it is unlikely. The days of playing for a draw from the outset of Test matches disappeared when it was decreed, belatedly, that at least 90 overs must be bowled in a day and when the effects of limited-overs cricket seeped into the subconscious of cricketers everywhere. Calculated aggression is the only way for England to hit back from Australia's devastating victory at Edgbaston, which is not to say that batsmen will not need discretion nor bowlers strict control.

On the contrary, the aim must be to build long partnerships and to bowl the right length and line to frustrate the likes of Michael Slater and Adam Gilchrist into getting themselves out. Secure catching is the other absolute essential if Australia are not to extend an unbeaten record at Lord's that goes back to Hedley Verity's triumph on a turning pitch in 1934. Atherton recognised the need for improvements in all departments yesterday when he faced the press, Vodafone cap characteristically askew, after what he called 'a more settled build-up' to the match by comparison with Edgbaston.

The return of Graham Thorpe, who held some spectacular catches here against Pakistan in May before England's progress came to an abrupt halt, and the inclusion of Dominic Cork and Mark Ramprakash, should sharpen fielding that has let the side down badly in the last two Tests. Twelve missed catching and stumping chances, not to mention the narrowly missed run-outs in both games, have been as big a reason as any for the successive defeats. It is true that Gough and Caddick bowled badly by their highest standards at Edgbaston but Steve Waugh acknowledged yesterday that it would have been a far closer contest if the 'big moments' had gone the other way.

Waugh, who has won eighteen of his twenty-five Tests as captain, leads a team of champions whose own fallible catching in the first Test was untypical. The incomparable Keith Miller, one of Bradman's 1948 Invincibles, unequivocally described it this week as 'the best team I've ever seen'. They will be unchanged today, having preferred Brett Lee to Damien Fleming despite Lee's recent twinge in the ribs, and where swing is often as dangerous as uneven bounce this seems an unnecessary risk for Australia to have taken. The pitch, dry on top, has been protected from the forecast showers and it is thickly grassed, so England will play all four seamers. Alec Stewart will be playing his sixteenth Test at Lord's with any suggestion of a stain on his character at last officially removed after the ACU concluded that there was 'no substantive evidence' against him.

Stewart has a Test average here of 53. Cork is the other England player with a special record at Lord's. It is now twenty-three innings since he took five wickets in an innings for England – before that he had achieved it five times – and against Pakistan, using this year's crop of Duke balls that are softer and have swung less, he lacked the nip and the outswing that is crucial to his success. He has made only two Test fifties but it was his batting that finally made possible the two-wicket win over the West Indies when he returned to the England side after an absence of nineteen months here last year; the catalyst for the run of success that followed.

DOMINIC CORK

He was, it now seems obvious, a meteor not a star, but he shone so vividly for a time. The rigours of the contemporary game took too swift a toll on his lean frame. Nor does it preserve a man's energy to live on your nerves as he has.

In 2001 Dominic Cork was a bull without horns, charging about with all the apparent gusto of the season five years earlier when he had run amok against the West Indies, but now finding only a mocking red cape and a succession of stinging darts in his back.

He had been a hero again the season before, settling the epic Lord's Test with the bat as certainly as he had won it with the ball in 1996. For a few seasons he was always a potential match-winner with his optimism, unbridled hostility, late outswingers and mean bouncers from a springy, classical action. Now, the menace and verve had gone from his cricket. The arm was lower, the swing came early in flight if it came at all. His batting had an even more fevered air than normal.

It was, is and always will be a cruel game. Perhaps Cork has the depth of character to come back but it is unlikely. In the Lord's Test Glenn McGrath, briefly put off his own game by Cork's ability to rile opponents, described him to a group of spectators on the boundary as a 'pussy'. He implied that he is a man whose mental strength, let alone his physical, was insufficient to stand the strain.

2001 v. Australia: 1 match; 26 runs at 13; 1 wicket at 84

It was on this ground, too, that in his first Test against the West Indies in 1995 Cork took 7 for 43 in the second innings, the best figures by an England bowler on debut for more than a century. At the age of twenty-nine, with Chris Silverwood, Alex Tudor and others breathing down his neck, it is now or never for him too.

England need some luck if they are to bring this series alive and it may have to begin with the toss and the opportunity to bowl first in cloudy weather. Like the tosses at Adelaide and Sydney in the last series, this will be an important one, not least in memory of Glenn McGrath's devastating 8 for 38 here last time. It will take much more than a call of heads or tails, naturally, to knock Australia from their perch, especially at Lord's where England have beaten them only once in the last twenty-five matches. The elder Waugh and Michael Slater have already made Test hundreds here: Mark Waugh, Hayden, Ponting and Martyn will all want to join them on the board.

Despite the unfortunate clash with the Open Championship, 120,000 tickets – capacity crowds for the first four days – have been sold and MCC officials estimate that they could have sold three times that number, rather more than the entire member-ship of the Conservative Party. The majority, surely, will vote for an England victory and a dream revived.

Thursday, 19 July

Second Test, Lord's (first day of five): England have scored 121 for 4.
Shane Warne was given a couple of exploratory overs yesterday but for the rest of a day of staccato bursts Australia seldom had less than three slips and two gullies, sometimes four and two. It was bad enough for England to lose the toss. To be obliged to bat between showers for short periods on a pitch that allowed

the fast bowlers plenty of bounce and movement off the seam was akin to soldiers trying to advance to the next rock under constant enemy fire.

Against fast bowling of unremitting hostility they did well to lose only four men before bad light ended the fourth of the skirmishes and play was called off at ten minutes past seven. In all, the weather allowed only 40 overs and one ball to be bowled and it was not until the fourth session late in a frustrating day that batsmen had any chance to settle without having half an eye on approaching clouds or the warning lights that denote approaching bad light.

All day the golden arrow below the Father Time weather-vane pointed resolutely towards the bands of gloomy weather blowing up from the west, absolutely what England had not wanted in a series in which they are already one behind – unless, of course, they had won the toss. Instead a rueful smile from Michael Atherton when the coin was finally spun after morning rain swiftly conveyed the amazing fact that Steve Waugh had won it for the eighteenth time in his twenty-six matches as captain and that England had lost for the ninth time in a row and the thirteenth in fourteen Tests against Australia.

Sometimes the toss matters, sometimes not. This was one occasion when it certainly did, but for 31 overs played in four different sessions Atherton looked capable of defying the ill star that often seems to hover over England at Lord's, playing with excellent balance and judgement until finally he left a ball from his great tormentor, Glenn McGrath, and was given out lbw as the ball jagged back a foot down the slope from the Pavilion End. Technology suggested that the ball might have gone over the stumps but in the instant that it happened bowler, batsman and umpire were probably of one accord: it looked out.

It was a crucial moment and decision because it left Graham Thorpe, struggling manfully in his first innings in any cricket for seven weeks, with Mark Ramprakash against Australian bowlers knowing that one more wicket would certainly make it their day. Brett Lee obliged with a wicked ball that left Ramprakash in the air before darting back up the slope through a wide open gate. It was a great ball to find against a batsman looking as relaxed as he ever has in a Test on what used to be his home ground. The painful fact remains that Ramprakash has now been out for 14 in his last four Test innings against Australia: it is a figure unlucky for some.

England's determination to bat positively was evident from the moment that play started an hour and a half late. McGrath had already shown he was going to get some movement both ways when Atherton boldly hooked the first bouncer of the day – and the sixth ball – for four. Thorpe later played an equally decisive hook but neither shot was typical because the three fast bowlers wisely pitched the ball up, mainly to an off-stump line, inviting the batsmen to take on the array of slips whenever the ball was aimed wider.

Trescothick picked up the gauntlet but not always with discretion. He had hit a couple of good shots off the back foot but also been missed by Mark Waugh at second slip off a no-ball from Gillespie before he edged to Adam Gilchrist, driving without moving a toe, let alone a foot, at a ball well wide of his off stump.

Atherton led from the front as he always did in his regular days as captain. Driving classically through the covers when the ball was in the right place, he gave a patient crowd something to cheer. Butcher played with similar judgement, especially in picking the appropriate ball to leave outside the off stump or to put away in front of point with the full face of the bat. When tea-time came and with it the honour for the teams of being presented to the Queen inside the Pavilion – it was too wet, alas, for the traditional scene to be enacted outside – England were 55 for 1.

There was sufficient time before Butcher fell in the third short session for the monarch to feel that she had had no influence on the Mother Country's further decline. Going back to a length ball delivered from over the wicket by McGrath, he edged to second slip where Mark Waugh held on to the one that counted, low to his left. It was his 157th catch in a Test match and it is as certain as the wind from the west that before this match is over he will have become the most prolific catcher in Test history. Mark Taylor, whose own 157 were caught almost exclusively in the next door position at first slip, was at Lord's and will be one of the first to congratulate him.

Soldiering on, Atherton and Thorpe had lifted the total to 97 over what was now a slow outfield before the fourth and final period in which Australia rammed home their advantage. Duncan Fletcher, the England coach, said at the close that England were still hoping for a total of 350, one that would take much getting even if the more cheerful forecast for today is fulfilled. His opposite number, John Buchanan, called it 'quite a benign pitch' and it is certainly one on which runs should come more comfortably if the sun shines and the outfield quickens.

The details of this day's cricket will fade, but not for the old lags of the *Test Match Special* team – Baxter, Frindall, Blofeld, Agnew and myself – the events of the tea interval. We were presented to the Queen in the Pavilion committee room, immediately after the players. Not only that, but *she* presented *us* with a cake. Dressed in mauve and looking much younger and more delicately pretty close-at-hand than her photographs suggest, she chatted amiably with us for a few minutes before handing over what proved to be a very tasty Dundee cake. Blowers did most of the talking, Aggers asked her if she had baked it personally – 'not personally but specially' she said, repeating the 'specially' to make us feel important – and I contributed only a rather corny reference to the monarch taking a wicket on these occasions (after several years of royal visits it was noticed that the presentation of the teams in front of the pavilion often preceded a wicket for England. In 1930 the prolific Bill Ponsford was caught off Jack White for 81 the very ball after shaking the royal hand, ending an opening partnership of 162. It made no long-term difference because Australia scored 729 and won the game by 7 wickets). I am sure she hears this observation every time she visits.

I think I had had a more natural conversation, one to one, when, as a young BBC correspondent, I had been presented to her at a party in Canberra before she opened the Australian Parliament in 1977. Strangely, that momentous occasion seemed to have slipped her memory now.

I almost missed the honour this second time. I looked up from my laptop at the start of the early tea interval only to realise that the rest of the team had left for the pavilion some time before without telling me. It was a dreadful moment. I sprinted round the ground, evading 30,000-odd milling spectators with the agility of an elusive wing three-quarter and arrived at the door of the committee room with glasses steamed up and body perspiring unpleasantly. Fortunately the others were still waiting to be summoned by Roger Knight, the MCC Secretary, and I was given a couple of minutes to compose myself.

The prince of cricketing raconteurs, J. J. Warr, used to tell the story of an MCC member passing beneath the window of the committee room in the days when the broadcaster and cricket writer E. W. Swanton was a member of the committee and women were strictly not allowed into the pavilion. 'I've just seen an extraordinary thing,' he told his companion in a startled voice: 'Swanton, in the committee room, talking to a *lady*.'

Several of Swanton's fortunate successors in the BBC radio broadcasting box, myself amongst them, metaphorically touched forelocks to the late Brian Johnston whose joyful commentaries had so much to do with the popularity of ball-by-ball commentary on the radio and the long tradition of presenting cakes to the wafflers and quaffers.

Royal visits to Lord's became regular events in the days of King Edward VII, the central figure in a famous painting of 1886 depicting the then Prince of Wales watching an imaginary match between England and Australia. The joint artists, Sir Robert Ponsonby Staples and H. Barrable, included amongst the other spectators not only the future Queen Alexandra but also Lily Langtry. It was Edward VII who allowed England cricket teams to play with the emblem of the crown and three lions (the footballers had to be content with three lions) and who watched the Australian Warren Bardsley score a hundred before lunch against South Africa in one of the matches in the pioneering but short-lived triangular Test series of 1912.

The present Queen's visits used to take place on the fourth day of Lord's Tests in the days before the expansion of Test fixtures made planning more difficult. In 1966 the Secretary of MCC, Billy Griffith, rang Buckingham Palace to ask whether the visit might be put forward because the West Indies seemed to be on the point of losing. The West Indies manager, Jeff Stollmeyer, expressed the view that the precaution was unnecessary and was right because Gary, later Sir Garfield, Sobers batted most of the day with his cousin, David Holford, and England subsequently failed to win.

Friday, 20 July
Lord's (second day of five): Australia, with 5 first-innings wickets in hand, are 68 runs ahead of England.

Mark Waugh's 108 at Lord's yesterday was an innings of unyielding discipline by a singular genius. Building as it did on another formidable feat of fast bowling by Glenn McGrath, it went a long way towards winning both the second Test and the Ashes for Australia, but a moment of inspiration in the field by Darren Gough, and a bouncer by Dominic Cork that skimmed Steve Waugh's left glove and finally gave some justification for a surfeit of short-pitched bowling, brought limited consolation for England late in the day.

It raised hopes that this time Australia's first-innings advantage might not seem insurmountable by the time that England go out to face the music a second time, but so very impressively did Damien Martyn and Adam Gilchrist resist all that was thrown at them in the last nine overs of the second evening that the writing seems at least to be pencilled on the wall already. The second new ball cannot be claimed for another thirteen overs, Australia have managed to score at virtually four runs an over without attempting anything risky and unless someone bowls out of his skin this morning the match may be gone beyond recall by lunchtime today.

In a game that has so far produced no more than variations on the Edgbaston theme, the brutal truth is that England are doing better but that it is not enough. Two missed chances either side of tea again handicapped them yesterday against opponents who can be guaranteed to punish errors; there were twenty-one no-balls bowled, twenty-nine fours conceded and too many instances when fielders dived over balls that the Australians would somehow have stopped.

Waugh's innings left seasoned observers wondering if there has ever been a right-handed batsman who has played off his legs with silkier timing, or, indeed, a team, even an Australian team, that pursues Test victories with a more voracious hunger than this one. Australia's bowlers allow no margin for error, their fielders have caught every legitimate chance in this match and the batsman whose innings formed the centrepiece of the day yesterday has a way of hitting fours off even the most blameless balls.

It is becoming a truism that they have no weakness beyond the one exposed in India against good spin bowling on helpful pitches. They have no Harbhajan Singh to bother them here and there is not enough in the pitch to turn Gough, Caddick, White and Cork into the match-winning quartet of last season. More to the point, perhaps, they are up against better players.

MARK WAUGH

If he were of royal blood, rather than from one of the many hot, flat, unlovely suburbs that lurk behind the glamorous centre of Sydney, he would be properly addressed as 'Your Insouciance'. There have always been batsmen who made the game look easy, from Reggie Spooner, who held the bat 'like a lady would hold her fan' to David Gower, who batted as if in his dinner jacket; but few who stroked the ball about as casually as Mark Waugh and none, surely, who looked so cool in every circumstance.

During his hundred later in the 2001 series at The Oval, in weather too hot for the taste of many of us, he wore a sleeveless sweater throughout. Like unmelting ice amidst all those sweating around him, he played his strokes with a languid grace, as if in slow motion. Time and again when Mark Waugh is batting one sees the long, unhurried swing of the bat and thinks that he is stroking the ball for one or two, only for it to hasten away from pursuing fielders like the hare from the greyhounds.

The bread-and-butter stroke for which he will always be fondly remembered is the easeful turn off his legs past square-leg. It would drive any bowler to the madhouse because he plays it, often, from as far across his stumps as middle and off.

There are days when he gives his wicket away idly – it is a telling fact indeed that his highest Test score, after twenty Test hundreds, was only 153 – and like all batsmen who make it look easy his occasional days of struggle are a surprise. But there are days, too, when he is almost impossible to bowl to.

2001 v. England: 5 matches; 430 runs at 86; 1 wicket at 69; 2 hundreds; 9 catches

When Waugh came to the wicket five overs after lunch yesterday Australia were 27 for 2 and Gough and Caddick were in full sail. When he left, thrown out by Gough from mid-on although he was off-balance and had only one stump to aim at, they were

25 runs in front with their captain well set and the other two Edgbaston centurions to come. Nothing would deflect Waugh from his double mission, to put right the little matter of not having made a Test hundred at Lord's and to add another layer to the foundations of victory. Yesterday nine of his fourteen fours were hit with wondrous timing through mid-wicket or square-leg, each a model of waiting for the ball to arrive before turning it off the full face of the bat with a twist of the wrists. It will be the image that all who have watched him will ever associate with the younger Waugh.

Until his partnership of 107 with his twin, England had gone some way towards compensation for a morning dominated by Australia's bowlers. McGrath and Lee, getting the ball to swing on a sunny morning, immediately made batting look perilous and only when McGrath distracted himself by trying to bounce out Cork did his performance from the Pavilion End drop below the impeccable. Stewart edged a ball that lifted and left him, Thorpe followed one that did much the same, and White, driving at a length ball, sliced it to gully.

White has had two miserable Tests so far. He has made four runs from three innings and lost the ability to swing the ball away from the right-handers. Cork has not done much better but there was a greater variety about his bowling and without suggesting anything like permanence he rode his luck with the bat to make 24 before Ponting caught a fierce cut at backward point. Only Ian Ward, showing again that his temperament is right for Test cricket however imperfect his technique, could get much satisfaction as England lost their last six wickets for 66 in 23 overs. Shane Warne, eager to get in on the act, finished it by bowling Caddick off his pads and Gough with a yorker.

IAN WARD

It took a period as an outcast from county cricket and a lucky break when Mike Edwards, the former Surrey player, asked him to play in a pre-season trial, for Ian Ward to get a second lease of life as a professional cricketer.

Jack the lad became, like Bunyan's Christian, a diligent pilgrim on the straight and narrow road. Progress season by season at The Oval was augmented by hard work in the winters in Perth under the eye of the former South African Test batsman, Peter Carlstein. A successful 'A' tour of the West Indies made him the next batsman to get his chance at Test level, although those who knew said that he was not quite good enough.

Against Pakistan and Australia he showed courage, a sound temperament, but a flawed technique. Back to the drawing board.

2001 v. Australia: 3 matches; 68 runs at 13.60

England were at least a hundred runs short of having anything realistic to play with but for a time Gough and Caddick raised hopes. Matthew Hayden fell in Caddick's excellent first over, caught at second slip off a ball angled across him. Ricky Ponting, though he hit his first ball for four through mid-on, went three overs later to a ball that bounced and left him, edging it to third slip.

Slater never fully settled, especially once Gough had rapped him on a finger, but on a day when the ball was swinging it made little sense, as Mark Waugh later suggested, to keep banging the ball into the middle of the pitch as they did. Slater eventually got an edge attempting a half-hearted pull that no doubt had something to do with the pain he was feeling from his injury, but the Waughs, though they never relish the barrage of short-pitched stuff to which they are so frequently subjected, invariably emerge from the battle with credit.

They both offered chances of sorts. When he was 59, off the last over before tea, Mark cut Cork hard to gully where White, diving right, could do no more than touch the ball with his right hand. That would have been a sensational catch but Gough would have expected to hold the caught-and-bowled opportunity from Steve when he was 14 more often than not.

Whether England win or lose, the Lord's Test is always fun. Brian Johnston always used to throw a party at his house in St John's Wood on the Friday night, and Pauline, his merry widow, has kept it going. So many of their old cricketing friends were there – Ted and Sue Dexter, Raman and Anne Subba Row, Alan and Betty Davidson, Ben and Belinda Brocklehurst and all the inheritors of the *Test Match Special* tradition.

ADAM GILCHRIST

You can imagine him as a schoolboy: bright, plucky, confident, smiling, liable to impetuosity but eager to help anyone: conscientiousness epitomised. As soon as the teacher had posed the question to the class, his hand must have been raised: 'Sir, sir; oh please sir . . .'

Keen as a whetted knife, Adam Gilchrist played in fifteen of Australia's sixteen Test wins in succession. Following a cult hero into a team as adulated as Australia's is not easy, but within a year or so of taking over permanently from Ian Healy, people throughout Australia were wondering why he had not done so earlier. A fit little terrier who never gave less than his best in any fight had been replaced by a Crufts Supreme Champion.

It has never taken Gilchrist long to prove his quality once he has got the chance. He had to move State to claim a regular place in a Sheffield Shield team and Perth's pitches, as hard and fast as an ice-rink, have sharpened his game to such a point that anything that gets in his path is liable to end up cut, let alone bowlers who pitch the ball short to him.

It suited Australia to blood him in one-day internationals. When the tour to England started he had already played in 113 of them, having blazed his way to 50 off 33 balls in the 1999 World Cup final at Lord's. He had needed only 28 balls for his 50 in Goa shortly before the trip to England and at Trent Bridge against Pakistan he drove so hard that, as Simon Briggs wrote, you could almost see the vapour trail.

In only his second Test, at Hobart against Pakistan in 1999, he had turned a game that his side had no right to win by making 149 not out in the second innings. A little more than a year later, his value to the Test side was already such that the series in India in 2000/01 could be said to have revolved around him. He rescued Australia on the first day of the rubber with a second Test century of rare daring, but they lost the two games in which he failed with the bat.

This buccaneering batting has been supported by wicket-keeping of high class, whether diving for catches standing back or whipping off the bails for Warne, Miller or MacGill.

Everything is done, moreover, with a schoolboy relish, almost with a smile. Whether or not he is destined to be the next captain, he may break all records for wicket-keeper/batsmen. There are times, indeed, when one looks at the pointed ears and wonders if he might not, like Doctor Spock, have powers beyond the range of a normal human.

2001 v. England: 5 matches; 340 runs at 68; 1 hundred; 24 catches; 2 stumpings

Saturday, 21 July

Those spurned chances yesterday were as nothing by comparison with the positive rash of mistakes that occurred at Lord's this morning. England were like so many nervous best men at a wedding, dropping the ring whenever it was called for. Butcher started it in the second over of the day, muffing a lowish chance that seemed from the commentary box at the Nursery End to hang obligingly in the air after Gilchrist had played forward to Gough. Next Gilchrist cut at Gough, Ward dived at cover, got the ball in both hands, and dropped it. Butcher missed a second, very difficult chance off Caddick before Gough's melancholy morning was completed by Atherton, missing a sitter in front of his chest at first slip when Gilchrist appeared to be trying to help him with a deliberate steer of the kind you see being taken in fielding practices off the coach's bat.

When finally Gilchrist top-edged a catch to Stewart, Gough was as glum as a wizard who has lost his spell-book. Everyone knew the game was up; the match on the way to being lost; the series to being thrown away. As if it wasn't hard enough to beat the Australians without helping them at every turn.

BRETT LEE

There is no doubt about Brett Lee's ability as a fast bowler. He runs like an Olympic sprinter and there is exemplary balance in his action. The eclipse of Shoaib Akhtar makes him the quickest bowler in the world. It is, however, no new discovery that speed is not enough at the highest level. A bowler also has to move the ball, in the air or off the pitch, because he is up against good batsmen on good pitches most of the time. Only when he swung the ball, especially at Lord's, did this fair-haired Adonis live up to his billing.

There was just a suggestion that his early success had gone to his head. There was more than a trace of the braggart about some of his gestures and expressions as he tried in vain to build significantly on the dramatic success of his start in Test cricket: a wicket with his fourth ball and another thirty in his first five matches. No doubt the impression was false, however. They do not let anyone get too big for his boots in the Australian dressing-room. Somewhere in the next series for the Ashes England's batsmen can expect to suffer revenge for his relative failure in this series.

2001 v. England: 5 matches; 24 runs at 6; 9 wickets at 55.11

By tea-time England's situation was beyond recall: three men out cheaply and, incredibly, Thorpe injured again. This time it was Lee who broke a bone, during a snarling spell in which, like Lillee before him, he seemed to be summoning up some deep hatred of his English progenitors from the depth of his Australian being.

Sunday, 22 July

Lord's (fourth day of five): Australia beat England by 8 wickets.

It is a matter of opinion whether the Australia team that is now two-up in the Ashes series with three to play is the best or merely one of the best that has ever taken the field at Lord's. It is not in doubt, however, that one of the invariable lessons of history is that teams with the best fast bowlers and the best close catchers will dominate all their opponents anywhere outside the Indian subcontinent.

Glenn McGrath and Jason Gillespie virtually finished the England batting on their own yesterday morning as England lost their last six wickets for 39 in 48 balls. To rub further salt into the wound it is more than likely that Graham Thorpe will miss the third Test as he did the first, this time with a broken right hand. Struck by a bouncer from Brett Lee during the first wave attack on Saturday afternoon, Thorpe sees a specialist today after what was officially described as an 'inconclusive' X-ray.

Broken bones and pulled muscles form part of the unchanging story of England's inferiority since Australia won the first of what now looks almost certain to be seven series for the Ashes since 1989. So, too, do missed chances at key moments of matches. Yesterday's was just another England collapse at Lord's, perhaps, but it had in common with all the others of recent times, not to mention those that England have inflicted on Zimbabwe, the West Indies and Pakistan here in the last two seasons, the combination of well-directed fast bowling and predatory catching.

Five of the six swept away below the clouds, after Alec Stewart had been leg-before to a breakback from McGrath in the sixth over, were caught behind the wicket: two by Adam Gilchrist, three by first, second and third slips, snapping up rapid edges. Mainly it is a matter of confidence, but partly one of technique, too. Duncan Fletcher has made it a priority since he became the England coach to improve the fielding, but at head height or above the Australian practice with torpedo-shaped balls gives them an easily discernible superiority. In their youth both Shane Warne and Ricky Ponting were outstanding players of Australian Rules Football, a game demanding frequent overhead catching; Mark

Waugh played Rugby League. It is one more thing for England to try in the quest to catch up.

As for trying too hard, cricket is no different from tennis or golf. England's situation on Saturday was synonymous with that of Colin Montgomerie's at Royal Lytham yesterday. Already having to make up for the fallibility of their batting in the first innings, they took the field heavy with tension. One dropped catch by Mark Butcher at second slip off the seventh ball of the day led to three more as Gilchrist, the man they most wanted to get out early, was allowed to hit Australia to their decisive first-innings lead. After the match Steve Waugh recalled how the same desperation to dismiss Viv Richards had led to Australian errors in the field against the West Indies in the 1980s.

That Australia lost two prime batsmen in getting the paltry 14 runs required before winning before lunch on the fourth day only underlined what might have been if England had not dropped the three catches off Darren Gough on Saturday morning. At the least it would have been a longer and closer match, although no one should be deluded into thinking that anything other than an Australian victory was likely once they had won the toss and bowled England out for 187 in the first innings.

England had five of their seven first-choice batsmen in this game but it is hard to think that even with Nasser Hussain and Michael Vaughan they would have dealt with McGrath, Gillespie and Lee. It was Gillespie, hyperbolically described by Australia's captain as the best bowler he has ever seen, who took the opportunity this time to complete a five-wicket analysis. With his short run-up, high action, exemplary use of the wrist and extraordinary ability thereby to hit the pitch with the seam of the ball every time, he became the third bowler in the match to follow the new fashion of raising the ball to the crowd.

McGrath had had his moment on Friday, Andrew Caddick on Saturday when none of the batsmen enjoyed facing him with the second new ball. Yesterday it was McGrath who again made the early incisions that count most, following the off-cutter which cut short a brief display of Stewart's stroke-making quality with a ball that lifted and cut away from Ian Ward to give Ponting the chance of a brilliant two-handed catch at face height to his right at third slip.

Craig White was able to leave the hat-trick ball but in McGrath's next over Cork played a fatally irresolute stroke. It is not impossible that it will be his last in a Test match. A day after the twentieth anniversary of Ian Botham's famous innings at Headingley, White now stirred a few lingering vestiges of outrageous optimism, chancing his arm to good effect and, with Caddick, obliging Australia to bat a second time before Gillespie's pace and bounce finished the job in six balls.

Australia have never lost an Ashes series after taking a 2–0 lead, something they achieved here for the fifteenth time. Their aim now will be to inflict a second 5–0 whitewash on England, last achieved in 1920–21 when English resources were depleted after the horrors of the First World War. First they will concentrate on securing the urn by shutting England out of the third Test at Trent Bridge next week. Not since 1948 has an Australian tour seemed quite so much like an extended march of triumph.

Monday, 23 July

It was said of the Roman Emperor Diocletian that he had 'made a desert and called it peace'. The Australians, too, are laying waste to English cricket at the moment and there is no peace in sight. Yesterday came melancholy confirmation that Graham Thorpe had broken a bone in the back of his right hand during his brief engagement with the enemy at Lord's on Saturday afternoon and that he will miss the Trent Bridge Test next week.

Having visited the same specialist in Windsor consulted two weeks before by the captain, Nasser Hussain, Thorpe, too, was told that he would be unable to play cricket for three weeks. Unless he defies the analysis by recovering three days sooner and playing in Surrey's four-day Championship match at The Oval on Wednesday 8 August, that would leave him only two one-day games before the fourth Test at Headingley. It is due to start on 16 August and quite possibly, given recent pitches there, to end two days later.

GRAHAM THORPE

He was the *sine qua non* of English success. A seemingly innocuous calf injury became a long-running saga and reflected no credit on the medical support for England players. When finally the best batsman in the land was pitch-forked into the fray, he was like a champion boxer who has not had time to prepare for the big fight against a challenger who was in prime condition. A ball from Brett Lee that seared into the back of his hand at 95mph marked the end for Thorpe and, in effect, for England.

2001 v. Australia: 1 match; 22 runs at 11

His experience of taking on McGrath, Lee and Gillespie at Lord's without having played an innings in a match for six weeks, was such that Thorpe cannot relish the prospect of rushing back to face them on a surface almost bound to suit them at Leeds. The chances must be that he will not return until the fifth Test at The Oval, by which time it seems equally likely not only that the Ashes will have been retained by Australia but that they will still be chasing the possibility of winning all five Tests.

I cannot remember England being in quite such a desperate plight since the days of West Indian omnipotence in the 1980s. In series against Australia the current position resembles the one in 1974/75 when Lillee and Thomson were breaking bones as well as wickets. It is by no means certain that Hussain will be fit to return for the third Test, starting in Nottingham next Thursday. Michael Vaughan is recovering from an arthroscopy operation to a knee but will not be ready to return until Headingley at the earliest and Matthew Hoggard is also more likely to play on his home ground than at Trent Bridge, if only because Yorkshire are by no means certain to pick him for the Roses match against Lancashire this weekend.

A spokesman for the ECB said yesterday that Hoggard has made a sufficiently good recovery from an injury to his left foot to be in contention for a place in Yorkshire's over-crowded fast bowling department for the games against Lancashire starting on Friday and for tomorrow's Cheltenham & Gloucester quarter-final tie against Warwickshire, also at Headingley.

Selection is, of course, Yorkshire's prerogative. They have been told that Craig White and Darren Gough, in common with all the centrally contracted members of the England team at Lord's (or at least, those still standing) will be allowed to play for their counties between now and next week. They have to choose not only from White, Gough and Hoggard but also from Silverwood, Sidebottom, Hamilton and 23-year-old Steve Kirby, whose first appearances for the county this season suggested that he might have some of the pace, fire, aggression and accuracy of Brett Lee.

The Australians have a phrase borrowed from horse-racing for men like Kirby; they call them 'fast bolters' and one such, Matthew Nicholson, was picked almost out of the blue to play England at the MCG in the last Ashes series. It will not encourage our own more conservative selectors that Nicholson has not 'trained on'. If Kirby is picked by Yorkshire despite all the England bowlers around him and were to have another eye-catching game or two this week after taking 7 for 50 on his first appearance for the county against Kent and following it up with 12 for 72 against Leicestershire, they would, nevertheless, have to consider him for the relatively quick pitches at Headingley and The Oval, gamble though he would obviously be.

In an ideal world Kirby would be allowed to settle down for a full season next year before being picked to play in Australia the following winter if the early performances have been repeated. England's current plight is truly desperate, however, and the temptation to unleash him sooner would be considerable if he continues to win matches for Yorkshire. It will not happen at Trent Bridge where the replacement for Dominic Cork, if there is one, is more likely to come from a group including Martin Bicknell, Alex Tudor, Chris Silverwood and Ashley Giles.

England will certainly consider one spinner, possibly two, at Trent Bridge, where they might expect a more docile pitch and some help for spinners. Although Craig White's brief flurry with the bat in the second innings at Lord's was hardly sufficient evidence on which to promote him to seven at the expense of Ian Ward, it would be no surprise if it happens.

Such is the supreme confidence, quality and efficiency of Australia as they have played throughout the tour so far, the truth is that only by giving an overnight passport to Harbhajan Singh and V. V. S. Laxman are England likely to be able to knock them off track.

The Australians now have five clear days before a match against Hampshire at the weekend which is expected to attract a capacity crowd to the new ground at Southampton. Not since 1953, when the television habit was in its infancy, has the demand to watch these Australians in the flesh been so great.

The players themselves are having the time of their lives, with the only exception, perhaps, of the brooding, deeply disappointed Justin Langer, who has slipped off the joyride and desperately wants to be allowed back on. For the rest it is high summer, with a heat-wave guaranteed by the forecasters for at least a week; the wives and children are in the capital and not going home until the weekend; and they are not just winning but doing it in style.

England 1st innings

			R	M	B	4	6
*MA Atherton	lbw	b McGrath	37	139	92	5	0
ME Trescothick	c Gilchrist	b Gillespie	15	48	36	2	0
MA Butcher	c ME Waugh	b McGrath	21	58	42	4	0
GP Thorpe	c Gilchrist	b McGrath	20	98	50	1	0
MR Ramprakash		b Lee	14	38	38	0	0
+AJ Stewart	c Gilchrist	b McGrath	0	17	10	0	0
IJ Ward	not out		23	96	67	2	0
C White	c Hayden	b McGrath	0	18	14	0	0
DG Cork	c Ponting	b Gillespie	24	44	28	3	1
AR Caddick		b Warne	0	13	11	0	0
D Gough		b Warne	5	6	4	1	0
Extras	(b 7, lb 8, w 2, nb 11)		28				
Total	(all out, 63.3 overs, 288 mins)		187				

FoW: 1–33 (Trescothick, 11.3 ov), 2–75 (Butcher, 24.4 ov),
3–96 (Atherton, 30.6 ov), 4–121 (Ramprakash, 39.2 ov),
5–126 (Stewart, 42.4 ov), 6–129 (Thorpe, 44.3 ov),
7–131 (White, 48.5 ov), 8–178 (Cork, 58.2 ov),
9–181 (Caddick, 61.3 ov), 10–187 (Gough, 63.3 ov).

Bowling	O	M	R	W	
McGrath	24	9	54	5	
Gillespie	18	6	56	2	(4nb)
Lee	16	3	46	1	(7nb, 1w)
Warne	5.3	0	16	2	(1w)

Australia 1st innings

			R	M	B	4	6
MJ Slater	c Stewart	b Caddick	25	111	62	2	0
ML Hayden	c Butcher	b Caddick	0	7	5	0	0
RT Ponting	c Thorpe	b Gough	14	14	12	3	0
ME Waugh	run out (Gough)		108	209	170	14	0
*SR Waugh	c Stewart	b Cork	45	146	97	7	0
DR Martyn	c Stewart	b Caddick	52	127	99	6	0
+AC Gilchrist	c Stewart	b Gough	90	170	121	12	0
SK Warne	c Stewart	b Caddick	5	7	4	1	0
B Lee		b Caddick	20	77	45	3	0
JN Gillespie		b Gough	9	13	14	2	0
GD McGrath	not out		0	1	1	0	0
Extras	(lb 9, w 1, nb 23)		33				
Total	(all out, 101.1 overs, 441 mins)		401				

FoW: 1–5 (Hayden, 1.5 ov), 2–27 (Ponting, 4.5 ov),
3–105 (Slater, 24.1 ov), 4–212 (ME Waugh, 51.3 ov),
5–230 (SR Waugh, 57.1 ov), 6–308 (Martyn, 81.5 ov),
7–322 (Warne, 83.2 ov), 8–387 (Gilchrist, 96.6 ov),
9–401 (Gillespie, 100.5 ov), 10–401 (Lee, 101.1 ov).

Bowling	O	M	R	W	
Gough	25	3	115	3	(6nb)
Caddick	32.1	4	101	5	(11nb)

White	18	1	80	0	(1nb)
Cork	23	3	84	1	(5nb)
Butcher	3	1	12	0	(1w)

England 2nd innings			R	M	B	4	6
*MA Atherton		b Warne	20	73	45	3	0
ME Trescothick	c Gilchrist	b Gillespie	3	23	20	0	0
MA Butcher	c Gilchrist	b Gillespie	83	231	159	12	0
GP Thorpe	lbw	b Lee	2	6	7	0	0
MR Ramprakash	lbw	b Gillespie	40	115	91	4	0
+AJ Stewart	lbw	b McGrath	28	45	41	5	0
IJ Ward	c Ponting	b McGrath	0	1	1	0	0
C White	not out		27	38	28	5	0
DG Cork	c Warne	b McGrath	2	5	3	0	0
AR Caddick	c Gilchrist	b Gillespie	7	19	8	1	0
D Gough	c ME Waugh	b Gillespie	1	4	2	0	0
Extras	(lb 3, w 2, nb 9)		14				
Total	(all out, 66 overs, 280 mins)		227				

FoW: 1–8 (Trescothick, 5.2 ov), 2–47 (Atherton, 16.4 ov),
3–50 (Thorpe, 17.6 ov), 4–146 (Ramprakash, 46.3 ov),
5–188 (Stewart, 58.2 ov), 6–188 (Ward, 58.3 ov),
7–188 (Butcher, 59.5 ov), 8–193 (Cork, 60.6 ov),
9–225 (Caddick, 65.1 ov), 10–227 (Gough, 65.6 ov).

Bowling	O	M	R	W	
McGrath	19	4	60	3	
Gillespie	16	4	53	5	(2nb, 1w)
Lee	9	1	41	1	(4nb)
Warne	20	4	58	1	(3nb, 1w)
ME Waugh	2	1	12	0	

Australia 2nd innings			R	M	B	4	6
ML Hayden	not out		6	17	8	0	0
MJ Slater	c Butcher	b Caddick	4	6	5	1	0
RT Ponting	lbw	b Gough	4	2	3	0	0
ME Waugh	not out		0	4	3	0	0
Extras			0				
Total	(2 wickets, 3.1 overs, 17 mins)		14				

DNB: *SR Waugh, DR Martyn, +AC Gilchrist, SK Warne, B Lee,
JN Gillespie, GD McGrath.

FoW: 1–6 (Slater, 1.5 ov), 2–13 (Ponting, 2.3 ov).

Bowling	O	M	R	W	
Gough	2	0	5	1	
Caddick	1.1	0	9	1	

Australia won by 8 wickets.

Seven

Trent Bridge Too Far

While the Australians were resting, I returned to the neglected scene of county cricket, watching Somerset beating Kent in the quarter-final of the Cheltenham & Gloucester competition before moving on to Cheltenham itself to see the first match of the only true cricket festival still in existence. At Canterbury I stayed at the Dormy House of Royal St George's Golf Club, so was able on the day after the game to have nine holes before breakfast all by myself on those glorious links on a still, perfect summer's morning with only the larks and the occasional tern or mistle-thrush for company. Before leaving for London the next day, 26 July, I wrote 400 words as requested on the *Wisden* computer's idea of the 100 best Test innings and had a quick swim in our ancient pool. On the way into town the sports editor apologetically asked me for an extra 400 words, which meant a foot on the accelerator, since I was supposed to be at the Park Lane Hilton by 7.30 for a dinner given by the National Sporting Club for the Australian team.

I dashed off a rewritten piece at the Oxford & Cambridge Club before hastening into my dinner jacket, only to see the following day that it was being advertised in colour at the top of the paper's front page and being given a lavish presentation on the front of the sports supplement too. News must be in short supply, but the editorial instincts were right: e-mails flooded *The Times* for the next few days arguing about the merits of various innings that had been omitted from the list.

With my shirt hanging out, metaphorically at least, I raced up St James's Street and Piccadilly, having filed my piece in a muck sweat. There were 1,000 people at the dinner and the adulation accorded to the team was only what they deserved. It was a hard night for most of the players because their wives and children were due to return home the following day. Glenn McGrath had his long arm round the shoulders of his pregnant English-born wife and Steve Waugh was close to his pretty wife, Lynette, also pregnant with their third child. They did their public relations job every bit as well as they play their cricket. They are a side with an aura at the moment and success is breeding still more success. I heard, however, that England are buying another piece of Australian cricketing property in the attempt to catch up: Rodney Marsh is to direct the English Cricket Academy when it finally gets going this winter after years of discussion.

I had to make what David Willis, Bob's extremely intelligent and well organised brother and director of the National Sporting Club, described as the 'keynote speech'. I tried to be funny most of the time and the audience was generous. Just as well, because I was followed by Stephen Fry, who raised extraordinary sums for the auction in aid of the Australian Professional Cricketers' Association. Fourteen thousand pounds, for example, for a case of bats signed by the teams who won the sixteen Tests in succession. Stephen (Fry not Waugh) was excellent company as my next-door neighbour at the table. Apart from adapting Evelyn (not Stephen) Waugh's *Vile Bodies* for the screen, he has been asked to direct the proposed film, his first in that role. He wants Maggie Smith to be the main character. *Vile Bodies*, which I read after Alan Gibson once recommended that I should read more Waugh and less Swanton, is as entertaining a novel as *Scoop* and *Decline and Fall* and I suppose it will become a best-seller again if the film succeeds, as in the hands of the brilliant Fry it no doubt will. He is engagingly modest, but I thought a good deal more confident and relaxed than when I last met him at a benefit dinner for Simon Hughes. That was shortly before he had his crisis of confidence and left the cast of a Simon Gray play soon after it had opened. It showed that no matter how copiously gifted you may be – and he is as intelligent a man who has ever trod the boards – the burden of expectation can suddenly seem impossibly heavy. Perhaps even the Australians will come to understand that soon.

And so to bed at the Oxford & Cambridge Club before driving to Cheltenham tomorrow to report the first day of the Festival. It was a bonus that Sussex were Gloucestershire's opponents when I planned this match three months ago and it is a further bonus that Sussex start the game as the leaders of the second division, but, sadly, my son Robin M-J will not be playing. It is now eight weeks since he last bowled but they finally got round to using cortisone in his badly torn muscle below the ribs and he is praying that he will be fit to return to the side next week. His only chance of making up for lost time as far as furthering his international ambitions is concerned will be to do really well all-round against the Australians when Sussex play them after the third Test. If he is fit, of course.

Friday, 27 July

It will attract yet more derogatory Australian comment about going back to old has-beens but Phil Tufnell is the obvious, one could almost say the only, direct replacement for Ashley Giles if England's first-choice left-arm spinner is ruled out on grounds of fitness for next week's third Test at Trent Bridge.

Giles played for Warwickshire yesterday in the Cheltenham & Gloucester quarter-final having been quoted as admitting that his troublesome left Achilles tendon is 'permanently inflamed and sore to touch'. He added: 'I can't say I'm 100 per cent fit.'

Added to the disappointing news yesterday that Nasser Hussain has not made a sufficiently good recovery from the finger fracture he suffered against Australia in the first Test in Birmingham seventeen days ago, the continuing doubt about Giles has left the England selectors with two very delicate decisions to make when they meet today for preliminary discussions – the final decisions will wait until after two more days of first-class cricket.

Hussain is not fit to play for Essex in their CricInfo County Championship match this weekend, which means that he will either have to play at Nottingham without having batted since having his left little finger broken by a ball from Jason Gillespie, or leave it to Michael Atherton to carry on as caretaker captain.

The news of Giles's condition is hardly a revelation because he bowled throughout the winter tours, and particularly in Sri Lanka earlier this year, with increasing pain from an injury that has plagued him for several seasons. His seven Test wickets in Sri Lanka cost him 44 runs each following his outstanding series in Pakistan where he topped the averages with 17 wickets at 24.00.

The selectors will have to take a pragmatic view on Giles's form and fitness, not to mention a medical one on his longer-term availability. The delicate question is whether he should have surgery to a long-term injury that responded only marginally to the rest it was given between March and June. I am afraid they took the wrong decision. He will now have to have an operation that will keep him out of cricket for at least four months. Thus the man whose name would have been almost the first on the team-sheet for the tours of India either side of Christmas may have to miss the trip.

Steve Waugh had a go yesterday at Marcus Trescothick for the naïve remarks in his newspaper column on Sunday when he said that Australia were 'playing the game at a different level to us or anyone else on the planet'. Unwisely, he added: 'They hit the balls to parts our batsmen cannot reach and when they bowl the level of pressure they create is far higher than anything I have experienced.'

Waugh said yesterday that no Australian cricketer would have dreamed of writing anything like that and of course he is right. In the middle of a Test that England were still fighting to retrieve these were comments for a journalist to make, not a player in the current England team. They suggested that those who have been calling for Trescothick to be thrust into the England captaincy before he is ready are simply foolish. In certain circumstances, perhaps, but not the ones that England find themselves in now.

Sunday, 29 July
No Tufnell; no Mullally; no Martin Bicknell; no Robin Smith. Eschewing the dramatic and persevering instead with the recent policy of changing the team as little as possible, the England

selectors have made only one unforced change to the team for the third Test in Nottingham this week. For a match which must be won if Australia are not to retain the Ashes for the sixth time since they regained them in 1989, Alex Tudor replaces Dominic Cork, becoming one of five Surrey players in the squad of thirteen.

Robert Croft, Usman Afzaal and Chris Silverwood are all included in the thirteen from whom the eleven will be chosen on Thursday, but in the case of the last two, both involved in practice before the Lord's Test, the duties are unlikely to go further than the nets. On what is expected to be one of the best pitches of the series for batsmen, an attack with some variety is essential so the final choice is likely to be for five bowlers, three of whom, White, Croft and Tudor, will be expected to consider themselves as all-rounders, whatever the Australian bowlers may be inclined to call them.

In one sense it is admirable that, even in extreme adversity, the selectors have refused to be deflected from longer-term team-building by the desperation of the situation they face. But there were temptations: Smith would have been the really opportunistic choice in view of what he and his Hampshire side have achieved by beating the Australian touring team over the weekend, albeit after a declaration by Steve Waugh designed to stretch his team before the third Test.

Smith, who made a battling hundred in the first innings to make the Hampshire victory possible, remains a player of high class and courage, although he is a relative liability in the field. To recall him now would revive memories of the return of Cyril Washbrook in 1956. In these peculiar circumstances, though, there would have been much to be said for it as a temporary measure before the established middle-order returns. I cannot see Ward, Afzaal or, had he been chosen, Owais Shah, giving the Australian bowlers as much trouble as Smith might have done. Mullally has pressed his case in the same game as a bowler who takes wickets by accuracy these days. Bicknell is bowling superbly as he has, more or less, for several seasons. His batting, too, seems to improve each year. He is quicker than he looks from his relaxed action, but the selectors are obsessed with his apparent lack of pace, forgetting that he always does something with the ball. They had picked him, however, subject to performances in the Benson & Hedges final, changing their mind when Tudor looked more dangerous in that game.

ROBERT CROFT

Feisty little Welshman with a bland, flat off-break, butting through the breezes in the mad June days . . .

'Croftie' is a great little trier but compared to Shane Warne or Muttiah Muralitharan he is indeed like the dirty British coaster alongside exotic craft from sunny lands afar. It is not his fault: he is a prisoner of his era, the type of cricket county professionals play and the pitches on which they learn their trade. He has made the most of ability with both bat and ball, working hard to improve and when he has had his moments of success – plenty for Glamorgan and one or two for England too – he has enjoyed them to the full.

2001 v. Australia: 1 match; 3 runs at 1.50; 1 wicket at 10

Tufnell has well over twice Croft's wickets at not a great deal more than half the cost this season. His is the most contentious omission for a game that England must try to win. In a match to be played on one of the older pitches on the Trent Bridge square, there is expected to be some help for spinners. Despite Croft's all-round qualities, Tufnell is much the more likely match-winner in home conditions, but his return to the dressing-room, if it does not come in dry weather at The Oval, is likely now to wait until the tour to India. Unless Giles recovers more quickly than expected and in the absence, sadly, of younger contenders, he can pack his toothbrush and cigarettes now.

Cork has been known to turn cricket matches and, once or twice, a Test series. After thirty-four Tests, however, despite a typically resilient all-round performance on Saturday when he knew that the sword was poised, the evidence of his two Tests this season is that he has failed to rediscover his outswinger (his figures have been 2 for 201 in 69 overs) and that his bold but fevered batting is unlikely to produce runs of significance against fast bowlers as good as Australia's.

Tudor, famously, scored 99 not out in his most recent Test, his third, against New Zealand two years ago. He has been a part of two tours since, to South Africa and as a replacement in Pakistan, without demanding or being given the chance to build on the positive aspects of three mixed performances so far. Against Australia in Perth in his first game, admittedly on the quickest pitch in the world, he made life distinctly uncomfortable for the Australian batsmen, Steve Waugh included. He finished with seven wickets from his two Tests in that series but bowled without rhythm against New Zealand and has been inconsistent since.

ALEX TUDOR

According to his father Alex Tudor was still growing in 2001. Perhaps it was not therefore such an insult to leave him out of the winter touring parties so soon after taking five wickets in a Test innings, sending him instead to the National Cricket Academy.

He is an enigma, this softly spoken, God-fearing, polite, friendly young fast bowler; a heavyweight boxer above the waist, a slender-legged antelope below. If he reaches maturity both physically and mentally he will be an all-round cricketer to treasure.

2001 v. Australia: 2 matches; 14 runs at 4.66; 7 wickets at 27.85

The fact is, however, that he picked up a couple of wickets even in that game against New Zealand at Edgbaston. His vibrant opening spell in Surrey's final at Lord's a fortnight ago confirmed that he is more likely to be inspired rather than frozen by a big occasion and there is no doubt about the quality and growing confidence of his batting. He is a better bowler when he opts for rhythm first, pace second, but one look at Glenn McGrath will remind him that one usually follows from the other.

Still unable to practice, let alone play in a match, Nasser Hussain will be fit, barring further mishap, for the fourth Test but the odds are against either Graham Thorpe (broken hand) or Michael Vaughan (knee) making it back in time for Headingley. Not until the final Test at The Oval, therefore, are England likely to be able to select their first-choice middle-order.

Wednesday, 1 August

England called the Somerset fast bowler Richard Johnson to Nottingham today after Tudor had reported stiffness in his side and Silverwood had suffered a recurrence of recent back trouble. Tudor is expected to play, after a few words from the manager and the coach to remind him that, as a fast bowler, he can never expect to feel completely fit. The strong suspicion is that his problem today is more a lack of self-confidence than physical injury. He need not be so diffident. He has great natural ability as a bowler, batsman and, Bambi legs or not, in the field.

Mental frailty in the English camp, or what the Aussies would call 'the wrong mindset', has been very much in the public domain again following the appearance under a journalist's door in the Australians' hotel at Southampton of a memo to the team from John Buchanan, quoting liberally from the teachings of the fifth-century Chinese general, Sun Tzu. Buchanan dismissed a conspiracy theory that it had been pushed under the door of the PA reporter, David Clough, on purpose (the memos had been distributed by hotel staff) and was happy to discuss his own theory that England players and management were making excuses for the events of the series so far.

There are those who believe that this tall, bespectacled Queenslander with the bushy moustache has made enemies who will unseat him before long, just as they did at Middlesex when he lost his job as coach in 1999 to Mike Gatting, who did no better as coach the following season. Buchanan must be doing something right because Australia have won eighteen out of twenty Tests since he became coach in succession to the world-weary Geoff Marsh. He is orthodox enough in his practice routines but a great theorist on the workings of the mind and a relentless analyst of the technical and mental deficiencies of opponents.

He was right to criticise Shane Warne's lack of fitness in India – the effect has been plain enough on this tour – but is rumoured to have offended the urbane and competent manager, Steve Bernard, and the long-serving physiotherapist, Errol Alcott, by seeking originally to replace them with men he knew better. Steve Waugh dismissed the Chinese philosophy lightly when he said yesterday, 'If anyone can decipher it, please let me know.' But he added: 'I like working with John because he's always challenging the players in different ways.'

Buchanan himself said: 'I don't think for one minute [the thoughts of General Tzu] are going to be a Bible for seventeen players. It's intended to focus their attention, to extend them and get them to think differently. If it struck a chord with a handful of them, it's made an impact.'

Thursday, 2 August

Third Test, Trent Bridge (first day of five; England won toss): Australia are 80 runs behind England with 3 first-innings wickets in hand.

This was more Headingley than Trent Bridge. Throughout the first day of the third Test the ball swung and seamed sufficiently under a pewter sky for the fast bowlers to be in a state of constant anticipation, like children on their way to the beach. Seventeen wickets fell in the 86 overs before the light faded, Marcus Trescothick alone could play an innings of lasting command, yet the truth was that only Glenn McGrath, Shane Warne and Alex Tudor bowled especially well until, late in a dramatic day, Andrew Caddick joined in the fun with three wickets in eleven balls.

The night is darkest just before the dawn. Could it be that, at last – and at the latest possible moment, because Australia were 48 for no wicket in reply to their own inadequate first innings score of 185 – England have bowled themselves back into the Ashes series? It may yet be no more than a chimera, but it can at least be said that they have finally emerged from a full day's play with the advantage.

It is not in any way yet a decisive advantage. Australia were bound to run into a squall somewhere on the voyage and with Adam Gilchrist at the helm they will be confident that they can sail back into calmer waters. Averaging 121 in the series after his two previous innings, he drove his first ball for four when he came in at 94 for 5 and even if his and the other two wickets that remain were to be hustled out this morning, a lead of 60 or thereabouts could prove insignificant.

If the forecasters are correct and the atmosphere freshens it will be fascinating to see what effect a change in the weather may have on the conditions that made life so tricky for batsmen yesterday. The pitch started dry and the bounce, although never especially high or low, was sufficiently uneven to keep everyone guessing from the first over. McGrath's first ball to Atherton bounced through high and was safely left; his second, pitching in the same place, flew through lower to hit him on the arm-guard. Up went umpire Hampshire's finger; out went the acting England captain with a sad little shake of the head and the bowlers' day had started.

The swing was no more lavish than the bounce, perhaps because most of the bowlers were at least as interested in exploiting the cracks, but when they gave it the chance all the quick bowlers got movement through the heavy air of a day on which a thunderstorm always seemed possible. Even in clear weather the ball generally swings a little here, influenced by the river on one side and the trees that line Fox and Hound roads on the other, but since the building of the Radcliffe Road Stand, the best of its kind anywhere in the world, the movement seems somehow to have increased.

The critical difference between England's performance in this game so far has been that the catches behind the wicket have been taken. Australia missed two chances, the first of them by McGrath at mid-on off Brett Lee when Alec Stewart had made three, an expensive one because Stewart went on to play one of only two innings of any substance. White was also missed in the slips but Atherton pouched two at first slip, the first of them taken securely in front of his throat to give Caddick the prized wicket of Steve Waugh.

Atherton added to the pressure on Australia by setting shrewdly balanced fields after Matthew Hayden had given the innings a rollicking start. The performances of the two elder statesmen were important but the great bonus for England with the future in mind was that Tudor did so well after the doubt about his appearance. Showing no sign of the stiff muscle in his side that had required a fitness test yesterday morning and the calling-up of an eleventh-hour replacement, he was fractionally fortunate to claim Hayden leg before in his second over but he made the ball talk off the seam after that and was unlucky not to add more than one wicket.

MATTHEW HAYDEN

Two images linger in the mind's eye of Hayden on his way to establishing his overdue place in Australia's Test team. One is of a fantastic catch taken in the deep at Lord's when he was merely a substitute on his first tour of England in 1997. The other is of an athlete built like a modern back-row rugby forward, going though his exercise routine on the outfield at Cairns, with the help of a huge rubber ball bigger even than Hayden himself. His enormous muscular power is the result of endless hours of monotonous physical labour that had one single-minded objective: to help him get to the top in cricket.

His batting was driven by the same desire to make himself the best. Practice, practice, practice has been his mantra; the bowling machine and a no less dedicated coach, John Buchanan, his chief allies.

The rewards came in abundance in the year of the Millennium. First he scored 1,270 runs from only twenty-two first-class innings for Northamptonshire, whom he captained from the front; then he started building another small mountain for Australia. In India before the tour of England he made 549 in three Tests and 303 in four one-day internationals. Virtue often has more than its own reward.

2001 v. England: 5 matches; 234 runs at 33.42; 4 catches

Teams bowled out before tea on the first day after winning the toss cannot normally expect to win Test matches unless either the pitch or the batting is poor. Given the unlucky dismissal of Atherton, and with three first-choice batsmen not available until the fourth Test, the story of England's innings is simply that, Trescothick and Stewart apart, they were outclassed by the magnificent McGrath and quite unable to get on top of Warne.

They are the leaders of an attack that has now taken more wickets – 1,024 between them – than any combination of bowlers in Test history. McGrath added five more to his bag of 330 with another superb example of controlled menace, consistently pitching the ball on the perfect length around the off stump. Butcher edged to third slip as a ball straightened when he was pushing to leg; Ward edged the first ball of his second spell from round the wicket; White was snared at forward short leg and Stewart steered an outswinger to second slip.

Warne, meanwhile, bottled everyone up from the Radcliffe

Road End in an unchanged spell of fifteen overs between lunch and tea, getting some turn and offering no gifts. By claiming Tudor lbw on the front foot – correct, according to the illogical new law – and Robert Croft caught at silly point in his next over, the maestro claimed his 100th wicket in twenty-one Tests against England.

The day-long mayhem placed Trescothick's batting in sharp relief. Neither Lee nor Gillespie could match McGrath's control and he punished them both, waiting for the short ball to hook or pull, or driving anything over-pitched. Three times he unveiled a brace of boundaries off Gillespie, each time following a pull with a drive. He had scored 69 from 93 balls with 13 fours when Gillespie had his revenge by finally drawing an indeterminate stroke from England's future captain.

Responding to all the early finishes in recent Tests the ICC has resolved to inspect grounds where referees report unsuitable pitches. Talat Ali, the official here, can hardly put yesterday's events down to an inadequate pitch, merely to a combination of circumstances.

Friday, 3 August
Trent Bridge (second day of five): England, with 4 second-innings wickets in hand, are 139 runs ahead of Australia.
The genius of Shane Warne turned a thrilling Trent Bridge Test Australia's way with stunning suddenness yesterday evening. In a day prolonged by frequent showers for an hour and a half beyond its scheduled close, Warne produced a spell of 4 for 11 in 36 balls to turn a promising-looking England score of 115 for 2 into a perilous 144 for 6. They lead by only 139.

To some extent it was a case of batsmen buckling under the high pressure of having to make a decent second-innings total in a match they have to win, but Warne has always been a master of exploiting not just a pitch which helps him but also any tension in his opponents. At times like this he is like a dog who knows the postman is nervous of being bitten.

The variations are nowhere near as baffling as they used to be before his two operations but the mesmeric accuracy, the natural cunning and the biting turn of his leg-break were all in evidence as he followed up the vital wicket of Michael Atherton by bowling Alec Stewart off an inside edge, having Mark Ramprakash stumped as he danced down the pitch in an ill-judged attempt to turn the tide, and finally claiming Craig White to a low catch off inside edge and pad.

As Adam Gilchrist remained to undermine the apparent strength of England's position on the first evening, so does Ian Ward, the last specialist batsman, to keep the small flame of English hope alive this morning. The ball is still moving around for the faster bowlers, but if anything batting became marginally less tricky in a fresher atmosphere yesterday, so England will somehow have to eke out another fifty runs or more if they are to set Australia a fourth-innings total that will turn the pressure back on them.

After a morning's cricket dominated by the brilliance of Gilchrist and the promise of Alex Tudor, the game reverted for two hours and more to a theme it knows and loves: Michael Atherton versus the rest. Relishing the challenge of hostile fast bowling as only he does and given determined support by Marcus Trescothick and Ramprakash, he kept the match in the balance and the spectators on the edge of their seats until for the second time in a thrilling match he was the victim of an erroneous decision.

It should be added at once that he had been extremely lucky not to be given out lbw by the same umpire, Venkataraghavan, when, having scored only 12, he was trapped in front by a nip-backer from Glenn McGrath. It has been no more an easy match for umpires than it has for batsmen. Having had this slice of luck to balance being given out caught behind off his arm-guard in the first innings, Atherton made a typically skilful, resolute fifty with nine fours before Warne claimed him caught behind with a leg-break that turned across the face of his bat but narrowly missed the edge.

MARCUS TRESCOTHICK

Sometimes it helps to have an arresting name. It stuck in the minds of regular readers of the *Cricketer* in the 1980s when the teenage Trescothick was always finding his way into the small print for deeds done in and around Keynsham. (It is well documented that he once reached his 4,000th run in the last game of the season, knocking off the runs against the clock to reach his personal goal and simultaneously to batter Keynsham to victory.) Nor was he ungrateful to his Cornish ancestors, not to mention a cricket-playing father, when Duncan Fletcher made a note of having seen him score a century of exalted excellence for Somerset against Northamptonshire in 1999.

By then 'Banger', fond of sausages and built a bit like one, was on the verge of rediscovering the prolific form of his carefree youth. He had quietly worked out a way to live and a method that worked against the best bowlers. Like so many others he had needed a winter in Australia to teach him that fitness and the right mental and technical preparation were essential.

Who knows whether or not it was a blessing that he had ironed out his faults in county cricket and came to England already the complete article? At once he exuded not so much confidence, still less arrogance, but self-assurance at the crease. At once he scored runs. Soon he was chipping in to team talks or suggesting tactical manoeuvres in the field: not too cockily, but usefully, sensibly and, like his batting, at the right time. This was not just a past captain of the England Under-19 team but a future captain of the full England side, no doubt.

After a year as an international cricketer he was a likeable West Country lad, still; but a national celebrity too. The dream in 2001 was that he might go one stage higher and become a national hero. In reality he experienced how much is needed to become one.

2001 v. Australia: 5 matches; 321 runs at 32.10; 4 catches

If this was unlucky for England, Trescothick's dismissal was trebly unfortunate. A precise stroke from the middle of his bat in Shane Warne's second over was intercepted by the back of Matthew Hayden's leg as he turned away in an attempt to avoid being hit. Diving forward, Gilchrist caught the rebound with admirable opportunism and the Australians were already celebrating by the time that the third umpire, David Constant, had confirmed to the umpires in the middle that the ball had not touched the ground. None of them was aware, until further television replays from another angle showed it, that Venkataraghavan, the umpire at the bowler's end, had missed a fractional no-ball as Warne's foot landed with the back of his boot on the line.

To make it even worse for Trescothick the umpires then took the players in as rain began to fall. Having been caught at short-leg in Russell Arnold's shirt in the Colombo Test in March, Trescothick must wonder if there are any more unlikely ways to be snared at short-leg off full-blooded sweeps. There is, however, nothing much new in cricket and Australians with long memories will see this as payback for the moment at Edgbaston, at a crucial stage of the Test that decided the 1985 Ashes, when Wayne Phillips was caught off a rebound from Allan Lamb's leg at silly point off Phil Edmonds. Phillips and Trescothick will not have agreed in the heat of each moment but these outrageous slings and arrows are part of cricket's esoteric charm.

There were two hours of thundery rain for the debate about technology to resume amongst pundits and spectators. A pressure pad on the popping crease to detect no-balls in the manner of Cyclops at Wimbledon may at least be worthy of experiment, but some means of letting the bowler's umpire know that he has missed a no-ball as soon as the television replay has detected it seems a more feasible means of allowing justice to be seen and done.

When the cricket began again it was Atherton who stood between Australia and the sudden burst of wickets that would surely settle the match and the series. Brett Lee was deployed to bowl flat-out from the Radcliffe Road End in an attempt to unsettle him as he had at Lord's. He soon beat Mark Butcher for pace and had Ramprakash caught behind off a no-ball but Atherton, the bit well and truly between his teeth, uppercut and sliced him to the third-man boundary and barely blinked when a bouncer glanced the grille of his helmet in front of his jaw.

It was paradoxical that in conditions the fast bowlers have relished, Warne should once again have intervened to steal the show. In the morning, however, it had been Gilchrist and Tudor who shared top billing, with a crucial little guest appearance from Jason Gillespie. Coming in after Lee had edged Tudor to first slip, he held up one end – and picked up runs with nudges and deflections – whilst Gilchrist unfurled one blazing drive after another when the ball was in the area he loves.

They put on 66 for the eighth wicket before Tudor, returning at the Radcliffe Road End, had him smartly caught by Atherton in front of his face and followed up with a well-deserved fifth wicket, courtesy of a brilliant left-handed catch by Butcher. If defeat follows today as it surely must, Tudor's performance will at least be one consolation.

Sunday, 5 August

Australia will have a different captain and a new batsman in the fourth Test at Headingley next week but if it knocks them out of their confident stride it will be surprising and, up to a point, irrelevant. The Ashes have gone to Australia again and with them a series clinched at 4pm on Saturday on the third day of the Trent Bridge Test after another irresistible demonstration of penetrative bowling and purposeful, entertaining batting.

The ethos of a whole team was symbolised first by the way that Shane Warne and Jason Gillespie left the field with their arms around each other after plucking out England's last four wickets in thirty-five minutes in the morning; then by the style and ease with which Damien Martyn and Mark Waugh knocked off the 69 runs still needed after Australia had effectively lost a fourth wicket when Steve Waugh was borne off on a stretcher.

Like the series itself, so long and enthralling in the build-up, so quickly and crushingly won by an unchanging, untroubled, confident and gifted all-round Australia XI against three different, diffident and unlucky England teams, it all happened so quickly. What should have been a long drawn-out struggle to score even 158, on a pitch still giving all the bowlers help, was over in fewer than 30 overs.

JASON GILLESPIE

'Dizzie', the simple, down-to-earth Aussie with the medieval face, is your man when the chips are down. His character showed most clearly at Trent Bridge, when it looked as though Australia might have to concede a first-innings lead, with uncertain consequences. He not only got his head down and batted with gumption and a simple, common-sense technique, but morally, by precept and example, played the leading role in the partnership with Adam Gilchrist that baled the water from the boat.

Some of his most heroic games as a bowler have also come in adversity. He was leonine when Brian Lara stole the Barbados Test during Steve Waugh's first tour as captain; defiant in India when V. V. S. Laxman was riding the crest of his wave; and again when Mark Butcher played his great innings at Headingley, where Gillespie himself had triumphed four years before.

He tended to pitch too short or, more often, too full on that one day when Australia came second, but he is on most days a devilishly fierce fast bowler, generating stinging bounce from his tall, raw-boned frame.

2001 v. England: 5 matches; 41 runs at 13.66; 19 wickets at 34.31

Waugh will definitely miss the fourth Test and probably the fifth at The Oval with a torn left calf muscle. Adam Gilchrist will take over, as he was required to do at Adelaide against the West Indies in the last Australian summer, and he will relish it, however much the combination of captaining the Test side, keeping wicket and batting might sap even his bright-eyed enthusiasm if he is eventually asked to take on those responsibilities for a long period.

Waugh's batting replacement will either be the little left-hander whom he described as being the best Test batsman in the world only eighteen months ago, Justin Langer; or the next cab off the rank, another left-hander, Simon Katich, who has been quietly living up to the huge promise he has shown since boyhood and an impressive spell at the Adelaide Academy.

Langer was bitterly disappointed to be dropped to accommodate Martyn, but the latter has shown beyond doubt that he is a mature batsman of the highest class and it is Ricky Ponting who has failed to take the chance to establish himself at three in the order. His last fifteen Test innings have produced only one fifty. Martyn at three, Katich at five, Ponting back at six (where he made 127 against England at Headingley in 1997) and the devastating Gilchrist at seven looks like the logical solution.

England would have given much for any such disruption to the Australian side at the start of the series, and even more to have been able to field their own chosen XI from the start. 'We peaked too early,' the coach, Duncan Fletcher, said in reference to the performances in Pakistan and Sri Lanka which had led quite naturally to the high expectations for England this summer. When they beat Pakistan at Lord's in May they already had Matthew Hoggard, Ashley Giles and Craig White out of contention with injuries. White has never regained his winter form; Giles made one Test appearance before having the overdue operation on his Achilles tendon; and Hoggard was only briefly fit again before requiring another prolonged rest because of a damaged foot.

Since then Nasser Hussain has missed two Tests, Graham Thorpe two and Michael Vaughan all three. Thorpe, the best batsman in England, was a crucial absentee. He had to take on the fast bowling at Lord's with no match practice after six weeks away from the game. Losing Hussain, Fletcher said after this fourth successive Test defeat, the tenth in succession in five-day and one-day cricket, 'was a big, big blow'. He added: 'It was very difficult for Atherton to come in in a situation like this.'

It would have been much harder still had Marcus Trescothick been asked to fill in. There is always a right time and place to promote the young. It is right for Australia to elevate Gilchrist and Katich now because theirs is a position of supreme strength. Even if it disrupts their rhythm in the last two Tests, or Katich fails (and I doubt he will) it will not do any long-term harm to him or to the team.

The pressure has eased a fraction with the Ashes won and lost but Australia still want to win 5–0 and England desperately need to stop the rot. Despite the strength of Australia and England's position, there is something to be said for getting at least one young equivalent of Katich into the England team at Headingley. The snag is that it would have to be at the expense of Craig White, who would be on his home ground and is a better player than his helpless performances in this series have suggested.

The future intentions of Mike Atherton and Alec Stewart need to be clear to the selectors before they decide, but Stewart has no serious rival as wicket-keeper/batsman – James Foster would be chosen on no more solid evidence than Chris Read was in 1999 – and of the two prolific current openers in county cricket, Richard Montgomerie is thirty, David Fulton twenty-nine.

No one would be happier than Glenn McGrath if Atherton were to be replaced. He has batted well and held some fine slip catches – eleven in five Tests this season with two missed. They will not abandon him as an opener now whether or not he tells them privately what his intentions are for the winter and beyond. He is not short of media offers for the future but says publicly: 'I have contracts with Lancashire and England until the end of the season; then I'll make a decision.'

After 113 Tests each, the odds are that both Atherton and Stewart will play no more Test cricket after the end of the season. Hussain, Vaughan and Hoggard are hoping to return for the fourth Test – Thorpe not until the fifth – with Ramprakash, Ward and Croft likely to make way.

The best team in the world has thrashed the side officially rated the third best. It is South Africa's turn now to try to shake Australia from the top of the tree. They will certainly give them a run for their money in the three-Test series at home and away this winter but England will have to do what Australia could not – beat India in their own conditions – to retain third place in the ICC World Championship; and it would be just England's luck for Chris Cairns, the best cricketer in New Zealand, to return after a long lay-off to make life hard for them after Christmas.

They were always going to need not only a lot of luck but also the ability to get through on team spirit when the chips were down to prevent Australia winning their unprecedented seventh Ashes series in succession. The injuries inevitably disrupted the spirit, and in that sense at least the luck, as usual, went with the side in the ascendant. When the final chance came before lunch on Saturday at Trent Bridge, Hayden should have been given out leg before to Gough's second ball of the innings.

If the experienced Venkat had lifted his finger then rather than when the innings had taken its shape, who knows for sure how it might have affected the morale of the two sides and therefore the cricket that followed. The luck factor has played its part this summer but it cannot cloud the true picture. Except in fast bowling, where England might be said to have at least as many young contenders, Australia have proved again that they possess far greater strength in depth.

A second XI chosen from, amongst others, Katich, Langer, Elliott, Cox, Blewett, Hussey, Maher, Lehmann, Bevan, Law, Harvey, Bichel, Bracken, Noffke, MacGill and Miller proves the point. In a way this is just as significant as the 'fact' – at least the general opinion – that they have five players out of eleven who deserve to be called great. Shane Warne, Steve and Mark Waugh, Glenn McGrath, and now, indubitably, Adam Gilchrist are in that category. Gillespie may be soon. None of England's leading men – Atherton, Stewart, Caddick, Gough, Thorpe, Hussain – quite is.

Without their preferred middle order the England batting has failed lamentably against the best Australian attack since Lillee, Thomson, Walker, Gilmour and Mallett (with Jenner and O'Keefe in reserve) outclassed England under Ian Chappell in 1974/75.

In six innings of this series, England have reached 200 only twice and their highest total, 294 in the first innings of the first Test at Edgbaston, owed most to the last-wicket stand of 103. Their longest innings, the 227 in the second innings at Lord's, has lasted 66 overs. Only Marcus Trescothick and, in one innings, Mark Butcher, has looked likely to make a century, but no one actually has.

By contrast Australia's batting strength has been the middle order from four to seven, comprising their four centurions, Gilchrist, Martyn and the Waugh twins. Between them Caddick and Gough, with help at Trent Bridge from Tudor (and a single wicket each for Giles and Croft) have so far kept Slater, Hayden and Ponting to averages lower than 30. Despite that, Slater had a critical influence on the mood of the series by hitting Gough's first over at Edgbaston for 18 runs and on Saturday Hayden made his 42 rapidly and assertively.

England's bowling and fielding pushed Australia hard in the first innings at Trent Bridge but the quest continues in the short term for a spinner capable of becoming a match-winner in Test cricket and for batsmen of anything like the class of Damien Martyn, who has not only fitted seamlessly into the side in this series but looks just about the best player of them all.

Martyn is one of several members of the current Australian team to have gone through the Academy programme in Adelaide. In his foreword to *The Winning Edge*, a book about the mental side of winning by Jack Potter, the first director of the Australian Cricket Academy, Shane Warne writes: 'I was lucky enough to be chosen as one of his earliest students. At that time Jack Potter's ideas were revolutionary. He knew that if Australia was to become the world's top cricketing nation, the players had to work harder than anyone else, and then some. While other countries sat back and watched, the Academy turned Australia's young hopefuls into athletes, through programmes of weight-training, fitness work, psychological preparation, injury prevention, record-keeping, target and achievement setting and – last but not least – technique training.'

Years too late England are to have an academy of their own under Potter's successor, Rodney Marsh, and in time it must help, probably too late to have an effect on the national side in Australia in only eighteen months' time or in the World Cup that follows in South Africa. Meanwhile, the battle has to continue on every front: in the schools and clubs and the 'Active Sports' programme which the ECB has started with some success this season in order to expand on the middle ground between school cricket and junior county teams; in those junior county sides themselves, where talent is being nurtured better, and young fast bowlers are being protected from too much work too young; on county staffs where young professionals are no longer in any doubt that theirs is a harsh, competitive environment; at the National Academy where the best of them should now begin to get the training to turn some of them into champions; and in the England team group itself, which has to find a way back to the path that Fletcher and Hussain were starting to mark out for them.

The area of greatest concern remains county cricket: its balance, its quality and its quantity. Fletcher, coming in from outside, makes no secret of his belief that they play too much and that the standard is insufficiently high for young players to make the transition to Test and international cricket without feeling out of their depth at first. Overseas players back him by calling as one man for more preparation and fewer matches.

If the two-division Championship is to continue, and regional cricket to be rejected except as a means of giving touring teams stronger opposition, it has to be accompanied by one less one-day tournament. One of the two knockout tournaments has to go, however much the accountants at the ECB and in the counties will bleat at the loss of gate, membership and television money. It will come back eventually if England stop losing in three days in home Test matches.

In addition, the liaison between the England managers and the counties on medical matters needs further refinement and championship fixtures need to be played between Tests rather than during them, both so that England players can test themselves if they have been injured and so that Championship cricket itself is not further devalued by an ECB that too often treats it with disdain.

As for the length of Tests themselves, the argument first made by this writer after the Headingley Test last year surely has to be taken more seriously now. Tests in England and Australia at least should now be scheduled over four days of 100 overs each, not five of 90, with a reserve fifth day available in case of bad weather. No one is going to book in advance on Sundays any more in any case.

England 1st innings

			R	M	B	4	6
*MA Atherton	c ME Waugh	b McGrath	0	2	2	0	0
ME Trescothick	c Gilchrist	b Gillespie	69	125	93	13	0
MA Butcher	c Ponting	b McGrath	13	46	29	1	0
MR Ramprakash	c Gilchrist	b Gillespie	14	29	18	3	0
+AJ Stewart	c ME Waugh	b McGrath	46	133	90	8	0
IJ Ward	c Gilchrist	b McGrath	6	32	20	0	0
C White	c Hayden	b McGrath	0	10	9	0	0
AJ Tudor	lbw	b Warne	3	18	17	0	0
RDB Croft	c Ponting	b Warne	3	10	10	0	0
AR Caddick		b Lee	13	29	26	2	0
D Gough	not out		0	16	10	0	0
Extras	(b 1, lb 9, w 1, nb 7)		18				
Total	(all out, 52.5 overs, 225 mins)		185				

FoW: 1–0 (Atherton, 0.2 ov), 2–30 (Butcher, 10.5 ov),
3–63 (Ramprakash, 17.3 ov), 4–117 (Trescothick, 28.2 ov),
5–142 (Ward, 36.1 ov), 6–147 (White, 38.4 ov),
7–158 (Tudor, 43.3 ov), 8–168 (Croft, 45.6 ov),
9–180 (Stewart, 48.4 ov), 10–185 (Caddick, 52.5 ov).

Bowling	O	M	R	W	
McGrath	18	4	49	5	
Lee	6.5	0	30	1	(5nb, 1w)
Gillespie	12	1	59	2	
Warne	16	4	37	2	(2nb)

Australia 1st innings

			R	M	B	4	6
MJ Slater		b Gough	15	75	49	1	0
ML Hayden	lbw	b Tudor	33	56	42	7	0
RT Ponting	c Stewart	b Gough	14	32	20	3	0
ME Waugh	c Atherton	b Tudor	15	65	44	3	0
*SR Waugh	c Atherton	b Caddick	13	38	30	2	0
DR Martyn	c Stewart	b Caddick	4	15	8	1	0
+AC Gilchrist	c Atherton	b Tudor	54	119	59	10	0
SK Warne	lbw	b Caddick	0	2	2	0	0
B Lee	c Butcher	b Tudor	4	41	14	0	0
JN Gillespie	not out		27	72	62	4	0
GD McGrath	c Butcher	b Tudor	2	2	4	0	0
Extras	(lb 3, w 1, nb 5)		9				
Total	(all out, 54.5 overs, 259 mins)		190				

FoW: 1–48 (Hayden, 12.6 ov), 2–56 (Slater, 17.1 ov),
3–69 (Ponting, 19.6 ov), 4–82 (SR Waugh, 28.6 ov),
5–94 (ME Waugh, 31.5 ov), 6–102 (Martyn, 32.2 ov),
7–102 (Warne, 32.4 ov), 8–122 (Lee, 39.1 ov),
9–188 (Gilchrist, 54.1 ov), 10–190 (McGrath, 54.5 ov).

Bowling	O	M	R	W	
Gough	15	3	63	2	(1nb, 1w)
Caddick	20	4	70	3	(3nb)
Tudor	15.5	5	44	5	(1nb)

White	2	1	8	0	
Croft	2	0	2	0	

England 2nd innings			R	M	B	4	6
*MA Atherton	c Gilchrist	b Warne	51	150	104	9	0
ME Trescothick	c Gilchrist	b Warne	32	71	55	4	0
MA Butcher	lbw	b Lee	1	6	9	0	0
MR Ramprakash	st Gilchrist	b Warne	26	75	70	3	0
+AJ Stewart		b Warne	0	5	2	0	0
IJ Ward	lbw	b Gillespie	13	53	39	1	0
C White	c SR Waugh	b Warne	7	35	24	0	0
AJ Tudor	c Ponting	b Warne	9	52	26	1	0
RDB Croft		b Gillespie	0	6	4	0	0
AR Caddick	c Gilchrist	b Gillespie	4	8	7	1	0
D Gough	not out		5	26	8	1	0
Extras	(b 4, lb 3, nb 7)		14				
Total	(all out, 57 overs, 243 mins)		162				

FoW: 1–57 (Trescothick, 16.3 ov), 2–59 (Butcher, 17.6 ov),
       3–115 (Atherton, 36.6 ov), 4–115 (Stewart, 38.2 ov),
       5–126 (Ramprakash, 40.2 ov), 6–144 (White, 48.5 ov),
       7–144 (Ward, 49.4 ov), 8–146 (Croft, 51.3 ov),
       9–156 (Caddick, 53.5 ov), 10–162 (Tudor, 56.6 ov).

Bowling	O	M	R	W	
McGrath	11	3	31	0	
Gillespie	20	8	61	3	
Lee	8	1	30	1	(7nb)
Warne	18	5	33	6	

Australia 2nd innings			R	M	B	4	6
ML Hayden	lbw	b Tudor	42	84	51	7	0
MJ Slater	c Trescothick	b Caddick	12	25	17	2	0
RT Ponting	c Stewart	b Croft	17	34	31	3	0
ME Waugh	not out		42	134	45	7	0
*SR Waugh	retired hurt		1	1	1	0	0
DR Martyn	not out		33	106	37	6	0
Extras	(lb 4, nb 7)		11				
Total	(3 wickets, 29.2 overs, 192 mins)		158				

DNB: +AC Gilchrist, SK Warne, B Lee, JN Gillespie, GD McGrath.

FoW: 1–36 (Slater, 5.4 ov), 2–72 (Ponting, 13.2 ov),
       3–88 (Hayden, 18.3 ov).

Bowling	O	M	R	W	
Gough	9	1	38	0	(2nb)
Caddick	12.2	1	71	1	(4nb)
Tudor	7	0	37	1	
Croft	1	0	8	1	

Australia won by 7 wickets.

Eight

Butchered

Nowhere in England are folk more like Australians than in Yorkshire. Local pride here goes far deeper than anywhere else. The broad acres are almost sacred. The symbolic story is the one about the Dales farmer who made friends with a visitor from Texas during an agricultural conference at Harrogate. One sunny evening he took the Texan to the highest point of his property and showed him the magnificent vista of rolling fields below, each one nibbled by healthy-looking sheep and separated from the next by a rough stone wall.

'I'm proud to say that every blade of grass you can see from here belongs to me,' said the farmer with swelling chest and rising emotion.

'Gee, that's nothing,' rejoined his companion. 'Where I come from it takes me three whole days to get round my farm in a station wagon.'

'Oh, bad luck,' said the dalesman. 'I used to have a car like that.'

Yorkshire is different; Headingley is different. The slope tends to unbalance visiting bowlers, but it is something more than that; something indefinable. If anything was going to knock the Australians out of their all-consuming stride it surely had to be here, with their captain unfit because of his torn calf muscle – and at the scene of the rudest shock in their cricketing history.

Thursday, 16 August

Fourth Test, Headingley (first day of five; Australia won toss): Australia have scored 288 for 4.

The toss was of no great importance, the new ball swung dangerously, the pitch had an unevenness of bounce that can only increase – but still England could not prevent Australia taking such a grip on the fourth Test that already it is hard to imagine their doing anything other than winning it. This time it was Ricky Ponting's turn to play the innings that made the difference. Saved from a third-ball duck by a blade or two of Headingley grass and a fuzzy action replay, he proceeded with hawk-eyed, quick-footed brilliance to his eighth Test hundred and his second on this ground.

Bradman, too, used to make a habit of scoring hundreds at Headingley. Ponting may be not much larger and he apparently picks the ball up every bit as quickly, but in most respects they are chalk and cheese. The young pretender will never have the same concentration, unyielding defence or calculated approach. He is a gambler on and off the field, aptly nicknamed 'Punter', and an entertainer *par excellence*.

RICKY PONTING

Small brown eyes set in a podgy face suggest a naughty schoolboy, always jumping off rocks, wriggling under fences and arriving late in the classroom with a cut on one knee and the mud on the other one all the more obvious for the fact that his socks have fallen down. Gradually and reluctantly, though, Ricky Ponting, the boy wonder from Launceston, Tasmania, has been obliged to grow up; to take himself and his profession more seriously than his instincts really wanted.

It was the penalty for choosing a team sport in which to make a living. Luckily for him, and he is the sort who makes his own luck by bravado, he has team-mates who recognise his genius and absorb his mistakes. If he had played golf instead – he plays off scratch and is gifted enough to have become a professional – he might not have been able to apply the self-discipline that being in a team environment demands.

Even teams lose patience, however, if a talented individual fails to conform; or rather to contribute as he should. 'Punter' Ponting's second tour of England was make or break for him. His form had fallen away towards the end of the season in Australia and he had not enjoyed batting against Harbhajan Singh on turning pitches in India. No one really doubted he would make a success of Test cricket again but in the unlikely event of sustained failure there were plenty of others waiting to take his place.

Dazzling strokeplay in the one-day internationals encouraged the tour selectors to take a punt themselves and to promote him to number three in the order for the Tests. Rather than sheltering a little longer at six in the order, he was asked to be that little bit more responsible, without changing the way he played. On the first day of the Headingley Test he finally repaid their faith, setting up what should have been another Australian victory on the ground where he had made his first Test hundred four years before. With nineteen fours and three sixes he exploded the beguiling myth that he might be just an exceptionally gifted flat-track bully.

Another inch and he would have been caught third ball for 0, but the Ponting luck prevailed and it was the last chance he gave on that sunny August afternoon. Few if any contemporary batsmen could have got into position so very early to hook short-pitched balls of 85mph into the stands.

2001 v. England: 5 matches; 338 runs at 42.25; 1 hundred; 7 catches

He reached three figures yesterday in nine minutes under three hours with three sixes and eleven fours. It was the pulled sixes that told, above all, what a wonderfully good eye he has. Mark Waugh, his patient and unselfish partner in a third–wicket stand of 221 in 46 overs, had a distinctly uncomfortable time when Gough and, especially, Caddick began peppering him with short balls in a not unsuccessful effort to unsettle him. He was eventually caught off the splice off a ball that lifted in the final over of the day. Yet Ponting simply swivelled inside anything short and lifted it over the square–leg boundary with the ease of a walker idly knocking the head off a thistle with his stick.

Once past 100 he enjoyed himself even more in the evening sunshine, blazing nine more fours off the back foot on both sides of the wicket as England's bowlers failed to appreciate that this is one batsman to whom bowling short of a length really is a waste of time. Finally defeated eight overs from the close by a ball from Alex Tudor that lifted and left him, his was an innings of great importance to him personally, after a series of cheap dismissals both before and after his promotion to first wicket down. His 144, the first time he has passed 17 in twelve Test innings, could prove decisive to the outcome of this game.

Having lost the toss as usual – he was not disappointed to do so and might well have been tempted to field anyway – Nasser Hussain used six bowlers in his vain attempt to break up the stand that developed once Caddick began to tire towards the end of an outstanding opening spell. Caddick alone posed any consistent threat: Gough was never as dangerous after the shine had left the ball, Tudor lacked the necessary accuracy and Alan Mullally did not possess anything like the essential venom to go with his accuracy on a pitch that needs energy on the ball if it is to reveal the devil below the surface. At the sort of slow-medium pace at which Trevor Goddard used to open the bowling for South Africa in the days before pace was a pre-requisite for earning the new ball in a Test, Mullally was steady enough but caused barely a moment's anxiety to anyone. He may yet move up a gear, but he looks suspiciously like the wrong selection.

ALAN MULLALLY

Alan Dulally, someone called him. If he were a racehorse he would need more reminders than most with the whip. Concentration is not his greatest virtue. Even in the fiercest battles in the middle he has a distracted air, like an Oxford don who has wandered into a busy rush-hour tube without his spectacles.

He is, however, immensely good-natured and he can be a very fine bowler when he attacks the stumps and hits a rhythm with his flowing, loose-limbed action. A persistent injury between his ribs, refusing to heal completely, has held him back for two years but he has also seemed to lack the constant direction he needs from an understanding captain.

2001 v. Australia: 1 match; 2 wickets at 49.50

As expected it was Robert Croft, and Richard Johnson – who might have bowled well in the conditions – who were left out of England's thirteen. Once the rain had cleared to allow a start at 2.15, those who took the field did so knowing that there is always a chance with the new ball at Headingley and for an hour or so they had every reason for optimism. To help his outswinger Caddick had a strong wind blowing across the ground towards the black spire of St Michael's, bowling down the slope from the Kirkstall Lane End. Initially, too, both he and Gough bowled a refreshingly full length.

A wicket looked possible at any stage as Michael Slater and Matthew Hayden launched the innings with customary gusto, helped on their way at once by a leg stump long-hop from Gough that Slater pulled and Mullally, sprawling like a felled giraffe, failed to stop on the fine-leg boundary. When he was 9 Hayden edged Caddick fractionally in front of Trescothick in the gully; when Slater was 11 he was dropped at square-leg by Mullally, pulling at Caddick; when he was 13 he top-edged Gough over Caddick's head at square-leg. Gough immediately conceded a totally unnecessary overthrow.

Just one of those days again, it seemed. But England did get themselves into the game before Ponting and Waugh claimed it so dauntlessly. In the twelfth over, Caddick's sixth, Slater was leg-before to a ball of full length that pitched on the off-stump and looked as though it would hit it. In the highly eventful fourteenth, Hayden looked plumb lbw to an inswinger, survived the appeal, but was out to the next ball which this time darted back off the seam. Three balls later, Ponting, walking into a drive as he does and number three batsmen should not, edged fast and low to Mark Ramprakash at third slip. He held the ball, diving right, in outstretched fingertips. Ponting stayed his ground; Venkataraghavan and David Shepherd consulted; the third umpire, Neil Mallender, was called upon to study the replay and, once he had seen the magnified image, decided it was too unclear to be sure.

If a guilty man was thereby rendered innocent, no one has ever made amends more gloriously than Ricky Ponting. He said at the close of play that dents are already appearing on the surface of the pitch and that Shane Warne would 'turn it square'. It looks ominous for England.

Friday, 17 August
Headingley (second day of five): England are 292 runs behind Australia with 8 first-innings wickets in hand.
If the absence of Steve Waugh went unnoticed in Australia's innings the return of Nasser Hussain certainly has not in England's. Stirred by his determination, and for the last two and a quarter hours of the second day braced by his example with the bat, the first four batsmen battled with great resolution against fast bowling of higher quality than their own.

With eight wickets left England need a further 93 runs to make Australia bat again. It has been, and is sure to continue to be, a tortuous uphill climb but Atherton, Trescothick, Butcher and Hussain all got their heads down in the shadow of another daunting Australian total. If there is a single reason why this has been an improved batting performance to date, it was that they left the ball better than they and their colleagues generally did in the first three Tests.

The results have been much less entertaining for a loyal Headingley crowd than Australia's innings of 447, to which Damien Martyn contributed his second felicitous hundred in a series in which he now averages 78. They have scored at 3 runs an over so far compared to Australia's 4.4, but that is largely because there were far fewer balls that invited an attacking stroke than were offered by all the England bowlers except the relatively tidy Mullally.

The pace of the game has dropped, perhaps, but to score decent totals in Test cricket it is necessary to build from sure foundations. Home spectators should be more than satisfied by the determination of the resistance shown so far. It has much to do with the character of the captain, Nasser Hussain. Without an innings in first-class cricket since breaking a finger in the second innings of the Edgbaston Test on 10 June, he played some stern and intelligent bowling from Glenn McGrath and Jason Gillespie with excellent judgement. No less important, he immediately signalled to Shane Warne that he would not be allowed to dictate terms unopposed on a pitch lacking the bounce he relishes.

NASSER HUSSAIN

Only the second university-educated England captain since Mike Brearley, Nasser Hussain has come closer than anyone to that Socrates of the cricket field. What has set him apart is care for his men.

It is ironic, because all the way to the top job he has been considered by most of his contemporaries a selfish man. As a young player he smouldered when cricket's injustices interfered with his ambitions, like a cat toying with a young bird who knew he could fly if only he could be left to learn for himself. Even in maturity he has given the impression of a man being played like a puppet on strings held by divine hands. If a pitch is keeping low, Hussain gets the ball that shoots into his feet in front of middle. If it is bouncing, he gets the one that lifts brutishly into his brittle-boned hands. If an umpire is having a bad day, he is the one who gets the illogical decision. As flies to wanton boys are we to the Gods; they kill us for their sport.

Yet he has persevered, this Madras-born son of a proud English immigrant and an English wife. Growing up under Joe Hussain's discerning eyes he was as much a leg-spinner as a batsman, who took wickets by the half-dozen but whose flight deserted him as he grew, as it does so many diminutive wrist spinners, in England at least. Whilst at Durham he played a fine innings in the cause of the Combined Universities that so nearly took his team, led by Michael Atherton, into the semi-finals of the Benson & Hedges Cup. For Essex he milked runs backward of square with wrists as strong as whipcord. Only when opportunities came to play for England did he drive himself to defy his Oriental instincts and to hit it straight through the V with the full face of the bat.

The first tour, to the West Indies, confirmed his talent and courage, but also his technical and temperamental imperfections. His first Test against Australia underlined the fact that both the raw talent and the ready anger might be melded into steel, like pig iron in the furnace. Another overseas trip, with the 'A' team to Pakistan as captain, showed his great potential as a leader. Then it was a question only of the right place and time.

It came after the World Cup in 1999 when the yeoman Stewart was demoted and it was Nasser's great good fortune that his appointment co-incided with a coach from Zimbabwe who shared his views about managing men. Without Duncan Fletcher the vicissitudes of cricket at the highest level might have brought out more of the devil and less of the saint. But his achievements have been his own, the product of a matured character, shrewd mind and God-given talent, all the more formidable an obstacle in the path of apparent Australian invincibility for the fact that, a few weeks before the Tests began his gentle wife, Karen, had given birth to their first child. Now there was perspective added to ambition.

2001 v. Australia: 3 matches; 177 runs at 35.40

England's first target today will be to avoid a follow-on; Australia's to give themselves the option, at least, of enforcing it. The pitch that Andy Fogarty and his staff have produced is firm and so far the variations in the bounce of the ball are not alarming, but they are sufficient to test the confidence of a middle order that is short of runs and inner confidence. Australia's advantage would have been greater still had not the camera quite possibly lied for a second time in the match when Mark Waugh appeared with the naked eye to have caught Trescothick low at second slip off McGrath when he had made only 4. One angle showed the ball bouncing well in front of his hands but it is hard to believe that fielders of old who felt themselves taking clean catches in similar situations were wrong as often as slow-motion replays now suggest.

One has to go back seven matches between England and Australia here, to 1975, to find the last time when one or other side did not make a total in excess of 400. The perception of Headingley in the last twenty years is that it is a paradise for seam and swing bowlers but if that is not a myopic view (Yorkshire folk would call it *southern* myopia) it is at least astigmatic. Between the wars it was batsmen who dreamed of playing here and creaming boundaries off perfect pitches across one of the fastest outfields of all. The truth about the square now is that on most occasions it gives everybody a reasonable chance.

Figures for scores on the ground in the last ten years show that at the six Test venues it is only at Old Trafford and Trent Bridge that the average of runs per wicket is higher. England's average for the last ten Tests at each venue is 35 at Trent Bridge, 33 at Old Trafford, 28 at Headingley, Edgbaston and The Oval (with Headingley fractionally higher than the other two) and 26 at Lord's. But for their opponents it is 41 at Old Trafford, 35 at Headingley, 34 at Edgbaston, 33 at Trent Bridge, 31 at The Oval and 27 at Lord's. For the volume of runs scored by both sides Headingley comes fourth behind Old Trafford, Trent Bridge and The Oval but it is 1,084 runs higher than Edgbaston and 1,567 higher than Lord's.

All that duly acknowledged, the fact is that it is far from the batsman's playground that it was. Ray Illingworth, who knows – what other former England captain will be spending the weekend preparing pitches for two matches on his own club ground as Raymond will be at Farsley – says that the square has not been the same since George Cawthray dug up some pitches and filled them with soil taken from the bed of the river Humber at Hull. He believes that the problems of pitches all round the country – patchy grass, a lack of life, no help for finger spinners or, often, for genuinely fast bowlers – are due to the over-use of heavy loam. Frankly I would trust the view of a man steeped in the game since boyhood to horticultural experts, no matter how many letters they have after their names.

There were no complaints about the pitch from Martyn as he reeled off a series of perfectly timed off-side strokes off either foot, but on a day that started badly for him Darren Gough began to have some of the luck that he has lacked in earlier Tests. Simon Katich, after a sound start to his Test career, left an inswinger as soon as Gough got his hands on the new ball and, at 396, Gough had the joy of seeing Adam Gilchrist driving low to cover where Trescothick dived forward to take a fine catch.

SIMON KATICH

Solid is the word for Katich; in build and in character. They had presented him with his first baggy green cap in Sri Lanka when he thought he was going to play as Steve Waugh's substitute. But the iron man returned to the side despite a broken nose, so Katich missed his chance and returned his cap with thanks. An Englishman might have put it aside for his benefit season.

Even Waugh could not play at Leeds, with a calf muscle lacerated in two places, so this strong left-hander won his cap genuinely this time. He did not set the city on fire, but everyone who has played with him believes he will claim a regular batting place for Australia soon. Like Waugh himself he can be relied upon when there is an emergency.

He will be all the more certain to be ready when the call comes for the fact that his progress has not been plain sailing. Having stood out for the maturity of his attitude as a young man, he captained the Academy and it was confidently predicted that one day he would also be a captain of Australia; but he missed most of the home season after his tour of Sri Lanka because of chicken-pox and a subsequent virus. A successful season at Durham in 2000 was followed by a brilliant one for Western Australia in which he scored six centuries.

One step forward; half backward. But he will get there.

2001 v. England: 1 match; 15 runs at 15

Three more wickets for Gough and one for Mullally followed in the first seven overs of the afternoon. Atherton and Ramprakash held good, low slip catches and Stewart an excellent one running back as Warne top-edged a hook before Atherton, diving left, parried a rapid edge to give Stewart the satisfaction of claiming the rebound.

Atherton and Trescothick were sorely tested at times in the opening overs but they were still together at tea, only for Atherton to get an outside edge to his *bête noire* immediately after the interval. Four overs later, when Trescothick tried to hook a ball that bounced towards first slip and succeeded only in getting a top edge, Butcher and Hussain were presented with the toughest of challenges. They met it with such judgement and determination that, once Hussain had escaped a perilously close lbw shout from McGrath before he had scored, the nearest Australia came to parting them was when a throw from Martyn missed the stumps at the bowler's end with Butcher a yard from the crease.

Butcher has sometimes lacked concentration, but seldom time, against the best fast bowling. Yesterday he made few mistakes, even against Warne, his sometime nemesis. As for Hussain, a careful and patient look at the bowling was followed by gradual expression of his more attacking instincts. The short balls were pulled or hooked if they were not ducked, and even two searing inswinging yorkers from Gillespie could not get through.

Sunday, 19 August
Headingley (fourth day of five): England require a further 311 runs to beat Australia with all second-innings wickets in hand.

At last, a five-day match. It might not have been so but for a liberal supply over the weekend of the showers that invariably attend Headingley Tests, but even with sunshine forecast for today and on a pitch on which the unpredictable bounce has duly become more dangerous for batsmen, England have a slim chance of denying Australia the victory they have once again deserved.

With 311 to win and all their second innings wickets intact, indeed, England have a theoretical opportunity to win, following a bold but in no way unexpected declaration by Adam Gilchrist yesterday evening. He gave his bowlers an excellent chance of finishing the job again today but in any case there would be no great mourning in Sydney and Melbourne if there were to be an unexpected sting in the tail. With the series and the Ashes already won, any reason for caution has gone and the truth is that Australia will have to bowl poorly or two or three England batsmen will have to play exceptionally well today for his gamble to fail.

There was an element of controversy about the course of the England second innings, all 2.3 overs of it. The final session began at 5.40 in a brief patch of sunshine on a day of frequent inter-ruptions that demanded extreme patience from what was origi-nally another capacity crowd. Several delicate decisions had to be made by umpires Venkataraghavan and David Shepherd about the fitness of the ground. The way that Jason Gillespie slipped as he tried in vain to stop the only scoring stroke during eleven minutes of tense cricket suggested that parts of the outfield, at least, were not completely fit for cricket to be played with 100 per cent safety.

It is another matter whether they should sometimes play anyway, for the sake of the paying public, even if fielders are required to tread with caution. But it was also, in a way, the issue here. Officials of the ECB, acutely aware of the fact that they had to hand back almost £2 million last year in refunds because Tests finished early, were anxiously watching to see whether there would be a requirement to compensate those who had bought all yesterday's tickets in advance. Had only one ball fewer been bowled, the cost to the board would have been £200,000.

Hearts were therefore in mouths when Venkat approached Shepherd to point out that three lights warning of the deteriorating visibility were shining. Much to everyone's relief – except, perhaps, that of eleven Australians – Mike Atherton blocked a stinging delivery high on the bat before there was a further consultation and the players walked off in gloomy light before another heavy shower made sure that the long-suffering spectators would not get anything else to watch. How many of them were aware of how close they had come to a 50 per cent refund is a guess, but at least the board has been able to show some largesse today. Entry will be free for juniors for what could conceivably be a very dramatic day's cricket and tickets will cost only £10 for adults, £5 for senior citizens.

There is, of course, a precedent for a remarkable last-day run-chase at Headingley – the 404 scored by Australia in 1948 despite the fact that the declaration had been delayed by Norman Yardley until the last morning. Unfortunately for English prospects today, the pitch looks like bouncing as steeply as it did for Bob Willis in 1981, even if it does not also turn for Shane Warne as much as it did for Jim Laker and company thirty-three years before.

It is much the most remarkable aspect of Australia's recent run that they have scored at a rate sufficient to give themselves every chance of winning even matches in which the weather intervenes. They have not played in a drawn Test match since September 1999, when two of the three games on their tour of Sri Lanka were shortened by rain after the painful collision between Steve Waugh and Jason Gillespie, and their subsequent defeat, in Galle. This is the twenty-second Test since that tour and Australia have won nineteen of them against six different opponents in four different countries.

To an extent England have earned their outside chance today by their improved batting performance in the first innings, but, staunchly as Mark Ramprakash played and brilliantly as Alec Stewart timed the ball in the late assault against the second new ball, there was a rather fevered air about the approach on Saturday. The signs for them in the 22.3 overs in which Australia extended their second innings from 69 for 1 to 176 for 4 declared yesterday were not encouraging.

DARREN GOUGH

'We peaked too soon,' said Duncan Fletcher as he tried to make sense of the rapid demolition of England's plans to regain the Ashes. Of his champion fast bowler, at least, it was true. In taking twenty-four wickets in six Tests in Pakistan and Sri Lanka, Darren Gough had achieved something very unusual indeed on the fast-bowling graveyards of the subcontinent. Dennis Lillee's Test figures on his only tour of Pakistan, at the same three grounds, were 3 for 312.

Against Australia he took five wickets in an innings only once. Even that was unconvincing and owed something to fortune. For Gough and for England, however, the luck had come too late for the fourth Test at Headingley. The Ashes had gone. It was dropped catches, at Edgbaston in the first Test but especially at Lord's in the second, that knocked the stuffing out of his bowling. That and, naturally, the Australian batsmen who would not let him get away with failures of line and length. Against Gilchrist, even his good-length balls on the off stump went whistling past mid-off with interest.

It was hardly fair, but that is cricket. Gough was a far wealthier man by the end of his benefit season of 2001 but certainly not a happier one. The dazzle had gone from the smile, the swagger from his step, the puff from his chest. The peacock had lost the gloss of his plumage.

Everyone knows, even in Yorkshire, where they disapprove of his move to his wife's county of Buckinghamshire, that 'Goughie' will bounce back. It is not in his nature to be down for long. He loves a confrontation, backs himself to win it, and more often than not, he does. His fast bowling has made every England side he has played for the stronger. No matter what the batsmen have to take from opposing quick bowlers, they know their man is going to give it back.

Assuredly he will be missed when he goes for good. He may even be the last of his type, too, because there are very few fast bowlers of under six foot still thriving on covered pitches round the world. Gough has all the fast bowler's skills and strengths: fierce pace, outswing with the new ball, inswing with the old, slower balls spun both from off and from leg. What is more, he uses them with intelligence. But his stock ball skids on to the bats of the best players on the best pitches. To hit the gloves he has to dig the ball in short. This seems to be the age of the taller man and only bowlers of Gough's skill and spirit can hope to compete.

2001 v. Australia: 5 matches; 82 runs at 13.66; 17 wickets at 38.64

Down the slope from the Kirkstall Lane End there was nasty bounce at times for Andrew Caddick and both bounce and sideways movement for Alan Mullally. Up the hill Darren Gough got a ball to dart back into the pads of Ricky Ponting to claim him leg before on the back foot after another innings replete with dazzling strokes. He got his runs at exactly a run a ball, hitting ten fours and another six deliberately hooked off Caddick over square-leg's head. The ball that got him out would have climbed over the middle stump.

For consistency none of the England bowlers could be compared to Glenn McGrath, whose twenty-first five-wicket haul in Test cricket took him to 350. He needs only five more today to overtake one of his boyhood heroes, Dennis Lillee. Lee bowled very fast after lunch on Saturday, although the 16 that Alec Stewart and Mark Ramprakash plundered from his first over after lunch hurried England past the follow-on mark after Nasser Hussain's fall to a shooter and Mark Butcher's mental aberration. No doubt England will approach this final day positively but at the scene of his first triumph in Test cricket, Jason Gillespie is highly unlikely to go without wickets again.

Monday, 20 August
Headingley (fifth day of five): England beat Australia by 6 wickets.
Headingley Cricket Ground's reputation for inspiring deeds of unlikely English heroism grew a cubit or two yesterday when

Mark Butcher, the 28-year-old Surrey left-hander, whose thirty previous Tests had suggested a very good batsman but hardly a great one, produced an inspired innings of 173 not out to win the fourth Test against Australia by six wickets. Inevitably it aroused memories of Ian Botham's 149 not out to help beat Australia against even larger odds in 1981.

This was the third successive England victory at Leeds and their highest fourth-innings score to win at home, surpassing the 263 for 9 against Australia at The Oval in 1902. That match, in which Gilbert Jessop made a hundred when Australia looked sure to win and the Yorkshiremen George Hirst and Wilfred Rhodes got the runs in a last-wicket partnership of 15 amidst unbearable tension, has an inviolable place in the game's folklore. So has the only match in which England have ever scored more than yesterday's 315 to win a Test in the last innings, when Jack Hobbs and Herbert Sutcliffe had to contend at first with a wet pitch before England scored 332 for 7 to beat Australia at Melbourne in 1928/29.

The odds were 16 to 1 against when England set out yesterday morning to try to score 311 more runs to win the fourth Test. Such was the alarming, almost frightening bounce of some of the balls bowled by Glenn McGrath and Jason Gillespie in the first half-hour of a sunny morning, they might have been 500 to 1 as they were here in 1981.

At 33 for 2, Australia could easily have bowled them out for 120, but the chestnuts were pulled from the fire by an innings of astonishing brilliance. Nasser Hussain's determination, phlegmatic approach and skill helped Butcher to play his natural game to such effect that when he was out with 101 still needed, Butcher went joyously on to win the game in the face of all reasonable expectations. Against high-class bowling and athletic fielding he cut, pulled and drove his way to a six (carved deliberately over third man) and twenty-three fours.

As the ball became softer and the variations in bounce fewer, the prospect of victory became steadily more credible. It was achieved in the end at twenty minutes past five on a tide of boundaries to which Mark Ramprakash and, briefly, young Usman Afzaal, contributed. As many as twenty-one overs were left unbowled, leaving the crowd that had packed Headingley for a fifth successive day – the gates were closed twenty minutes before lunch – pinching themselves with pleasure that England had pulled off the second-highest winning fourth-innings score in their history.

It has denied the Australians their dream of a five–nil clean sweep but nothing became them so much as the manner in which they took their defeat. To a man they applauded Butcher when he reached his hundred and again when he had won the match. The stand-in captain, Adam Gilchrist, had declared to set England their target, as he might not have done if the Ashes had still been at stake, but this was, nonetheless, a wonderful consolation for England after a summer in which luck had hitherto deserted them. Headingley restored it as it so often has.

In thirty previous Tests there had been only hints that Butcher was capable of quite so consistently commanding an innings as this. He has always been an impressive player of fast bowling; brave, a shrewd leaver of the ball but with all the shots needed and a very straight bat in defence. What he has lacked before has been a secure method against the best spin bowlers and the concentration to move on from promising starts, despite his two previous centuries – at Brisbane against Australia in the last Ashes series and here against South Africa the following season.

MARK BUTCHER

When the autobiography of Mark Butcher is published – and given another season like the one he had in 2001, it probably will be – it might well be subtitled 'The Man Who Stopped McGrath'. Or perhaps 'The Man Who Stopped the Whitewash'. Until Mark Butcher repelled him at Headingley on the sunny afternoon of 20 August, the odds still were that Australia would win the fourth Test and go on to take the series 5–0. Boldly hooking and cutting as McGrath, up the slope from the Football Stand End, strove to get extra bounce from the pitch in what everyone sensed was the crucial spell of bowling, Butcher seized with equal alacrity on any over-correction, hitting him down the ground with clinical drives from the middle of a broad bat. The five-over spell cost 28 runs and by tea the force was irresistibly with the muscular left-hander.

What a joy it was to see full, yet controlled, expression given to the natural talent that flows from this most good-natured of men. It was only just, however, his most remarkable performance of the summer. Earlier he had suddenly taken almost a handful of wickets with a shrewd mixture of inswingers and outswingers at Edgbaston. Soon after, he had appeared live with his guitar on Radio 5 Live and sung one of his own compositions with the feeling and tunefulness of someone who could easily have made a living in the world of pop music.

Such is the mixture of gifts given to this son of a marriage between a Bajan mother and a father whose own left-handed batting had won him an England cap and should have brought him more. It was Alan as coach, and caring parent, who nursed his son's technique through the winter of 2000/01, whilst Mark was trying to retrieve his form and to recover from problems with his own marriage to Alec Stewart's sister. Early in the season that followed he was worried about keeping his place in a Surrey side full of Test cricketers, but the injury to Graham Thorpe gave him another chance at the level all professionals covet. He might have known that his luck was going to turn when Adam Gilchrist dropped him before he had scored in the first innings of a series in which he ultimately finished with more runs than anyone on either side.

Domestic worries had contributed to his loss of form in South Africa in 1999/2000 but he had already shown Australians his talent, establishing himself by helping Mike Atherton to save the second Test at Lord's in 1997, then recovering from a nasty blow on the head and a desperate start to the tour of 1998/99 by making 116 in the first Test at Brisbane.

Time will tell if he is destined, more than most, to suffer lows as well as celebrating highs. A smoker and a drinker, attractive and attracted to the ladies, he has always enjoyed the '*après* cricket' but if he can channel the energy mainly towards his batting for the rest of his career, McGrath will not want to bowl at him.

2001 v. Australia: 5 matches; 456 runs at 50.66; 1 hundred; 4 catches

'It will be remembered for a long time,' said Hussain of his innings, with proper British understatement. In fact it will be remembered as long as cricket is played. In all the circumstances it was scarcely less remarkable than Ian Botham's 149 not out in 1981. If not in quite the exalted class of Graham Gooch's heroic 154 not out to beat the West Indies on a much worse pitch in 1991, it will certainly be mentioned in the same breath. It is, too, the happiest of coincidences that his score matches Bradman's on the day that Australia scored 404 to win at Headingley in 1948.

Yesterday's events have to some extent laid the bogey of that painful defeat and should end the constant temptation to recall the famous victory after following on here in the Botham/Brearley/ Willis game. More importantly, it puts a fairer perspective on this summer's events. Australians could begin to understand yesterday how Hussain's side did so well in the previous twelve months. They will, too, be keener than ever to have Steve Waugh back at The Oval on Thursday after what, looked at one way, is the third defeat in twenty-two games; but viewed less charitably is the third defeat in six.

The spirit of England's approach, if not for a long time the substance, was evident from the first ball yesterday. Michael Atherton pulled it, a short delivery, through mid-on for four. Two balls later he was out, defeated by the great bowler yet again and by a ball that lifted and left him to brush his top glove on the way through to Gilchrist. He departed with one of those wry smiles that signalled there was nothing he could have done to change his fate.

Hussain now watched impassively from the balcony as the two left-handers, Butcher and Trescothick, did their best to survive the fearsome opening salvoes. Butcher quickly showed that he would attack when he could by splicing a cut high over the slips off McGrath but in the eighth over of the innings and the fifth full one of the morning Trescothick got a ball from Gillespie that would have made a giant blanch. It reared past his face and climbed high over Gilchrist before hitting the boundary after one more bounce.

Trescothick went in Gillespie's next over, slicing a drive hard to the gully where Hayden made a sharp catch look simple. It was the courage of Butcher and Hussain in playing every ball so strictly on its merits that was so impressive about the early stages of their match-winning partnership. Hussain, who has played better in this match than at any time since his first tour in charge in South Africa, cover-drove the first half-volley he received for four and put his bat under his arm as if it were a rolled-up newspaper about to be read in the sunshine on a park bench. Body language, they say, tells so much.

Butcher, perky but controlled, was no less inclined to bow before Australian pressure that, Ashes won or not, lost nothing in its fierceness by comparison with the previous Tests. A decisive hook for four off McGrath persuaded Gilchrist to bring on Shane Warne for the first time at 59 for 2. When, an over later, Gillespie was given a turn up the hill, Hussain swivelled to pull him high over square-leg and the wall that separates the ground from Cardigan Road.

These were the moments that changed the mood. The ball was not recovered and its replacement seemed not to bounce so fiercely. Batting became easier. The occasional snicks refused to go to hand as they had done earlier in the series. At lunch England were 118 for 2 and the third-wicket pair had put on 96. Everything depended now on McGrath's afternoon spell. For once he found a foeman worthy of his steel: if Butcher was not cutting him past cover or over the slips, he was pulling or on-driving him, freely and handsomely.

Hussain bravely bore the brunt of a furious and admirably sustained spell of an hour and a half by Brett Lee. In one over he exceeded 90mph with every ball but it was Gillespie who eventually claimed England's captain, to a catch down the leg-side. It changed little because Ramprakash played no less well in Butcher's support, getting firmly forward and showing not a trace of his supposed temperamental frailty.

The game was all but won when he edged Warne so low to Waugh at slip that replays suggested, once again, that the ball had touched the ground first. It showed something of Ramprakash's innate decency that he walked without waiting for the television verdict. But it was in keeping with a delightful match that had defied the weather and been played highly competitively but without a moment of nastiness. For that the Australians were largely responsible and deserving of Hussain's grateful verdict: 'They play the game in the right way.'

Australia 1st innings			R	M	B	4	6
MJ Slater	lbw	b Caddick	21	49	40	2	0
ML Hayden	lbw	b Caddick	15	65	37	1	0
RT Ponting	c Stewart	b Tudor	144	211	154	20	3
ME Waugh	c Ramprakash	b Caddick	72	225	147	9	0
DR Martyn	c Stewart	b Gough	118	186	135	18	0
SM Katich		b Gough	15	78	42	3	0
*+AC Gilchrist	c Trescothick	b Gough	19	30	20	4	0
SK Warne	c Stewart	b Gough	0	12	8	0	0
B Lee	c Ramprakash	b Mullally	0	9	4	0	0
JN Gillespie	c Atherton	b Gough	5	11	17	1	0
GD McGrath	not out		8	6	6	2	0
Extras	(b 5, lb 15, w 1, nb 9)		30				
Total	(all out, 100.1 overs, 449 mins)		447				

FoW: 1–39 (Slater, 11.1 ov), 2–42 (Hayden, 13.6 ov),
      3–263 (Ponting, 59.3 ov), 4–288 (Waugh, 66.3 ov),
      5–355 (Katich, 84.3 ov), 6–396 (Gilchrist, 90.5 ov),
      7–412 (Warne, 94.1 ov), 8–422 (Lee, 95.4 ov),
      9–438 (Gillespie, 98.5 ov), 10–447 (Martyn, 100.1 ov).

Bowling	O	M	R	W	
Gough	25.1	4	103	5	
Caddick	29	4	143	3	(6nb)
Mullally	23	8	65	1	(3nb)
Tudor	18	1	97	1	
Butcher	1	0	7	0	(1w)
Ramprakash	4	0	12	0	

England 1st innings			R	M	B	4	6
MA Atherton	c Gilchrist	b McGrath	22	80	54	4	0
ME Trescothick	c Gilchrist	b McGrath	37	98	73	4	0
MA Butcher	run out		47	164	110	5	0
*N Hussain	lbw	b McGrath	46	137	97	7	0
MR Ramprakash	c Gilchrist	b Lee	40	132	102	5	0
U Afzaal	c Warne	b McGrath	14	22	18	2	0
+AJ Stewart	not out		76	160	83	10	1
AJ Tudor	c Gilchrist	b McGrath	2	11	4	0	0
AR Caddick	c Gilchrist	b Lee	5	19	13	1	0
D Gough	c Slater	b McGrath	8	7	6	2	0
AD Mullally	c Katich	b McGrath	0	17	13	0	0
Extras	(b 2, lb 3, nb 7)		12				
Total	(all out, 94.2 overs, 428 mins)		309				

FoW: 1–50 (Atherton, 18.4 ov), 2–67 (Trescothick, 22.4 ov),
      3–158 (Hussain, 54.2 ov), 4–158 (Butcher, 55.5 ov),
      5–174 (Afzaal, 60.5 ov), 6–252 (Ramprakash, 83.5 ov),
      7–267 (Tudor, 86.2 ov), 8–289 (Caddick, 89.4 ov),
      9–299 (Gough, 90.5 ov), 10–309 (Mullally, 94.2 ov).

Bowling	O	M	R	W	
McGrath	30.2	9	76	7	
Gillespie	26	6	76	0	(1nb)
Lee	22	3	103	2	(5nb)
Warne	16	2	49	0	(1nb)

Australia 2nd innings			R	M	B	4	6
ML Hayden	c Stewart	b Mullally	35	144	99	6	0
MJ Slater		b Gough	16	36	23	2	0
RT Ponting	lbw	b Gough	72	91	72	10	1
ME Waugh	not out		24	52	28	3	0
DR Martyn	lbw	b Caddick	6	28	20	1	0
SM Katich	not out		0	7	6	0	0
Extras	(b 5, lb 7, nb 11)		23				
Total	(4 wickets dec, 39.3 overs, 182 mins)		176				

DNB: *+AC Gilchrist, SK Warne, B Lee, JN Gillespie, GD McGrath.

FoW: 1–25 (Slater, 8.2 ov), 2–129 (Ponting, 28.2 ov), 3–141 (Hayden, 31.4 ov), 4–171 (Martyn, 38.1 ov).

Bowling	O	M	R	W	
Gough	17	3	68	2	(2nb)
Caddick	11	2	45	1	(4nb)
Tudor	4	1	17	0	
Mullally	7.3	2	34	1	(5nb)

England 2nd innings			R	M	B	4	6
MA Atherton	c Gilchrist	b McGrath	8	12	12	2	0
ME Trescothick	c Hayden	b Gillespie	10	43	30	2	0
MA Butcher	not out		173	315	227	23	1
*N Hussain	c Gilchrist	b Gillespie	55	197	117	6	1
MR Ramprakash	c Waugh	b Warne	32	74	51	5	0
U Afzaal	not out		4	10	6	1	0
Extras	(b 14, lb 16, nb 3)		33				
Total	(4 wickets, 73.2 overs, 329 mins)		315				

DNB: +AJ Stewart, AJ Tudor, AR Caddick, D Gough, AD Mullally.

FoW: 1–8 (Atherton, 2.6 ov), 2–33 (Trescothick, 9.6 ov), 3–214 (Hussain, 54.3 ov), 4–289 (Ramprakash, 71.2 ov).

Bowling	O	M	R	W	
McGrath	16	3	61	1	
Gillespie	22	4	94	2	(1nb)
Warne	18.2	3	58	1	
Lee	16	4	65	0	(2nb)
Waugh	1	0	7	0	

England won by 6 wickets.

Nine

The Captain's Return

Poor Mark Butcher probably knew that his sudden fame would soon be tempered by reality. He had forty-eight hours to savour or to fear the consequences before he and the rest of the team were confronted by the prospect of another five-day match. Dispensing with Mullally and Tudor – neither, apparently, fully fit – England refreshed their attack with James Ormond, the big outswing bowler from Leicestershire, and, possibly for the last time, with Philip Tufnell. His forty-second cap was reward for taking 55 wickets at 24 for Middlesex in the season to date; Ormond's first owed something to his ability to bowl useful off-breaks and to bat presentably when he put his mind to it.

Australia made two changes as well. Against the odds, through sheer will-power and after days of agonising invasive physiotherapy from the best in the business, Errol Alcott, on the two tears in his left calf, Steve Waugh fulfilled his dream of playing one more Test match in England.

Waugh and Nasser Hussain combined to write a book of diaries on the last Ashes series in England. Captains now – and still writing diaries – the influence of their characters on the teams under their command had been evident from the events of the last seven weeks. Partly because it has all been so compressed – too much so, thanks to the relentless demands of the revised international programme – the fifth Test was only the second time that they tossed the coin together.

The fact that England won at Headingley only after Australia had dominated the game for four days and declared was sufficient evidence, surely, that Australia would have won the Ashes anyway unless providence had smiled very emphatically in the other direction. Nevertheless, there was more than a hint at Headingley of how much tougher a fight England would have given them if Graham Thorpe had played more than one game and Hussain had not broken a bone for the second time in the season in the second innings at Edgbaston.

The rot had started in Hussain's absence against Pakistan at Old Trafford and his stiffening presence was missed, both in terms of defiant batting and moral fibre, during the six one-day defeats that preceded the first Test. Still more so, without question, in the games at Lord's and Trent Bridge that followed it.

Who knows whether Waugh would have declared like Gilchrist, or whether his tactics in the field would have been any different during Mark Butcher's *tour de force*? What is certain is that Australia could only be the stronger for their captain's return, both because his batting and experience of leadership would improve the side in themselves, and because Gilchrist would be released (like Botham under Brearley) to bat and keep wicket without any constraint.

Slater's absence lessened the spectacle. If this was to be the end of him after seventy-four Tests in which he had scored 5,312 runs at 42, scoring seven of his fourteen hundreds against England, he will be remembered as one of the great entertainers. Had he scored more than 176 runs in this series (six more than Hayden and 77 of them in his influential first innings at Edgbaston) his individualism within a closely-knit team would have been overlooked. Like Butcher he is great company, enjoys himself off the field and plays all the strokes on it.

Slater was admonished after a tantrum on the field in India and fined after missing a bus on this tour, although he was now officially dropped on form. The media awaited him with open arms as it did the estimable Michael Atherton. All who knew him believed that this was to be his last Test too, although he refused to say so until the dust had settled.

How much dust there would be was a matter of guesswork. The pitch was well covered by dry, thick, almost white grass. It looked much like all the Oval Test pitches of recent years whereon England had prospered more often than not, including in their last two games against Australia in 1993 and 1997. The ball had not turned as much as usual here for Saqlain Mushtaq and Ian Salisbury this year – one good reason why Yorkshire were about to take the Championship from Surrey – and it would take some broiling sun over the next few days for it to be as arid as it was when Tufnell took 11 for 93 four years ago. That, of course, would suit Shane Warne admirably.

Hussain said on the eve of the match that it was his personal opinion that Australia should be rewarded for their 'very fine cricket this summer' by being allowed to take home the original Ashes urn, bequeathed to MCC, rather than the cut-glass replica. Whether they win the series 4–1 or 3–2, there is no chance of that, much to Waugh's disgust. He really should not be provoked like this.

Thursday, 23 August
Fifth Test, The Oval (first day of five; Australia won toss): Australia have scored 324 for 2.

Henry Lawson, most revered of the early Australian poets, first suggested a phrase long ago for players like Justin Langer. The epitome of 'the great little Aussie battler', he responded to his first opportunity of the series by making a century that sent the clearest of messages to those who had left him out of the side. His opening partnership of 158 with Matthew Hayden, much the largest of the series, put Australia firmly in the box seat yet again, setting up fluent innings by Ricky Ponting and Mark Waugh that left Jimmy Ormond with mixed feelings at the end of an impressive first day as a Test cricketer.

JUSTIN LANGER

What a moral tale there was in Justin Langer's tour of England. To some extent his career had prepared him for what happened. It took him years to claim the place in the Australian batting order he coveted. Any place would do but, nugget of deeply mined Australian gemstone that he is, he persevered. Six years after a promising start in Adelaide in 1992/93 he finally earned a regular place at number three.

No wonder he was profoundly disappointed to be dropped when he was still averaging 39 in Test cricket. Having played for Middlesex for two seasons and captained them in 2000, he had come to love Lord's. He dreamed of making a century there wearing the green and gold. He would give his life for the honour of Australia.

It did not happen. He made a point of celebrating Damien Martyn's success. Hard as he tried to impress when his rare opportunities came against the counties, he failed. It seemed about to be the biggest disappointment of his life. But, come the bugle's call, Justin was the first into line.

2001 v. England: 1 match; 102 runs at 102; 1 hundred

In making 102 before retiring hurt Langer showed both his sterling character and the unyielding vigilance of his batting method. No contemporary batsman smells the leather quite like he does, playing the ball under his feet whether he has rocked back to stop a short one or danced down to the pitch of the ball against a spinner. He it was who was chiefly responsible for taking the initiative away from Phil Tufnell on a white featherbed of a pitch that is taking spin already.

Steve Waugh, duly resuming his role as captain after his own little battle against the odds, had little doubt about batting first when Nasser Hussain lost his ninth successive toss. He knows that Shane Warne (with an even blonder rinse to catch the camera's eye for the occasion) is four wickets away from 400 and that the greater the rough from the footmarks, the less likely he is to be denied his next step on the road towards Courtney Walsh. In the event it was a thankless day for bowlers, not just because it was so vilely muggy but also because the ball would not swing much for anyone. Apart from bowling too many no-balls, England's bowlers stuck to their job with concentration and determination but the only consolation on a chastening day for them was that Ormond swung the ball more than anyone else.

Bowling fast – well past 80mph – swinging the ball late in flight and getting bounce from the sturdiness of his build and a braced front leg, Ormond bridged the oft-mentioned gap between county and Test cricket in a comfortable half-stride. It may be easier for bowlers than for batsmen but the fact is that if you are made of the right stuff and possess the talent, it is less of a chasm than is so frequently claimed. It will greatly enhance his chances of selection for England that he showed for three overs that he can also turn usefully to off-breaks.

JAMES ORMOND

Rolling in to bowl, sturdy frame carried on bandy legs, James Ormond evokes images of the sheriff riding into a dusty town in the Wild West with a six-shooter on either hip. 'He shoots hard and he shoots to kill,' you can hear the folk saying as he dismounts and makes for the bar with eyes looking neither to right nor left. 'Folks around here don't give him no lip if they know what's good for 'em.'

If the Earldom of Ormond is a guide, he probably hails, a few generations back, from Ireland. His own upbringing was in Warwickshire. A cheerful soul who loves a party, it has taken him time to shake off the inevitable injuries, to learn to work hard for the rewards and to fulfil the early promise. With a good strong action he is quick enough for Test cricket and swings the new ball.

Hard labour no doubt awaited him in India but he deserved his first senior tour for England after taking his chance at The Oval in the final Test. Picked ahead of a man of similar qualities in Richard Johnson, he showed for a few overs the ability to bowl off-breaks, a craft first explored in the nets at Grace Road.

Like the former Surrey and England swing bowler Geoff Arnold, they call him 'horse'. He should settle for becoming as good a bowler as Arnold.

2001 v. Australia: 1 match; 35 runs at 17.50; 1 wicket at 115

But this was a batsman's day and it belonged utterly to Australia. It would be quite wrong to portray Langer's innings of four hours twenty minutes as a struggle, dogged though it was, but it was somehow in keeping with its grittiness that he should have been stopped in the end not by the fall of his wicket but by a blow to the head from a bouncer by Andrew Caddick.

Initially trying to hook a ball six overs after tea, but changing his mind in mid-hit, he was struck close to the left ear and fell like a shot deer before being helped off, both literally and colloquially a bleeding hero. Langer said that he felt as though 'he had been hit on the ear by Lennox Lewis'. Taken to a local hospital for a precautionary scan, he returned with a clean bill of health, deeply satisfied at having made his eighth Test hundred in his first Test in England and prepared to resume his innings today if either of the Waughs will let him in.

It is the last time he will use this particular helmet, one that he had loaned to a group of climbers from South Australia, one of whom died on the expedition. 'I thought it was a bad omen,' he said. Now he knows, but happily his own damage was nothing worse than a cut.

Taking over from Michael Slater, who has been offered counselling by the Australian Cricket Board for his personal problems, Langer's previous seven centuries had come in two years of more or less unalloyed success at first wicket down. A lapse of form last winter, and Damien Martyn's relentless brilliance, pushed him to the fringe. The quintessential team man, it will further have eased Langer's pain to know that by the time that bad light stopped play Australia were already more than a third of the way towards the 903 for 7 that England made here in 1938.

What is more, they have once again contrived to score at four runs an over, buying themselves time to win the match should the weather intervene as it did twice, for very brief periods, yesterday. Having bowled through the last day at Leeds, and come out second best, Australia's bowlers must have been more pleased than usual to put their feet up for another day whilst Langer and Hayden, alias Little and Large, led their team to 66 for no wicket from 24 overs by lunch.

They were interrupted only by a fussy decision by the umpires to come off for the lightest possible sprinkling from heavy grey clouds. Immediately after this break Hayden was extremely lucky not to be given out to an inswinger of full length from Andrew Caddick, but the big Queenslander began to impose himself more forcefully after that, driving straight to balls that were not half-volleys once he knew that he could trust the bounce.

Hayden got to fifty first but Langer bustled in behind him a few minutes later, reaching his first landmark with a drive over mid-wicket as Tufnell tossed up the bait. In his first bowl for England since the New Year Test in Cape Town last year, Tufnell had some moral victories in the air but not until the forty-third over of an innings now thoroughly launched did he strike. Having swept him profitably enough from outside the off stump, Hayden middled a stroke on bended knee straight to deep square-leg.

PHIL TUFNELL

When the artful dodger came out to bat for England in both innings of the Oval Test he was cheered to the rafters; a folk hero. He batted with his usual feebleness, but just to have felt that warmth of support will have reassured him. It has been an up-and-down career to the background of a sometimes stormy domestic life but the public seems to like the image of a beer-drinking, cigarette-smoking wastrel, if only because they know he can laugh at himself, and because he has won a few matches for England.

Of very few who have played over the last twenty years can that be said. He was savaged by the Waugh brothers in what may turn out to have been his final Test but to have taken five wickets in a Test innings five times is something of which to be proud.

2001 v. Australia: 1 match; 7 runs at 7; 1 wicket at 174

When Ponting had made 1 Tufnell appealed for an lbw that would have been given on a luckier day but Ponting was soon striking the ball cleanly on either side of the wicket in another delightful exhibition of carefree batting. Mark Waugh joined in with equal pleasure on a pitch giving him plenty of time. All the more credit, therefore, to Ormond for getting a ball to bounce sufficiently for Ponting, looking to force it off the back foot, to edge it to first slip.

Friday, 24 August

The Oval (second day of five): England, with 9 first-innings wickets in hand, are 561 runs behind Australia.

They were playing the great unfinished symphonies of Schubert and Bruckner at the Proms last night but none of the England team will have been hurrying down to the Royal Albert Hall. To them it must have seemed that the Australian first innings was never going to end. They were roasted at The Oval like chickens on the spit.

For a substantial portion of the second day's play, indeed, they must have wondered if they would ever separate the Waugh brothers, let alone take ten wickets. In the event they took four, only two of them yesterday, before Steve Waugh declared to give his bowlers eighteen overs in which to try to capitalise on his country's third highest total at The Oval. Shane Warne's ability to rip leg breaks past the best batsmen without bowling full tosses or long-hops like ordinary wrist spinners made sure that the gesture was not in vain.

Had he wanted to, Waugh could have gone on long past the 695 in 1930 and the 701 four years later. Australia won those matches by massive margins but both were timeless games in order to get a result in series that were level. This time Waugh judged that he needed time to win the game, rather than pressing on to something really gargantuan and taking wickets partly by means of exhausting his opponents. The speed and authority of England's reply last evening, however, as Trescothick and Atherton reached 50 off 64 balls and ten fours whistled across the fastest of all fast outfields in the first eleven overs, suggested that anything is still possible in this encounter, even that result which no contemporary Australian cricketer ever seriously contemplates, an old-fashioned draw.

England's first innings against Sri Lanka here in 1998 occupied 158.3 overs and almost the identical number of minutes as Australia's on the first two days of this match – but England scored 445 all out, Australia 641 for 4 declared. The rate of their scoring, well over four an over again here, has been the main reason for their winning so many games, just as it was when Sri Lanka defied expectations by winning the game three years ago having themselves made 591 off 156.5 overs.

For much of yesterday this was once again a tale of two Waughs. Two of Australia's greatest run-scorers they may be, but they are as different in temperament as any twins can ever have been. It was entirely in character that, having put on 197 together for the third wicket, the second-highest of their nine century partnerships together in Tests, Mark Waugh, batting with supreme ease, should have given his wicket away for a mere 120 whereas the captain, batting in acute discomfort after opening up the tear in his right calf muscle, carried remorselessly on.

The younger of the babies born thirty-six years ago in Bankstown has now scored twenty Test centuries but has gone on to 150 only once. Steve has made more than 150 against every Test country he has played. They are not so much chalk and cheese as granite and cream. Together they make a mixture altogether too rich and potent for English bowlers on most pitches, let alone

one as true as this. The Oval in sunshine in August is not far from being the batsman's true paradise.

Steve's innings was one of trademark resolve, calculated, above all, to shut England out of the game for good. There will be no second-innings declaration this time, even if, by some exceptional batting, Australia are to be required to bat again. Warne, naturally, poses the biggest threat on a surface already taking spin and with plenty of rough for him to work with. He struck in his third over yesterday, spinning a leg break of perfect length past Mike Atherton's forward defensive. Steve Waugh has been saying for weeks that he thought young Brett Lee would reach his best form at The Oval but Colin Miller would probably have been a better selection in these conditions.

Waugh's 157 not out, his ninth Test hundred against England and twenty-seventh in all Tests, two short of Bradman, was either selfish or courageous, sadistic or masochistic, according to your point of view. He was in pain from the start yesterday and the longer he batted the more he had to hobble. He was obliged not to run quick singles or, if possible, twos – let alone threes. Therefore, he scored more slowly than he might have done. With batsmen as good as Slater and Katich in the touring party, it could at least be argued that he should have continued to rest the muscle he damaged in Australia's second innings at Trent Bridge, but it is his side, on which he has stamped his own individual brand, and he wanted to be here to lead it from the front, collecting whatever Ashes trophies are offered at the end of the match as a player clad in white rather than a plain-clothes bystander.

He was 77 not out at lunch to his brother's 92 but the partner-ship should have been broken in the first over of the day at the start of a superb new-ball spell by Andrew Caddick that ultimately brought him no reward. Having just reached 50, Mark Waugh edged an outswinger at perfect catching height to Mark Butcher at second slip but he dropped it, just to his right by his waist. James Ormond, given three overs with the new ball ahead of Darren Gough, could not match Caddick's accuracy and soon the fours were rippling again.

Waugh junior played with familiar lordly ease, reeling off sump-tuous strokes almost in slow motion as Phil Tufnell tried in vain to tie him down by bowling over the wicket into the rough. Steve Waugh was obliged to be more unorthodox because of his injury. Eventually it was Gough who bowled Mark as he drew away to carve through the covers. It was the stroke of a man sated on bread and honey.

Justin Langer was perfectly fit to resume his innings after his blow to the head the previous evening but, not unreasonably, Adam Gilchrist was promoted instead. His first boundary was a glorious drive past mid-off but he had not really reached top gear when Hussain rather belatedly called upon Usman Afzaal, renowned in his teenage years as an exceptionally accurate left-arm spinner. He revealed himself now at least to be an intelligent one by tossing his third ball in Test cricket wide of the off stump for Gilchrist to drill it to extra cover.

Whilst Waugh's amazing eye enabled him to keep the boundaries flowing, Damien Martyn proceeded to give another master-class of orthodox batting, one reverse sweep excepted. It enabled a declaration earlier than expected, for which Trescothick at least was grateful. He drove, cut and hooked his way to a rapid 50, but there is still a long way for him and for England to travel to save the follow-on, good though the pitch is; indeed, probably too long.

Saturday, 25 August

On the best pitch of the series, England made their highest total today and when stumps were drawn they were tantalisingly close to saving the follow-on. They need a further 33 runs, with two wickets in hand, but they will be harder to get tomorrow morning than they would have been this evening, with Mark Ramprakash in control, the bowlers tired after a long day in the sun, and Darren Gough enjoying himself with the bat for a change.

Ramprakash has scored the second England century of the series and the second of his Test career. What a world of hope and heartache lies behind that bald statement. It is a mystery why his first major innings in Barbados did not enable him to break free from the shackles that so often seem to accompany him to the crease. He has cared so much, tried so hard, but until now it was a long story of failing to do his natural talent full justice.

MARK RAMPRAKASH

Pale as a sick child he often looks when he walks out to bat in a Test. He looks so vulnerable. But he can mix it with the best of the world's bowlers: he proved it from the very outset of his tortuous career. He is a batsman of virtuous purity. If you want to know how to bat, indeed, watch Mark Ramprakash. He does most things right, but, above all, when he leans into his drives he gives an object lesson in the art of transferring the weight into the path of the ball in order to hit it hard without effort.

It is the essence of timing for any sportsman, be it Beckham weighting a cross, Wilkinson a kick between the posts, Woods a one-iron down the fairway or Ramprakash stroking a four along the ground through extra cover.

The 2001 season was his happiest in England although it began with a controversial move after he had earned a handsome benefit at the end of thirteen seasons for the county who found and nurtured his talent. In a way Ramprakash did not so much switch Middlesex for Surrey as Lord's for The Oval. He scored all four of his hundreds in the 2001 season on this bountiful square, three for Surrey, one for England. In eight games there he made 859 runs at an average of 66. Away from Kennington his aggregate was 235 in five matches at an average of 26.

His intense, highly-strung nature is well documented. But he would have been better if he had believed deep down that he was a great player. Self-deprecation has led to a bit too much respect for famous opponents. If it was in his nature to be a showman, he could have been as big a heart-throb as Imran Khan. The English-born son of an academic from Guyana and his English wife, he chooses rather to be a private man, sober and domestic.

It is something of a travesty that his overall Test average was so modest as his fiftieth Test for England approached but there was still time to put the record straighter.

2001 v. Australia: 4 matches; 318 runs at 39.75; 1 hundred; 3 catches

Today he battled through, never playing really freely until late in the day when Warne, after another outstanding piece of bowling from the Vauxhall End, finally began to offer some full tosses. He had been on virtually without a break since the first over of the day, when he spun a ball round Trescothick's front leg to hit his off stump.

Butcher and Hussain then had a promising partnership, both playing positively against Warne and making the most of the attacking fields and the fast outfield. The square at The Oval stretches almost the width of the field, so anything hit square fairly whistles away over the cut pitches. But McGrath allowed no such indulgences. Probing mainly outside off stump, he finally got Hussain to nibble and Mark Waugh, diving left, very nearly caught him at second slip. McGrath's opening spell was 9–5–5–0.

Warne, much more generous, was, of course, the perfect partner; always close to his next wicket. He duly had Butcher before lunch, clipping one of his favourite strokes off his legs with the spin, but this time via his pad and into short-leg's hands.

So Ramprakash came in with a little matter of 338 to make to save the follow-on. Despite an early cover-driven four off Warne he had made but 12 by lunch, when the captain was 49 not out. When he fell rather tamely in early afternoon, the ball spinning from the foot of a defensive bat to give his old Essex team-mate an increasingly rare Test wicket, poor 'Ramps' was left in the middle, as he so often has been before, looking exposed and younger than he is.

Perhaps it helped that he had a genuine youngster to nurse at first and one who was not afraid to express himself. Usman Afzaal played his natural game, full of shots, too loose for Test cricket, but sometimes it can be easier than the county game, when the sun is shining, the fields are so close to the bat and the pitch is as good as this one. Experienced, unfulfilled Test batsman and hopeful novice enjoyed a free-scoring afternoon, helped by too much that was over-pitched from Gillespie and Lee.

Ramprakash had still scored only 43 when McGrath intervened, surprising Afzaal with his pace off the pitch as he hooked and top edged to long-leg. Now, however, in the last two hours of golden light, this craftsman finally produced his long promised work of art. Wickets fell at the other end, but he drove boundary after boundary and reached the longed-for hundred with a sweep from Warne seven overs from the close. Gough hugged him, the crowd rose to applaud, the Australians patted him on the back and only the meanest of his critics could have said: 'About time too.'

It was his eighty-first innings in his forty-sixth Test. But Australians had never quite been able to understand why he was not an automatic selection for England. He averages 40 against them, better than any of the other batsmen in this side.

Sunday, 26 August

The Oval (fourth day of five): England, following on 209 runs behind, need 169 runs to make Australia bat again, with 9 wickets in hand.

There is nothing like a Bank Holiday weekend, especially one linked to a Test match, to bring rain from a clear blue sky. The volatility of the weather during the last Test of the summer came to England's rescue yesterday after the fall of Mark Ramprakash had signalled the end of a spirited, ultimately vain attempt to avoid the follow-on.

Caught behind driving at a flier from Glenn McGrath, Ramprakash's had been a noble innings that only became truly fluent in its later stages on Saturday as Shane Warne began to tire. Using only his vigorous leg-break and the 'scrambled' ball that skids on straight, Warne showed above all in recording his best Test figures outside Australia that an indomitable will to win has as much to do with his success as his natural skill and acquired cunning.

Australia still have a minimum of 90 overs today in which to try to force the win that, once again, they deserve. It is a shade of odds that even McGrath and Warne will not find sufficient help from a dry but still firm and reliable pitch to bowl England out in time, and sufficiently cheaply, to win their twentieth game in twenty-three Tests. It would be unwise to rule out the possibility, however. Despite a dropped slip catch by Steve Waugh yesterday and an injury to his brother Mark that may keep him off the field today, the hunger of a tired side is still evident from the aggression of their cricket in this game. For Warne, now past 400 Test wickets, it has already been another triumph.

For the moment the only certain effect of the loss of 66.5 overs on Sunday is that it has removed even the remote possibility of England building a sufficiently large second-innings total to turn the tables. Because fewer than twenty-five overs were bowled yesterday – play was abandoned at 4.40pm after an ethereal mist had turned into steady rain – Surrey and the ECB must refund £220,000 to the capacity crowd, half the cost of the tickets that were sold well before Christmas last year. Money back is compensation but only small consolation. At least tickets will be reduced today to £10 for adults, and free to members and all spectators under sixteen.

When play began yesterday in the sort of swirling air associated more with deerstalkers on Scottish hills, England needed another 33 runs to avoid the follow-on and thereby enhance their chances of achieving a draw by the most honourable route. Ramprakash started as he had finished in the golden light of Saturday evening after his happiest day in Test cricket since the magnificent innings in Barbados in 1998, but he was out with 18 still needed.

Five overs and a few brave shots later, Adam Gilchrist smartly stumped Gough off a bottom edge to record his hundredth Test victim in his twenty-first Test, two fewer than any other wicket-keeper. It is surprising, given the success of Warne and Stuart MacGill, that this was only the seventh stumping so far. Even more so that Gough had never previously been stumped.

Alas for Michael Atherton there was nothing so unusual about the way he fell in his last Test innings. A superb cut and decisive pull reminded McGrath why it is that he has enjoyed becoming Atherton's master as much as he has Lara's. In his third over, however, he once again found an outswinger of perfect length, Atherton was forced to play and the ball carried on off the seam to take the edge.

Warne took the catch at first slip before Atherton took the long walk back. One can guess his emotions: sadness that he had not been able to produce one last major innings for England; resignation to the supremacy of McGrath, now getting him for the nineteenth time; and reluctant pride, demanding acknowledgement, with a shy, dignified wave of the bat, of the standing ovation given to him jointly by the crowd and the Australians. Long live the chivalry of cricket.

MICHAEL ATHERTON

Hard as a pebble, stoical as a pilgrim, Mike Atherton may be seen as the last of a breed if every side sets out in future to follow the recent Australian lead by trying to score at least four runs an over in Test cricket. Three an over for his team, one and a half for himself, was much more in accord with his idea of proper, combative, see-saw Test cricket in which the job of the opener on the days when he was blessed with the luck to play a long innings was to wear down opposing fast bowlers and then to take the rewards soberly later in the day, punishing the bad balls stylishly enough with cuts and cover-drives, but working the gaps for singles, too, before indulging in some hooks against wearier bowlers when the new ball was taken.

The drily humorous, quick-witted, single-minded son of an able Lancashire headmaster of few words and a chirpy, outgoing mother, Michael was so good for Lancashire and England junior teams in his days at Manchester Grammar School that an England future was confidently expected even before he made his mark in his first match for Cambridge University. Yet he no more than tolerated the fame his ability and determination brought him and refused to exploit it for money. Instead, he took the heavy cares of the England team on to a back not quite broad enough.

I played against him once at Sir Paul Getty's beautiful ground at Wormsley. Much to Mike's pleasure and amusement I holed out second ball to mid-off. If he therefore concluded that this particular pundit couldn't play, the pundit himself saw the Atherton that might have been. Opening the batting with that brilliant stroke-player, John Crawley, he set himself to hit almost every ball for four and against respectable bowling came close to achieving it. In similar vein Crawley did well enough too but, normally so elegant, he looked crude by comparison.

Athers batted then with a range and authority he seldom allowed himself in professional company. One dazzling display of uninhibited strokeplay in a One-Day International against the West Indies at Lord's showed it was within his powers but, like Geoff Boycott and Ken Barrington before him, he trained himself to play to limitations imposed by what he perceived to be the needs of his team and his own success as a professional. Despite his inherited degenerative back disease, kept under control in recent years only by daily muscle-relaxing tablets and frequent injections of cortisone, he scored more than any other Test batsman in the decade of the 1990s. It was an achievement worthy of his greatest quality, endurance under fire. For it was his lot to play in an era of more or less outstanding fast bowling partnerships: Wasim and Waqar; Donald and Pollock; Ambrose and Walsh; Srinath and Prasad; Cairns and Nash; Reid and Alderman; Hughes and McDermott; McGrath and Gillespie.

If he overcame them during his 115 Tests, there were still the high-quality spinners: Shane Warne, Mushtaq Ahmed, Saqlain Mushtaq, Muttiah Muralitharan. With his famous soft hands, the ability to play the ball late and the shrewdness to hit it only in the areas he believed to be safe, he played them better than any other English contemporary. Of his sixteen hundreds only one, when he was still a fresh-faced subaltern, was against Australia, made on a turning pitch at Sydney. He got an edge to Ian Healy behind the wicket shortly before reaching even that century, but it was not given out. That rugged Queenslander chuntered about something-something non-walking Poms for some time under his breath until Atherton silenced him with withering logic: 'Oh come off it, Ian. When in Rome . . .'

He never played in a winning series against Australia, but he did against all the rest and his hundred against the West Indies at The Oval in 2000 gave him profound satisfaction.

The crowd rose to him again when they knew he was going to retire a year later. This, after all, was the man who had captained England more often than any other. Stubborn, self-assured, pragmatic, grudging in his praise of any opponent, he was also principled, a warm companion, never boastful and one of the pluckiest batsmen who ever played. He might now allow himself the joys of family life. Bat and gloves have been replaced by fishing-rod and golf clubs: he will catch the fish and hole the important putts.

2001 v. Australia: 5 matches; 221 runs at 22.10; 7 catches

England will be playing their Tests this winter without two other stalwarts of recent years. Alec Stewart and Darren Gough had both requested, justifying themselves yesterday through the medium of newspaper columns, that they should be allowed to miss the tour of India before Christmas. Both, however, had hoped to go to New Zealand from February to April. Between them the England management and senior ECB officials, having battled at the request of several players to find an itinerary that allowed everyone to get home for Christmas, have told them that as far as the Test series are concerned it must be all or nothing. Neither Stewart nor Gough will be named in the teams announced from Lord's tomorrow.

Both will face a battle to get back into the Test side, Stewart more obviously so in view of his age, thirty-eight. They remain, however, the best in the country in their particular specialities. That is not to say that whoever is chosen to replace them will not have established a firm hold on a place before the Sri Lanka and India tours to England next season.

Like Graham Thorpe last year after he had voluntarily missed the tour of South Africa, Gough may have to wait before reclaiming a Test place but, again like Thorpe, his proven class will be wanted sooner or later. It has been greatly to England's benefit in the last two years that he and Andrew Caddick have played together in every Test since the start of the series in South Africa in 1999 but Gough has bowled only 321 overs in first-class cricket this season for 39 wickets, 31 of which have been for England.

Duncan Fletcher and Nasser Hussain, England's coach and captain, decided that it would neither be fair, nor conducive to team spirit, to replace Gough and Stewart with younger players in India, only to ditch them for New Zealand. Yesterday both men were implicitly criticised for wanting to have their cake but not their curry. 'The selectors' approach to this issue has been flexible,' said an ECB statement. 'Test-only contracts have been offered to certain senior players in order to allow them to rest from the one-day programme and this offer remains on the table. However, the selectors feel it would set a dangerous precedent to allow players to pick and choose which elements of a winter tour they are prepared to undertake.'

The fact is that players have been doing so for as long as cricket tours have been regular winter events. Sir Alec Bedser, to give but one prominent example, was not chosen for a tour of India in order to keep him fresh for what were then considered more important series. It is equally true that when senior players drop out, chances are opened up for younger players. It is a healthy exercise and ultimately beneficial for all concerned, but players like Atherton, Stewart and Gough cannot be replaced overnight and the combined result of their decisions is that the chances of winning in both India and New Zealand were significantly reduced.

Monday, 27 August
The Oval (fifth day of five): Australia beat England by an innings and 25 runs.
Game, set and match. Silencing any lingering voices of doubt about their exalted place in history, Australia finished the 2001 Ashes series as they had begun it, with an innings victory and another vivid demonstration of their formidable all-round talent and tenacity. Shane Warne and Glenn McGrath had started the process with eight wickets between them on the first day of the first Test at Edgbaston; now they completed it with eight more at The Oval on the last of the fifth.

SHANE WARNE

Shane Warne revived a faded art and gave it a dramatic new lease of life. He has been a benison for cricket, for Australia and for the variety that adds spice to life.

He is a wizard; a playboy; a lover of life; a man's man; a husband and father; the best leg-spinner of his lifetime; the most prolific wicket-taker of all the wrist spinners; a charmer off the field; a con-man on it, drawing umpires as well as batsmen into his web; smiling as he plans the downfall of each batsman according to his lights.

Two operations have changed his methods. The googlies are rarities now but he has added a ball that goes straight on, although it looks like a leg-break, to counteract the growing number of players who like to sweep him. He remains incredibly accurate and now that both his right shoulder and his spinning fingers are strong again, he will face South Africa once more with confidence. His third tour of England was a personal triumph. He ripped and dipped the ball as of old, and although for once he needed to contribute little with the bat, much to the consternation of a confident and competitive cricketer who believes he is capable of a Test hundred, he caught brilliantly at first slip.

2001 in England: 5 matches; 31 wickets at 18.70; 5 wickets in an innings three times, 10 in a match once; 6 catches

There was a satisfying natural justice about that symmetry. McGrath, with thirty-two wickets, and Warne, with thirty-one, have complemented the performances of a group of devastatingly good batsmen throughout a series in which this Australia side has shown itself to be even stronger than those who won the previous six against England. McGrath passed Dennis Lillee's 355 wickets yesterday and with 358 now has more than any other Australian fast bowler. Warne moved on past Curtly Ambrose's 405 to 407, with only Walsh, Kapil Dev, Hadlee and Wasim Akram ahead of him.

The two great bowlers destroyed the main England batting in the morning, reducing them at the nadir to 55 for 5 and buying themselves the time to enjoy the process of finishing the job on a beautiful Bank Holiday afternoon. Such was the Australian supremacy in the end that Steve Waugh deliberately withheld McGrath in order to try to give Jason Gillespie and Brett Lee their share of the spoils. Only when a spirited ninth-wicket partnership by Darren Gough and James Ormond threatened to take the game beyond tea did he recall McGrath for the *coup de grâce*, duly delivered just after 3.30pm as if with a forehand and backhand sweep of his sword.

Metaphorically, indeed, the corpses lie strewn across the cricket fields of England, so supremely good has the Australian perform-ance been from the day of their arrival. They might have won five-nil had Damien Fleming played in Lee's place at Headingley; and even more easily had Colin Miller been the fourth fast bowler here, but they have been building for the future from their posi-tion of strength, which is exactly what they wanted to do. The figures suggest that Lee has failed in his first Ashes series but he is surely going to be a major force when McGrath retires. It could be argued that his one savage spell on the Saturday afternoon at Lord's was as influential as any, putting Graham Thorpe out of the rest of the series with a broken hand.

No doubt the team ethos would have drawn something extra from Lee and Gillespie had McGrath, officially Australia's man of the series, missed four of the games as Thorpe did. It is clear enough now that Australia would have won even if England had been able to field a first-choice XI throughout. Never have they possessed such strength in depth, certainly not four years ago when they were forced because of injuries to call on the modest Tasmanian all-rounder Shaun Young for the fifth Test at The Oval. The equivalent this time would have been Ian Harvey, who would walk into the England team along with half the Australians in county cricket.

GLENN McGRATH

In the eyes of almost every young cricketer who ever plays, fast bowling seems to be all about fear. Glenn McGrath, the quiet assassin of the greensward, has proved (once again) that in the end it is about taking wickets.

Heir in method and accuracy to Brian Statham and Curtly Ambrose, he may very well be the best fast bowler of them all. Once he took his wickets with a sneer, now he smiles more. He seems to have realised that he is good enough not to be so nasty.

An apt word for the way he used to be, although I hate it, is shitty. He was forever chuntering, either berating himself for slipping below the level of perfection; or niggling cynically away at the batsman; a Scrooge of a bowler railing against the world. It looked mean, it sometimes caused him to lose his cool and his control, and, whether or not that was so, it let both himself and his team down. The greater the pity, because those who know him like him very much.

Perhaps it was the season for Worcestershire, one of unremitting success, in 2000, that softened the hard edges. Getting to 300 wickets in the Perth Test of the following Australian summer against the West Indies, only six years after his first really successful Test match against England on the same ground, also seemed to relax him. Again, something seemed to happen when he above all the rest of the bowlers bore the heat and burden of defeat in India early in 2001. He, and the Australian team generally, discovered in that land where almost everyone seems to love cricket that the game really was bigger than winning or losing. More than that; you could actually gain friends and greater respect in honourable defeat. 'If you can make a heap of all your winnings; and risk them on one turn of pitch and toss; and lose, and start again at your beginnings; and never breathe a word about your loss . . .'

He came to England needing to prove nothing, but every time he and his team most wanted him to lead the attack, to make a mark early or take a critical wicket, he obliged. He had the courage to say in public that Michael Atherton would be his first target, just as he had before bowling against Brian Lara. In both cases he might have been made to look a braggart but he was as good as his word.

Or his bowling was. At the start of the series he had got Atherton out thirteen times; by the end it was nineteen. If Atherton's young opening partner, Trescothick, plays 100 Tests, as with luck he will, he may well consider that to get out only twice in the series to McGrath was something about which to be very proud. Twenty-five of his thirty-two wickets in the series were batsmen from the top seven in the England order.

It is all done so simply. A straight, unhurried approach, an easy swing of the arm, a high delivery over a braced front leg, a firm but never tense wrist behind the ball, and complete control of the length and direction he has pre-ordained with a calculating brain.

Of course it is not as easy as he makes it all look. He has had his injuries, including early back trouble; but he works to a rigorous exercise schedule to enable him to keep on running in. He still has plenty of miles on the clock of his smooth-running wicket machine; but he will be happy enough, when the time comes, to go back to the New South Wales country farm with his English wife and his young family, keeping an eye on thousands of sheep and hunting wild boar for his recreation instead of batsmen.

2001 v. England: 5 matches; 32 wickets at 16.93; 5 wickets in an innings four times

The left-handed Butcher and Trescothick set out hopefully yesterday before a decent crowd that grew almost to capacity by lunchtime. For four overs they suggested that the 209 needed to make Australia bat again might not be beyond them but in the fifth, with six runs added, Butcher, seven days on from his finest hour, pushed too firmly at a leg-break from Warne and was taken at silly point off pad and bat.

Two overs later the game was as good as won. First McGrath, immediately after Ricky Ponting had missed Trescothick off an edge to second slip, produced a ball quite unlike any other in the match. Spitting like fat from the frying pan, it reared towards Trescothick's head from not far short of a length and lobbed from his protecting hand to the bowler. Warne followed up by claiming Hussain leg before, half-forward to the ball that goes straight on.

McGrath versus Usman Afzaal was man versus boy. He would have gone round the wicket if he had needed to, but he did not, drawing the young left-hander into a forward plunge and taking the outside edge for Ponting, diving right in the injured Mark Waugh's normal position to make amends for his earlier miss.

At last now there was some resistance from England as Mark Ramprakash and Alec Stewart, bristling with defiance and timing the ball beautifully, put on 40 for the sixth wicket in twelve overs before lunch. Neither, however, could master the virtuoso Warne. Mainly over the wicket, but round when he felt the need, he wheeled tirelessly in from the Vauxhall End until inspiration began to desert him at the end of the innings, always with three or four round the bat. He constantly varied the trajectory and the line and whenever he wanted to he turned the leg-break viciously from the rough outside the right-hander's leg stump.

Four overs from lunch he struck again as Ramprakash had to pull out of a cut to a high bouncing leg-break and could only steer it to gully. Stewart had done enough to show how England will miss him this winter when he, too, was confounded by the conjuror. Five times he padded away balls pitched into the foot-marks from round the wicket but the sixth was aimed cunningly shorter, Stewart failed to reach it with his front leg and it spun a yard to knock the bail from the off stump.

Lee successfully hounded Caddick again, hitting his leg stump at 90mph before Gough and Ormond batted splendidly to pro-long the entertainment for almost an hour in their partnership of 58. Gough, who will be missed even more than Stewart, even managed three fours in an over from McGrath, the last a cheeky little pull off his nose, before Ormond's stout effort ended with an outside edge and Tufnell flashed at his second ball.

This twentieth Australian win in twenty-three Test matches broke the previous longest sequence by any side without a draw (twenty-two by England in the nineteenth century). They had beaten England at The Oval only once since administering the famous humiliation of 1948, when the Chappell brothers made hundreds in 1972. This time it was the Waugh twins whose glorious batting set up the victory after Justin Langer's outstanding innings on the first day.

Australia 1st innings

			R	M	B	4	6
ML Hayden	c Trescothick	b Tufnell	68	183	125	9	0
JL Langer	retired hurt		102	260	186	12	1
RT Ponting	c Atherton	b Ormond	62	126	102	8	0
ME Waugh		b Gough	120	252	176	16	2
*SR Waugh	not out		157	312	256	21	1
+AC Gilchrist	c Ramprakash	b Afzaal	25	48	32	2	1
DR Martyn	not out		64	62	54	10	0
Extras	(b 10, lb 13, w 1, nb 19)		43				
Total	(4 wickets dec, 152 overs, 624 mins)		641				

DNB: B Lee, SK Warne, JN Gillespie, GD McGrath.

FoW: 1–158 (Hayden, 42.2 ov), 2–292 (Ponting, 72.5 ov),
       3–489 (ME Waugh, 123.1 ov), 4–534 (Gilchrist, 134.3 ov).

Bowling

	O	M	R	W	
Gough	29	4	113	1	(7nb)
Caddick	36	9	146	0	(7nb, 1w)
Ormond	34	4	115	1	
Tufnell	39	2	174	1	(5nb)
Butcher	1	0	2	0	
Ramprakash	4	0	19	0	
Afzaal	9	0	49	1	

England 1st innings

			R	M	B	4	6
MA Atherton		b Warne	13	56	39	2	0
ME Trescothick		b Warne	55	82	57	11	0
MA Butcher	c Langer	b Warne	25	70	60	4	0
*N Hussain		b ME Waugh	52	128	88	8	0
MR Ramprakash	c Gilchrist	b McGrath	133	365	232	18	0
U Afzaal	c Gillespie	b McGrath	54	97	76	9	0
+AJ Stewart	c Gilchrist	b Warne	29	61	49	3	0
AR Caddick	lbw	b Warne	0	2	1	0	0
J Ormond		b Warne	18	38	27	2	0
D Gough	st Gilchrist	b Warne	24	98	71	4	0
PCR Tufnell	not out		7	23	15	1	0
Extras	(b 3, lb 13, w 1, nb 5)		22				
Total	(all out, 118.2 overs, 514 mins)		432				

FoW: 1–58 (Atherton, 12.4 ov), 2–85 (Trescothick, 18.5 ov),
       3–104 (Butcher, 30.1 ov), 4–166 (Hussain, 50.1 ov),
       5–255 (Afzaal, 71.6 ov), 6–313 (Stewart, 86.2 ov),
       7–313 (Caddick, 86.3 ov), 8–350 (Ormond, 94.5 ov),
       9–424 (Ramprakash, 113.3 ov), 10–432 (Gough, 118.2 ov).

Bowling	O	M	R	W	
McGrath	30	11	67	2	
Gillespie	20	3	96	0	(3nb, 1w)
Warne	44.2	7	165	7	(1nb)
Lee	14	1	43	0	(1nb)
Ponting	2	0	5	0	
ME Waugh	8	0	40	1	

England 2nd innings (following on)			R	M	B	4	6
MA Atherton	c Warne	b McGrath	9	23	20	1	0
ME Trescothick	c & b McGrath		24	69	43	3	0
MA Butcher	c SR Waugh	b Warne	14	36	29	2	0
*N Hussain	lbw	b Warne	2	13	7	0	0
MR Ramprakash	c Hayden	b Warne	19	81	63	3	0
U Afzaal	c Ponting	b McGrath	5	26	22	0	0
+AJ Stewart		b Warne	34	98	67	6	0
AR Caddick		b Lee	17	51	46	2	0
J Ormond	c Gilchrist	b McGrath	17	78	57	1	0
D Gough	not out		39	79	57	6	0
PCR Tufnell	c Warne	b McGrath	0	2	2	0	0
Extras	(lb 2, nb 2)		4				
Total	(all out, 68.3 overs, 283 mins)		184				

FoW: 1–17 (Atherton, 5.3 ov), 2–46 (Butcher, 14.2 ov),
3–48 (Trescothick, 15.5 ov), 4–50 (Hussain, 16.6 ov),
5–55 (Afzaal, 23.5 ov), 6–95 (Ramprakash, 36.2 ov),
7–126 (Stewart, 48.6 ov), 8–126 (Caddick, 49.1 ov),
9–184 (Ormond, 68.1 ov), 10–184 (Tufnell, 68.3 ov).

Bowling	O	M	R	W	
Lee	10	3	30	1	
McGrath	15.3	6	43	5	(1nb)
Warne	28	8	64	4	(1nb)
Ponting	2	0	3	0	
Gillespie	12	5	38	0	
ME Waugh	1	0	4	0	

Australia won by an innings and 25 runs.

Conclusions

It has freely been called the best cricket team that has ever played. What is certain is that the Australia team that won the 2001 Ashes series by four matches to one was the best in the world and certainly amongst a handful of the strongest sides ever to tour England. Amongst post-war sides, it proved itself to be at least the equal both of Bradman's unbeaten 1948 side and of the best of the many powerful West Indies combinations, the 1980 team unit which chose its fast bowlers from Roberts, Holding, Marshall, Garner and Croft and whose top batsmen included Greenidge, Haynes, Richards, Kallicharran and Lloyd.

Nothing stops international cricket for long these days and within months of the team's return home they were due to face challenges at home and away from a South Africa side quite capable of upsetting the champions if they should play at their best, Australia should not, and the luck should favour Shaun Pollock's team rather than Waugh's.

Whatever the future held, Waugh's Australia deserved to be called a great team not just because of what he and his players achieved on the field but because of the way they played the game. The declarations that led to the only defeats in first-class matches showed the largesse that only real champions possess. The manner in which they accepted defeat at Headingley was not just magnanimous, but spontaneously so. To be hard-nosed on the field is part of the business of winning in contemporary cricket but to reveal a generosity of spirit when things for once do not go according to plan is a sign of true quality.

In these two areas, of playing cricket that is entertaining as well as efficient, and of restoring the game's chivalry in a cynical world, Mark Taylor set the pattern but Waugh has developed it into a matter of policy. Under his leadership Australia have enhanced cricket.

It is, naturally, easier to play within the spirit of the game when you know you have strength in reserve. The Australians made their mistakes but their brilliance in catching, running and throwing enabled the bowlers, with two true champions in McGrath and Warne, to get full value for their skill and relentless accuracy; and the pace at which their batsmen scored sets them apart.

The pity, to me, is that it all happened so quickly, with matches following one another breathlessly, leaving little time to savour the outstanding performances. It is an inevitable consequence of the ICC's new ten-year Test programme that there will be too many matches and a general overkill, dictated, of course, by the insatiable demands of television. The dangerously independent Asian Cricket Council have added to the overload by staging their own extra and separate championship.

Australia's brilliant campaign started at Edgbaston with McGrath and Warne all but bowling England out on the first day only for Stewart and Caddick to suggest that there was a sting in the tail. Slater rubbed in the balm at once and, having inflicted some wounds of his own, made way for Steve Waugh, Damien Martyn and Adam Gilchrist to show that Australia would not release their grip once they had got on top.

Both at Edgbaston and Lord's they were helped beyond calculation by dropped catches but it was at Trent Bridge where the gulf was most marked, first when Gilchrist and Gillespie rescued Australia on the second day, then on the third when the England tailenders, given a similar chance to turn the game, failed lamentably to battle it out against Gillespie and Warne.

It had been like that for Australia throughout the trip; every crisis turned to their own advantage. Apart from offering their opponents the chance to win after third-innings declarations at Southampton and Leeds, they lost only an early one-day game to

Middlesex, but that was no more than a cheeky little Peugeot catching a Bentley unprepared at the traffic lights. When they needed to change gear in the one-day tournament itself, they sauntered effortlessly to the front, thrashing Pakistan in the final as easily as they had England on the way. Only in the first game of that series at Bristol, when they got the runs in the final over, were they stretched.

England missed that opportunity and they went on missing them in the weeks that followed until Butcher's innings permitted a glimpse at least of what might have been. Inspirational as it was, it was played only when the main issues had been won and lost.

As the Australians returned to their laurel wreaths, thoughts turned once more to what could be done to strengthen the professional base from which England draws its players. Throughout the season of 2001 domestic cricket had been continuing along the lines laid down two years previously when the ECB, having canvassed widely if not necessarily wisely, decreed that the 1999 County Championship would be the last to be played on equal footing by the first-class counties. The top nine in that year's Championship went into a first division in 2000, the bottom nine into the second, from which a fairly generous lifeline was offered by providing for three promotions each year.

The first season of two divisions unfortunately coincided with the introduction of centrally contracted England players. This had a direct positive impact on the national team but a negative one on county cricket, depriving matches of a certain amount of glamour but one team in particular, Yorkshire, of any realistic chance of winning the title.

The new system has undeniably produced competitive cricket and matches that remain of urgent importance to most of the counties for most of the season. In some cases it has sharpened up the performances of teams and individuals. It has, however, been at the cost of what used to be one of county cricket's greatest virtues, the variety of different grounds, pitches and opposition. Overseas professionals for thirty years or more have identified this variety as the very best aspect of the county game, the thing that rounded their game and completed their cricketing education. By contrast, only half the counties played against McGrath and Warne in 2000, only half faced Muttiah Muralitharan and Saqlain Mushtaq, or, for that matter, Darren Gough and Andrew Caddick, on their rare appearances, in 2001.

A review group under the chairmanship of the former Essex off-spinner, David Acfield, but otherwise composed of those who tend to put financial considerations before cricketing ones, was watching the course of events throughout the season with a view to recommending possible changes to the system to the First Class Forum in December. Any reorganisation would not, however, take effect until 2003.

They had to consider that, if the present structure continues, players, spectators and England selectors will get increasingly less experience; but the biggest disadvantage of two divisions is the probability that sooner or later it will drive some clubs out of business. It was predictable from the outset that the majority would soon claim that three promotions and relegations each season are too many for divisions comprising only nine teams and that only two should go up and down in future. That would only increase the likelihood of the rich getting richer, the poor poorer.

There are, of course, many who feel – usually from behind the desks of relatively affluent clubs with a Test ground to bolster their finances – that fewer counties would be an advantage. To my mind, they are wrong: this is a time when the game needs to expand, not to contract.

Some £29 million of the ECB's annual income of £50 million is ploughed back into the counties and there is a strong case for the hefty proportion of that large sum which goes into the wages of the players to be reduced, either by a cap on the total salary expenditure for all clubs and by a reduction to perhaps fifteen full-time professionals per county, or by stipulating – and enforcing – that one specified percentage of the annual distribution should go towards the development of cricketers under twenty, and another towards improvements in ground facilities for players and spectators, thus leaving a smaller sum for salaries. But to reduce the number of counties playing first-class cricket is not going to assist either greater participation at the grass roots or the quality of the cricket at the top. In time it would simply reduce the flow.

The old argument that six first-division sides suffice in Australia does not wash, because the population of England and Wales, more than three times Australia's, can comfortably accommodate eighteen first-class sides. These eighteen 'centres of excellence' provide the conduit to the top of the game and as good a means as any for co-ordinating youth and recreational cricket in their area. It is not the ideal system but it is the one that has evolved: provided all counties continue to develop their own revenue sources in a professional manner, there is nothing to be gained by pushing any of them over the edge.

My solution would be to refine the system of two divisions in order to retain what it has injected into the county game without prolonging the disadvantages beyond 2003. At the same time I would scrap the Benson & Hedges Cup as it exists and commence a long-overdue experiment in regional cricket.

Not only would touring sides play regional combinations in future (by playing weakened teams against tourists the counties have brought that upon themselves) but a new, self-contained tournament for the best players in the country, divided into six regions, would take place in the first three weeks of the season. They would play a straight league of five two-day, 200-over matches under Australian Grade rules. The remaining players – including some who would not otherwise have had a chance to play first-team county cricket – would contest an equally self-contained competition. Both tournaments would start around 20 April and conclude at the end of the first week in May, after which England contracts would be announced.

The Championship would then be played in two halves: initially between all eighteen counties divided into geographical groups to save expense on travel and reduce the number of games; then in two divisions as now. Overall each county would play thirteen games rather than the present sixteen. Crucially, all eighteen counties would start each new season on equal terms. The aim would be to retain sharp competitiveness without putting clubs out of business. County staffs would be pruned to about sixteen players, with a second-eleven competition played from early July, after exams, by young, part-time professionals and university students.

The benefits of bringing together the best England-qualified cricketers in a regional tournament ought to be obvious and press and public would soon see the worth of such a tournament, especially if it were sponsored and televised. It would give additional impact to the early weeks of cricket seasons that tend to limp into the sporting calendar as poor relations of a rugby union season that is approaching its climax and a football season that never ends.

A five-year trial for a short early-season competition containing five two-day games each for the six regions would give a fair indication of its value. After that everyone would be in a better position to judge whether regional competition should be extended or not. It is not ideal, from the point of view of mixing established England cricketers with their rivals, that the competition should be held so early in the season, especially if a winter tour has ended late, but the trial has to start somewhere. If necessary established England fast bowlers or other key players in need of a rest would simply have to miss the tournament in some seasons.

The Championship would then start (using 2001 dates as a model) on 9 May with five games each for counties playing in three regional divisions of six. The groups divide neatly and fairly into North (Durham, Yorkshire, Lancashire, Derbyshire, Nottinghamshire and Leicestershire); West and Midlands (Glamorgan, Gloucestershire, Somerset, Warwickshire, Worcestershire and Northamptonshire) and South (Essex, Kent, Surrey, Middlesex, Sussex and Hampshire). The top three in each region would form the first division in an eight-match competition in the second half of the season; the bottom three in each would form the second division.

No system is perfect and there are, arguably, two drawbacks to this one. First, the clubs in the second division would have no promotion to play for in the second half of their season, nor would first-division clubs have to fear relegation, but this would be offset by much higher financial incentives for the players, paid from the ECB's sponsorship and broadcasting revenue, augmented by money saved in travel and second-eleven expenses, and lower salary costs for fewer professionals. Every game would carry prize money for a win and there would be additional prize money, steeply graded, for the top three in each division, with significantly greater rewards for the first division starting at £150,000 for the champions.

The second drawback is that marketing games in advance would be difficult if the opposition in the second phase of the competition is not known until a relatively short time before the event, but dates would be prescribed and home games would be allocated as evenly and quickly as possible. This is no different from the present problem faced by counties who do not know whether they will be involved after the quarter-final stages of the knockout cups.

Under this plan, in which the Norwich Union and Cheltenham & Gloucester competitions would remain as at present, urgent competition would start with the first ball of the season and very probably not finish until the last. Despite having three fewer games in the Championship there would be a greater variety of opposition. The burgeoning transfer system would be avoided and local sponsorship encouraged by the fact that everyone would start with an equal chance of winning the first division of the Championship at the outset of each season. This competition accompanied by the Tests and One-Day Internationals would form the bedrock of every future season.

Meanwhile, the long overdue inauguration of a National Academy offers hope that young players with the talent, but not yet the strength or the know-how, to play Test cricket successfully, will in future be matured more swiftly.

Rodney Marsh, a stalwart of one of the best of all Australian sides, was appointed to be the director of the Academy on 8 July 2001. The first sixteen English 'students' left for Adelaide at the end of October, their ages ranging from eighteen to twenty-five. They were about to benefit from the accumulated wisdom of a man who was not only one of the toughest of opponents but who had also directed the Australian Academy in Adelaide for the last ten years.

The results have been demonstrably excellent. Over half the current Australian side spent time at the Academy, which is credited with the transformation of Shane Warne's career amongst others. Jack Potter, the first director, laid down the ground-rules aimed at developing what one might call 'whole' cricketers but Marsh further developed the idea of giving his young charges specialist advice from past experts in their field. Warne's mentor was Terry Jenner, while Brett Lee had expert guidance from Marsh's old friend Dennis Lillee.

There is no more passionate Australian patriot than Marsh but no one, also, keener to see England competing again on level terms. He has been notably more conciliatory in his remarks about English cricket since his infamous suggestion that English bowlers were no better than 'pie-throwers'. His son, Daniel, who captained the Academy side when his father was director, made a good impression as a batsman and fielder, if less so as a left-arm spinner, when playing as the overseas player for Leicestershire in 2001, until he broke his cheek-bone.

Marsh was the rugged presence behind the wicket in the sides led by Ian and Greg Chappell when Dennis Lillee and Jeff Thomson hit their peak together in the mid-1970s. They overwhelmed England and the West Indies in successive seasons and it was only when Lillee, Marsh and the younger Chappell retired from Test cricket in 1984 that performances dipped. The finishing school for the most gifted players at Adelaide played a significant part in building the period of sustained success that followed the winning of the World Cup in India under Allan Border as captain and Bobby Simpson as coach in 1988.

Marsh succeeded Potter after being sacked by Kerry Packer as a Channel Nine commentator in 1991 for outspoken remarks. It is probably the best thing that has happened to him since his retirement after a seventeen-year career in which he played in 96 Tests and finished with 355 dismissals as well as scoring three Test hundreds.

His main purpose will be to mature England's talented young players earlier by guiding them technically, temperamentally, tactically and, not least, in the whole approach to the life of a professional cricketer, including the food they eat and the way they conduct themselves in public.

Hugh Morris, the ECB's Performance Director, was chiefly

responsible for recruiting Marsh and setting up the first year's programme. The Adelaide centre will act as the host until there is room for the government-financed centre at Bisham Abbey, which has been on the drawing board at Lord's for years. The ECB and Sport England are still hopeful that Bisham Abbey will act as the base for the Academy from the winter of 2002–03 onwards, but gaining planning permission for the proposed facilities has been a problem and seventeen alternative sites were still under consideration when the plans were finally unveiled in July.

All this was a pathetic illustration of the British government's general failure to give sport its due place in society. For years successive governments had allowed playing fields to be sold for building by local authorities, almost daily thereby exaggerating the difference between young Britons who have to get into cars and travel miles to find any decent facilities while for Australians there is invariably something suitable around the next corner.

It was asked, when England's football side suddenly beat Germany 5–1 in a World Cup qualifying game, what it was that their new Swedish coach had done for them. It might have been asked again when the Ryder Cup team was finalised two days later. What used to be the 'Great Britain and Ireland' team but now encompassed Europe, had a disproportionate nub of three Swedes in the side of ten.

It was no coincidence. The amount of money spent on sport in England is 67 pence per person per year; in Australia it is £2.56; in France (the reigning European and world football champions) £5.16; in Sweden, where they churn out not just champion golfers but also tennis players by the dozen (and a decent football side too), it is £18.51.

Still, the National Academy was at last a statement of intent. The sixteen selected players lacked a genuine all-rounder but otherwise comprised several gifted young batsmen; three very fast bowlers, another of great potential and a fifth, Alex Tudor, who had taken five wickets against Australia at Trent Bridge and made 99 not out against New Zealand; a wrist-spinner; a finger-spinner and two wicket-keeper/batsmen. They were due to spend two months in Adelaide before Christmas, training, practising and studying, before returning in the new year to play a mixture of four-day and one-day games, mainly against State second elevens. The essential aim was to deliver individually tailored development programmes to each of the fortunate young cricketers and the academy will eventually be staffed with what Morris describes as 'high-quality technical coaches' under the direction of Marsh and his assistant, the former Lancashire captain, John Abrahams. The coaches and players will be supported by some of the best sports scientists and medical experts in the world.

Matches abroad are intended to be part of the programme even when the Academy finds an English base, but it is a shame that the £500,000 a year that is to be spent on the project, as part of the £2 million four-year agreement with the lottery-funded Sport England, is coming at the expense of the 'A' tours which broadened the experience of virtually all the current England team at an earlier stage of their development. Despite modest payments to the players themselves, the cost of some recent 'A' tours had also reached something close to £500,000 and Tim Lamb, the ECB's chief executive, has ruled out any more of them for the foreseeable future.

If the official quest to make England the best team in the world by 2007 is to succeed, there may be a case for diverting some of the 45 per cent of the ECB's overall income from all sources that is currently redistributed to the counties, but if it has to be either the academy or 'A' tours, there is no question that the academy has to be given its chance. Its prime business is to mature the talented young English players who too often fail to develop, for a variety of reasons, in county cricket.

The concept had been developed from research undertaken over the previous two years into all the best components of the most successful cricket academies in Australia, South Africa and New Zealand, not to mention academies from other relevant sports. Morris anticipates that 'nearly all future England players will have been through the National Academy structure'. That assumes that the selectors will, in future, be able to identify all the best players before the age of twenty-three, which is a dangerous assumption. For every late developer there is a younger talent that flatters to deceive. In Australia there is no sentiment when it comes to selection and no stigma attached to anyone who has made an unanswerable case in 'Shield' cricket without having been to the Academy. Those emulating the system here must beware the premature labelling of cricketers. The fact remains, however, that great players invariably make their potential known at an early age, whatever country they play for.

Marsh has no doubt that what he is about to undertake will help England towards the ECB's target of making them the best side in the world by 2007. 'My major target over the next three years,' he said, 'will be to develop a base of perhaps twenty players who, in three, five or seven years' time, will be very good Test and One-Day International cricketers, so that when the selectors sit down to pick a side it will be damn difficult to choose between them.'

Roll on that day. England may be, as Waugh said, 'the place to play', but unless the country's team beat Australia soon, and repeat it a few times to show that they mean it, it will become like the blue hills of Housman's *Shropshire Lad*:

> Into my heart an air that kills
> From yon far country blows:
> What are those blue remembered hills,
> What spires, what farms are those?
>
> That is the land of lost content,
> I see it shining plain,
> The happy highways where I went
> And cannot come again.

Series Averages

England

Batting	M	I	NO	Runs	HS	Avge	100	50	Ct/St
MA Butcher	5	10	1	456	173★	50.66	1	1	4
MR Ramprakash	4	8	0	318	133	39.75	1	0	3
N Hussain	3	6	1	177	55	35.40	0	2	0
AJ Stewart	5	9	1	283	76★	35.37	0	2	13
ME Trescothick	5	10	0	321	76	32.10	0	3	4
MA Atherton	5	10	0	221	57	22.10	0	2	7
J Ormond	1	2	0	35	18	17.50	0	0	0
U Afzaal	3	6	1	83	54	16.60	0	1	0
AR Caddick	5	9	2	101	49★	14.42	0	0	1
D Gough	5	9	3	82	39★	13.66	0	0	0
IJ Ward	3	6	1	68	23★	13.60	0	0	0
DG Cork	1	2	0	26	24	13.00	0	0	0
GP Thorpe	1	2	0	22	20	11.00	0	0	1
C White	3	6	1	38	27★	7.60	0	0	1
PCR Tufnell	1	2	1	7	7★	7.00	0	0	0
AJ Tudor	2	3	0	14	9	4.66	0	0	0
AF Giles	1	2	0	7	7	3.50	0	0	0
RDB Croft	1	2	0	3	3	1.50	0	0	0
AD Mullally	1	1	0	0	0	0.00	0	0	0

Bowling	O	M	R	W	BB	Avge	5i	10m
RDB Croft	3	0	10	1	1–8	10.00	0	0
MA Butcher	14	4	63	4	4–42	15.75	0	0
AJ Tudor	44.5	7	195	7	5–44	27.85	1	0

D Gough	155.1	24	657	17	5–103	38.64	1	0
U Afzaal	9	0	49	1	1–49	49.00	0	0
AD Mullally	30.3	10	99	2	1–34	49.50	0	0
AR Caddick	177.4	24	748	15	5–101	49.86	1	0
DG Cork	23	3	84	1	1–84	84.00	0	0
AF Giles	25	0	108	1	1–108	108.00	0	0
J Ormond	34	4	115	1	1–115	115.00	0	0
PCR Tufnell	39	2	174	1	1–174	174.00	0	0
C White	46.4	7	189	1	1–101	189.00	0	0
MR Ramprakash	8	0	31	0	–	–	0	0

★ = not out

Man of the Series: MA Butcher

Australia

Batting	M	I	NO	Runs	HS	Avge	100	50	Ct/St
SR Waugh	4	5	2	321	157★	107.00	2	0	2
JL Langer	1	1	1	102	102★	102.00	1	0	1
ME Waugh	5	8	3	430	120	86.00	2	1	9
DR Martyn	5	7	2	382	118	76.40	2	2	0
AC Gilchrist	5	5	0	340	152	68.00	1	2	24/2
RT Ponting	5	8	0	338	144	42.25	1	2	7
ML Hayden	5	8	1	234	68	33.42	0	1	4
MJ Slater	4	7	0	170	77	24.28	0	1	1
SM Katich	1	2	1	15	15	15.00	0	0	1
JN Gillespie	5	4	1	41	27★	13.66	0	0	2
GD McGrath	5	4	3	11	8★	11.00	0	0	1
B Lee	5	4	0	24	20	6.00	0	0	0
SK Warne	5	4	0	13	8	3.25	0	0	6

Bowling	O	M	R	W	BB	Avge	5i	10m
GD McGrath	194.2	56	542	32	7–76	16.93	4	0
SK Warne	195.2	41	580	31	7–165	18.70	3	1
JN Gillespie	174	42	652	19	5–53	34.31	1	0
B Lee	120.5	18	496	9	2–37	55.11	0	0
ME Waugh	13	1	69	1	1–40	69.00	0	0
RT Ponting	4	0	8	0	–	–	0	0

★ = not out

Man of the Series: GD McGrath